W9-BYV-754

CONTEMPORARY ISSUES IN ACCOUNTING REGULATION

CONTEMPORARY ISSUES IN ACCOUNTING REGULATION

Edited by: **Stuart McLeay**
University of Wales, Bangor, UK

Angelo Riccaboni
Università di Siena, Italy

KLUWER ACADEMIC PUBLISHERS
Boston / Dordrecht / London

Distributors for North, Central and South America:
Kluwer Academic Publishers
101 Philip Drive
Assinippi Park
Norwell, Massachusetts 02061 USA
Telephone (781) 871-6600
Fax (781) 681-9045
E-Mail <kluwer@wkap.com>

Distributors for all other countries:
Kluwer Academic Publishers Group
Distribution Centre
Post Office Box 322
3300 AH Dordrecht, THE NETHERLANDS
Telephone 31 78 6392 392
Fax 31 78 6546 474
E-Mail <services@wkap.nl>

 Electronic Services <http://www.wkap.nl>

Library of Congress Cataloging-in-Publication Data

Contemporary issues in accounting regulation/edited by Stuart McLeay, Angelo Riccaboni.
  p.cm.
Includes bibliographical references and index
ISBN 0-7923-8440-7 (alk.paper)
  1. Accounting, 2.Accounting--Law and legislation. I. McLeay, Stuart, 1946-II.
Riccaboni, Angelo, 1959-

HF5635 .C7529 2000
657--dc21

00-061053

Printed on acid-free paper.

Printed in the United States of America

CONTENTS

FIGURES

TABLES

CONTRIBUTORS

Oriol Amat Salas	Universitat Pompeu Fabra Barcelona
Apostolos Ballas	Athens University of Economics and Business
John Blake	Central Lancashire University
Gillian Butler	University of Aberytay, Dundee
Bernard Colasse	Université de Paris Dauphine
Jill Collis	Kingston University

Juliet Cottingham   Kingston University

Louise Crawford   University of Aberytay, Dundee

Robert Day   Bournemouth University

Roberto Di Pietra   Università degli Studi di Siena

David Dugdale   Bristol Business School

Doreen Gilfedder   Dublin City University

Dimosthenis Hevas   Athens University of Economics and Business

Roger Hussey   Bristol Business School

Robin Jarvis   Kingston University

Stuart McLeay   University of Wales, Bangor

David Neal   University of Wales, Bangor

Ciaran Ó hÓgartaigh   Dublin City University

Angelo Riccaboni   Università degli Studi di Siena

Klaus Schredelseker   Universität Innsbruck

Peter Standish   Université de Paris Dauphine

Marco Trombetta   London School of Economics

PREFACE

The papers included in this volume were amongst those prepared for and presented at the Workshop on Accounting Regulation, which was held at the Certosa di Pontignano, Siena, Italy in March 1998. The Workshop was organised by the Department of Business and Social Studies in the Università degli Studi di Siena.

This book covers a number of different areas relating to the study of accounting regulation. The various papers include assessments of the role of the State in regulating accounting and investigations into the process of setting accounting standards, as well as papers that develop a theoretical perspective on the need for regulation and others that report on empirical analyses of corporate behaviour in the regulated environment. Earlier versions of some of the contributions to this book (Chapters 1, 2 and 5) have been published as articles in the Journal of Management and Governance.

The first three chapters consider institutional frameworks where the role of the State has been paramount. Bernard Colasse and Peter Standish examine the evolution of the French approach to standardisation, from its initial codification up to the recent and far reaching reforms. The tension between the power of the State and the forces of the market is played out here in the context of a financial reporting regime that, having traditionally served the needs of the public authorities, has had to adapt rapidly to globalisation in order to keep abreast of the situation within which regulated enterprises operate. Apostolos Ballas, Dimosthenis Hevas and David Neal present an equally compelling essay that also links the history of the State with the outcomes of its regulatory system. In this case, the research study is located in Greece where the French model of a national accounting plan is applied, but with greater emphasis on the coordination of fiscal policies. The third chapter looks at Italy where, with Roberto Di Pietra, we explore another codified system. However, in contrast to France and Greece, accounting regulation in Italy has evolved in the absence of a national accounting council or any other form of delegated standardisation agency. The outcome is a more overt political dimension to accounting regulation, which remains under the direct control of the public legislature.

Chapters 4 to 6 provide an assessment of the public interest in standard setting, based on the experiences to date in the UK and Ireland. Robert Day sets the scene by questioning the very meaning of 'public interest', and explores this notion in the context of the earlier 'private' Accounting Standards Committee and the present 'public' Accounting Standards Board. The extent of public participation in the standard setting process is documented by Doreen Gilfedder and Ciaran Ó hÓgartaigh who examine over 1500 responses to discussion papers and exposure drafts concerning 21 ASB projects. The results show that in the UK, as the USA, there is a relatively high degree of involvement of preparers of accounts. Amongst these, larger companies are more likely to be active lobbyists, which leads the authors to warn standard setters against the possibility that the process may be interpreted as merely a discourse of the powerful rather than as one of public consultation. In a contrasting study in chapter 6, Juliet Cottingham and Roger Hussey concentrate on a specific issue in order to describe the way in which the standard setters manage the complex process of keeping a project on the agenda, and the factors that can lead to its progress or delay. The case of Related Party Transactions provides considerable insight into the changing nature of public concern, and emphasises the crucial role of the standard setters themselves in assessing the level of public support in the face of opposing positions taken by powerful interest groups.

Chapters 7 and 8 provide an introduction to the theoretical framework of accounting regulation. Marco Trombetta argues that the optimal regime of international regulation does not necessarily exclude the possibility of reporting different sets of accounts in different capital markets. One of the reasons why different accounting treatments are required in different countries is because the choice that exists is genuinely controversial. In this context, it is shown how a regime that permits mutual recognition of alternative accounting treatments (or in some circumstances a regime where firms may select their preferred set of accounting regulations) may be preferred to strict adherence to a single set of internationally accepted standards. Chapter 8 deals with issues of market efficiency. Klaus Schredelseker simulates a market characterized by asymmetry of information and beliefs and also by different levels of skills and capabilities in interpreting financial accounts. Market efficiency is shown not to depend directly on the level of mandated public information, even after recognising differences in the analytical skills of those who use the accounts which firms produce.

The final chapters of the book are concerned primarily with the behaviour of companies in the light of regulatory demands. John Blake and Oriol Amat Salas investigate creative accounting and outline some of the regulatory controls that may be introduced. They also report on the attitudes of auditors in this respect, based on a survey which was conducted first in the UK and then in Spain. In chapter 10, Jill Collis, David Dugdale and Robin Jarvis examine the arguments for and against the deregulation of financial reporting by smaller companies. Their survey of small and medium-sized companies reveals that the information in annual reports may be disseminated more widely than is appreciated by regulators. They conclude that the drive to reduce compliance costs may have the effect of reducing the usefulness of financial statements to third parties such as customers and suppliers who depend on the statutory accounts as a primary source of information. The last chapter focuses on accounting treatments in a specific setting, that of hydro electricity generation, and looks in particular at the link between price control regulation and the accounting policies of firms operating in that industry. This study by Gillian Butler and Louise Crawford involves international comparisons across a number of different countries where the regulatory environments differ considerably, and it shows how depreciation methods are able to vary significantly even in an industry where the assets are fairly similar in nature.

To conclude, we wish to thank the various authors for contributing with enthusiasm to this collection of research papers, thus providing a book that offers a number of interesting perspectives on the study of accounting regulation. Finally, we convey our sincerest thanks to Antonella Casamonti for her efficient typing and correcting of the camera ready copy of this book and to Gail Hughes for her useful suggestions for improvement to the style and use of the English language in the initial drafts of each chapter. We also acknowledge the support of Professor Giuseppe Catturi who, on behalf of the Università degli Studi di Siena, made possible the use of the excellent facilities at the Certosa di Pontignano where the 1998 Workshop on Accounting Regulation was held.

Stuart McLeay

Angelo Riccaboni

1

STATE VERSUS MARKET: CONTENDING INTERESTS IN THE STRUGGLE TO CONTROL FRENCH ACCOUNTING STANDARDISATION

Bernard Colasse and Peter Standish

INTRODUCTION

This chapter seeks to identify contending interests in the struggle to control French accounting standardisation and to understand their motivation for involvement. It covers the period from 1941 when the first serious attempt was made to develop and put in place a national accounting code, the *Plan comptable général* (PCG), to be applied generally by commercial and industrial enterprises. It then deals with steps taken by the post-war state in 1946–47 to revalidate the concept of a national accounting code and to create an institutional framework for this purpose. Thereafter, attention is given to successive major instances of reorganisation of that framework, culminating in the reforms of 1997 and those approved subsequently. It further includes a detailed analysis of the involvement of interested parties in the operation of the authority charged with accounting standardisation. The essential problematic issue is whether the French approach to accounting standardisation can be sustained, given the profound attachment of the state to the values of the *Etat colbertiste*.

The chapter is organised as follows. As the basis for subsequent application of concepts and institutional arrangements to the matter of accounting standardisation, the next section considers the nature of the state and the exercise of state power as it has evolved and been regarded within France. We then characterise the French approach to accounting standardisation with particular attention firstly to the nature and objectives of accounting standardisation embodied in the PCG and secondly to the role and process of the National Accounting Council, the *Conseil National de la Comptabilité* (CNC), and its predecessors in the implementation of accounting standardisation in France. This is followed by a closer examination of the evolution of the French approach to accounting standardisation from 1941 to the recent institutional reforms, marked by the initial war-time attempt to implement a national accounting code, post-war adoption of the PCG in 1947, subsequent revisions to the PCG in 1957, 1982 and 1986, and its proposed revision in 1997. Finally, conclusions are drawn regarding the sustainability of the French approach to accounting standardisation.

FRENCH GOVERNANCE: RELATIONSHIPS BETWEEN STATE AND CITIZENS

The evolution of French governance, in terms of its institutions and relationships between the state and its citizens, exhibits elements that have persisted or persistently been reasserted, and others that have exhibited instability or been marked by turbulence. In broadest terms, national governance concerns relations between the state and the governed, as well as between members (whether individuals, companies, or other entities) of a particular national society. The subject of interest here is a subset of those relations, namely those concerned with control over the allocation and use of economic resources for which accounting serves as an agreed instrument of financial performance measurement in the discharge of control. The analysis assumes heterogeneity of interests and priority rankings of the relevant parties in those relations. For purposes of social cohesion and avoidance or mitigation of conflict between parties, there need to be institutional arrangements and processes more acceptable to the parties than would be the absence of mitigating arrangements and processes, or the imposition of unacceptable alternatives.

The relationships under consideration go to the heart of the disposition of property arrangements in a society, as well as concepts and practices of custodianship and accountability of property. Experience shows that, across a wide spectrum of national societies and under varying social and political conditions, these relationships tend to exhibit a conservative character, marked by discourse, if not necessarily by behaviour, concerning propriety in financial affairs and legitimation of control. Accounting processes as the instruments of measurement and control are affected by the same broad considerations, as are the accountants who perform those processes. Thus, even in societies that undergo political turbulence, accounting and accountants have not been observed as subjects of revolutionary inspiration or as primary objects of change, but are repeatedly seen as instruments for the preservation or reassertion of social order. These considerations are relevant to France, with its history of political turbulence yet repeated reassertion after the passage of revolutionary waves of more conservative values and social arrangements. We conclude that, for the purposes of analysis, it is more fruitful to concentrate on certain enduring or reasserted tenets and attitudes of French life implicated in the management of property claims, rather than on revolutionary phases and ideas for revolutionary reordering of social and political arrangements.

Of the relationships relevant to this chapter, that between the state and its citizens is of paramount interest. If the state is characterised in terms of its political masters and their functionaries, and of administrative structures and programmes, its priorities in terms of access to resources are taken to be, firstly, that it secure sufficient revenue and assets to meet the demands of its masters and functionaries for compensation and perquisites of office. Secondly, it requires revenues and assets sufficient to impose its authority on the citizenry and secure compliance to an acceptable level with its demands. Thirdly, and especially in present-day conditions, it requires revenues sufficient to be redistributed among the citizenry in response to politically legitimated programmes of governance. Attainment of these priorities means that the state has an overriding interest in the efficacy of its taxation system and of related information systems for monitoring compliance by the citizenry with obligations to the state. Those obligations may refer directly to relationships between the state and its citizens. They may also refer to relationships among citizens of interest to the state for purposes of preserving social cohesion. Where the state imposes modes of accounting on its citizenry, this may be termed state-ordained accounting. Accounting which evolves spontaneously between citizens for purposes of recording relationships of resource exchange may be termed commercial accounting. The objective here is to examine the ways in which the demands of the French state upon its citizens have been expressed through its approaches to accounting standardisation.

The interest of the French state in accounting regulation and standardisation has a long history, dating from the original national French law to specify accounting requirements for enterprises, possibly the first in the world, the 1673 *Ordonnance de Colbert*. Certain aspects of its accounting obligations were in essence retained and developed in the 1807 *Code de commerce* and visibly remain in the current *Code de commerce* (Standish, 1997, Ch.3). These are examples of state-ordained accounting, superimposed in the first place upon well-established practices of commercial accounting (Bérard and Lemarchand, 1994). In the case of France, its state-ordained accounting is here termed 'Colbertist accounting' after its progenitor, Jean-Baptiste Colbert, Finance Minister, 1661–1683, to Louis XIV. The long-standing if rather fitfully exercised interest of the French state in accounting has persisted as from the time of the French Revolution through repeated, and at times violent, constitutional change associated with political turbulence.

Experience and memory of this turbulence have led to a wary relationship between the French state and its citizens, with the state, particularly beginning with the time of Colbert (Miller, 1990), exhibiting a characteristic need to be informed on the behaviour and actions of the citizens and to exercise control. Its instruments for doing so are a bureaucracy which absorbs possibly the highest proportion of working population of any European country and a dense thicket of regulation and administrative process, much remarked upon but never seriously contested.[1] Notwithstanding political turbulence and constitutional upheaval, many of the state administrative and judicial arrangements and institutions exhibit continuity and stability, such as the top echelon of state financial controllers, the *inspecteurs des finances*, and the highest civil and criminal courts, respectively the *Conseil d'Etat* and the *Cour de Cassation*, all three dating from the Revolution or early years of the Consulate (Bernard and Colli, 1984, pp.793–796; Sautel, 1982).

Through its bureaucracy and institutional structure, the state wields awesome power over the individual citizen. Nevertheless, in the democratic dispensation that has most often been applied in France since 1871, the state has learned to maintain its priorities but avoid large-scale social coercion. Instead, in many respects the French state assumes the role of social master, with the citizens as apprentices allowed to benefit from state tutelage and benevolence, and a feeling of fruitful involvement in formation of social policy. The discourse of this social pact between rulers and ruled lays emphasis on the concept and condition of solidarity. As a principle, solidarity partly stems from aspects of the French Revolution (Schama, 1989) but more particularly from the emergence of ideas on social priorities and organisation in the late 1800s, articulated in France in relation to economic affairs by Méline, at times Minister for Agriculture and later Prime Minister (1896–98) (Méline, 1905). Part of his programme concerned promoting mutual self-help, to be facilitated by the legislative authorisation of new forms of legal structures, notably achieved by the 1898 Law for friendly societies, *sociétés de secours mutuel*, and the 1901 Law for non-profit associations, *Contrat d'association*. In other words, solidarity finds practical expression in terms of collective obligation and approaches to social welfare through organisations of mutual support (Bourgeois, 1896; Hayward, 1961), an approach that has powerfully influenced the development of French structures and processes for health and other forms of insurance, as well as pension arrangements. Mutual organisations evolving from these sources have also provided the citizenry with possibilities of sheltering to a degree from the ever-watchful state through financially significant ways of conducting affairs on terms that attract tax concessions and less structured accounting requirements.

Solidarity is also bound up with strongly held ideas of the role and nature of public services, such as education, energy and transport, to be provided by the state as a demonstration of its power in performing its cardinal role as architect of social solidarity (Cohen, 1996, pp.181–190). Solidarity, mutuality and over-arching state power provide the foundation and motivation for social and managerial practices widely regarded in France as preferable to those attributed to competitive capitalism, which are frequently seen as socially corrosive and to be mistrusted (eg. Forrester, 1996). It is not even clear that tenets of competitive capitalism have deep roots within French business enterprise, with its long record of seeking protective regulation and, wherever obtainable, state financial support.[2] So far from the state operating as a pervasively threatening element in personal life, as was true in the *Ancien Régime*, modern French governments reveal anxiety when unable to placate vested interest groups, knowing from experience the rapidity with which demands for or resistance to change can escalate to breaking point and social disorder (Hoffman, 1974, pp.68–76). As a result French life offers many examples of deflected market forces, some deplored, others rationalised as a preferable alternative form of capitalism (Albert, 1991).

In these conditions of tension between the state and the forces of economic competition, the citizenry remains anxious that social solidarity be maintained. A favoured device for promoting this is through construction of representative bodies, exemplified by numerous state-ordained consultative councils giving representation to the widest possible range of interest groups. We term this the Versailles syndrome in reference to court life under the *Ancien Régime*, designed and managed to control the nobility by ensuring its commitment to a kind of permanent house party at the court of Versailles. Interpreted in a present-day context, the syndrome expresses, first, the need of the state to manage its relationship with potentially fissiparous social groups through elaborate consultative processes and, second, the need of the citizenry to avoid exclusion from involvement in those processes. Involvement ordinarily operates on the basis of voluntarism in return for the privilege of inclusion granted by the state. The Versailles syndrome is more than a condition of proximity or for mere exchange of views. It is a quintessential element of state policy and practice in France applied to the direction of economic life, along with repeated policy initiatives and actions that mark the state as an entrepreneur in its own right, undertaking major risk investments on its own account, setting broad strategies for key activity sectors from the viewpoint of national interest and, if need be, intervening directly in the strategic and financial direction of major private sector enterprises. This stance and practice constitute the programme of the Colbertist state and make up what is generally described as *dirigisme*.

The Versailles syndrome is a necessary condition for the non-coercive practice of *dirigisme*, itself essential for construction and maintenance of social cohesion. It may be desirable but is not crucial that consultation take the form of serious intellectual engagement between the parties. The stance of the state toward social solidarity and consultative processes is profoundly technocratic, shaped by enduring aspects of the formation and career paths of French state functionaries. For example, a high proportion of senior French civil servants are products of the celebrated *grandes écoles*, notably the *Ecole Polytechnique*, the *Ecole des Mines*, and in the post-war period, the *Ecole Nationale d'Administration* (ENA). The same cadre, frequently following career periods in the civil service, is heavily represented at senior executive levels in state enterprises and private sector groups. The intellectual force of this technocratic class, with its comparative advantage in utilising political and high-level commercial networks, means that consultative processes may be one-sided vis-à-vis less knowledgeable community representatives. Nevertheless, the Versailles syndrome applies to many fields of French life and is associated with long-standing and stable arrangements.

The foregoing is essentially an inward-looking view of French experience and values, now increasingly under test in the contemporary context of financial globalisation, broad international consensus on acceptance and strengthening competitive and capitalist structures and values, and possible attrition of the power of the state. When considered in that context, two related issues are relevant to accounting standardisation; namely, the role of French securities markets in expanding the number and capitalisation of listed French companies, and the problem of supplementing state pension schemes in the face of a rapidly ageing population. At present, the number and capitalisation of listed French companies (see Table 1.1), are substantially lower than in the UK, an economy and population of similar size. Furthermore, the average capitalised value of listed companies has a highly skewed distribution, resulting from privatisation of former state enterprises and the sparse flow of new smaller listings. Until now, French equity markets have played only a limited role in pension funding. What is lacking, as widely noted, is an equity investment culture, backed by firmer corporate recognition of governance issues and a focus on shareholder value.[3]

As related to financial markets, globalisation refers to the rapid interplay of

Table 1.1 Selected French securities market data

	1991	1992	1993	1994	1995	1996
No. of French listed companies:						
Principal market	547	513	472	459	444	406
Second market	288	271	254	265	266	280
Capitalisation of listed securities (F.bill.):						
Shares	1,803	1,809	2,692	2,415	2,445	3,073
Bonds	2,908	3,194	3,877	3,690	4,133	4,606

Source. Commission des Opérations de Bourse, 1996 Annual Report (English version), Table 1, 82.

securities investment decisions across national boundaries. This emphasises the cleavage between securitised assets and a underlying real assets. The former are associated with mobility, liquidity and pricing in international markets, with arbitrage as the mechanism for exploiting market imperfections. Real assets are associated with factories, physical infrastructure and labour markets, developed in response to asset location and technical modes of exploitation. Individual governments have declining power to control securities markets, understood as mechanisms for matching buyers and sellers. Those markets depend increasingly, as regards financial communication, on information quality assurance supported by international accounting standardisation and audit performed by major accounting firms. Neither of these assurance elements owes anything significant to the French or any other individual state, other than possibly the USA. Governments, however, are still very much expected to be concerned over social repercussions associated with real asset control and use. Popular and professional discourse in France suggests that the state has long felt uneasy about the role of securities markets as threatening loss of state control *Dirigisme* is primarily concerned with strategics related to real assets. On its record, the role of the modern French state has been one of massive financial commitment to obtain and sustain control over real assets, as in the 1981–1982 round of nationalisation or subsidies for selected icons such as Air France, Thomson, and Crédit Lyonnais. The conceptual framework for addressing the implications of international securitisation and its relationship to real assets has not as yet been fully addressed in France.

The implications of these issues are that until quite recently developments in international financial accounting and reporting evoked little interest in France. Instead, Colbertist accounting retained and even developed certain distinctive features unmatched in other OECD nations, with the PCG standardised chart of accounts as the most prominent example. The aspect of globalisation of greatest pertinence here is at the microeconomic level, in terms of the competitiveness of particular companies and industries. Financial accounting and reporting are key elements in the financing and investment strategy and technology of the firm. As French companies have seen the advantage gained by foreign competitors resulting from the application of different accounting technologies, for example, in terms of easier access to more liquid securities markets and improved credit ratings, pressures to adopt internationally accepted accounting standards have grown within France. These have been powerfully supported by the expertise of major international accounting firms, with their comparative advantage in interpreting changing international conditions to French companies. For the state, these are anxious developments, not only because of their implications for adoption of unfamiliar modes of accounting, but more fundamentally because as market-driven pressures, they threaten the very rationale for much of the process and content of Colbertist accounting.

THE FRENCH APPROACH TO ACCOUNTING STANDARDISATION

In this section, the foregoing argument is applied to analysis of the objectives of the French state for accounting standardisation and the nature of the resulting process, considered over the period 1941–1997. Drawing on the framework of Tilly (1984, Ch.4), the analysis is directed at the macrohistorical level, seeking to take overall account of particular big structures and large processes, which in Section 4 are then subjected to comparison in terms of evolution across discrete sub-periods within the overall period. Attention is also given to a microhistorical level, in terms of examination of individual and group encounters with the structures and processes under consideration. The analysis proceeds by regarding the French approach to accounting standardisation as exemplifying certain attributes held to be applicable to nation states in general. The attributes are derived from Bendix (1978), especially Ch.1, as summarised in Tilly (1984, p.93). As applied in this instance to France, the attributes are that, first, despite demonstrated experience in other states with approaches to accounting standardisation, France has worked out its own fate, meaning in this arena its individual approach to accounting standardisation, which is substantially independent of other states; second, that previous French institutional history and beliefs of the periods under consideration have placed tight constraints on possible solutions to recognised problems; and third, that pivotal events in the history of French accounting standardisation have not been modifications in the structure of authority but the expression through that structure of changes in dominant ideas, beliefs and justifications.

Colbertist accounting in the service of the French state

As previously observed, the French state may be said to have invented state-ordained accounting. Its essential condition is that it be imposed in terms of hierarchy of authority from the top downwards. The opposite condition is that of commercial accounting evolving as a bottom up process in response to needs of individual enterprises and the market place in general. As forms of commercial accounting were practised in France prior to the 1673 *Ordonnance* of Colbert, it was open to the state to follow the same road as, for example, England, where accounting regulation was unknown before the 1701 Act of Union with Scotland, and for long afterwards. Instead, having opted for Colbertist accounting, France reasserted this approach with the 1807 *Code de Commerce*, and in modern times with each successive and more elaborate version of the PCG, together with associated legislation and regulation for its application.[4] Except for the adoption by certain major French groups of consolidated accounting ahead of the 1985 adoption into French law of the Seventh Directive, there has been no modern significant instance of financial accounting and reporting practice in France developing technologies ahead of regulation.

There is no necessary reason for state-ordained accounting to express a constant set of concerns, in so far as the state adopts changing priorities and exhibits the capacity to adapt to changing circumstances. The 1673 *Ordonnance* of Colbert imposed on traders, merchants and bankers an obligation to keep certain accounting records and, in the case of traders and merchants, the significant additional obligation that their books of accounts be registered with a designated civil authority (Standish, 1997, Ch.3). At that time, the interest of the state in accounting regulation was limited to the promotion of social cohesion through construction of a system of information-based validation of financial claims arising in commercial affairs and resolution of disputes between parties over financial contracts. The absence of a linkage between the *Ordonnance* and taxation reflects the fact that revenues of the state were obtained without recourse to business profit taxation.[5] With the broader assumption of responsibilities for economic and social management by modern governments, the position changed. The motivation for the first attempt to develop and apply a national accounting code, which commenced in 1941 and resulted in the so-called 1942 PCG, was two-fold (Standish, 1990; Standish, 1997, Ch.2): first, the code was seen as indispensable to the needs of price surveillance and control, to be achieved through standardised enterprise classification of costs and revenues; second, standardised classification would form the basis for improved national economic statistics of enterprise financial performance.[6]

In the immediate post-war period, state priorities relevant to accounting were principally concerned with national economic management, seen as requiring support through national economic planning and development of national statistics. A further general concern was the national shortage of accountants and limited capacity in the educational and professional training system for raising the supply and level of accounting skills. This shortage was of particular concern to the state for its effect on administration of the expanded public sector and on management of commercial enterprises receiving state subventions, then widely provided as part of reconstruction post-war programmes (Standish, 1997, pp.77–80). The essential objectives for Colbertist accounting at that time were therefore limited to creating and fostering the application of a relatively simple national accounting code, the 1947 PCG. In light of other historical aspects of standardisation in France, notably as applied to standardisation of the written language, it may be said that the form of the PCG was intended to promote its acceptance and utilisation by relevant parties as a national accounting language.

As the phase of post-war reconstruction passed, new priorities emerged (Standish, 1997, Ch. 2.6). A linkage between a national accounting code and tax compliance by business enterprise, foreseen by the tax administration during the development of the 1942 PCG, was formalised in 1965. Measures to palliate concerns of the private sector, reflecting the priority attached to social cohesion, were addressed from 1959 by instituting of a process for adaptation of the PCG to meet the needs and preferences of specific trade and industry sectors. From 1969, with the establishment of the *Commission des Opérations de Bourse* (COB), the state began to recognise the importance of financial accountability in promoting the role of securities markets. Throughout this period, and up to the present, the state has, however, maintained full control over the process and outcomes of accounting standardisation in France, in other words maintaining the central characteristics of Colbertist accounting.

The Conseil National de la Comptabilité and the Versailles syndrome

The characterisation of the Versailles syndrome is used in this section to explain and interpret the establishment and composition of successive government commissions and agencies for accounting standardisation in France. The bodies in question and their dates of establishment are as follows:

    1941   Commission du Plan Comptable (1941 Comm)
    1946   Commission de Normalisation des Comptabilités (1946 Comm)
    1947   Conseil Supérieur de la Comptabilité (CSC)
    1957   Conseil National de la Comptabilité (CNC)
    1997   Comité de Réglementation Comptable (CRC)

The argument is that institutional arrangements adopted throughout the period either conformed to the characteristics of the Versailles syndrome, or otherwise were rapidly modified or replaced by arrangements that did. The institutional process for accounting standardisation has been examined in terms of involvement of the recognised constituencies interested in its outcomes. Two categories of data have been analysed: first, membership composition of the successive bodies and, second, the 1992 composition of specialist CNC standing commissions used to develop accounting standards or interpretations for approval by the CNC. The latter data were selected, first, given the institutional stability attributable to the CNC at that stage of its 35-year existence and, second, given that no data as yet exist to throw direct light on the current mode of CNC involvement of its constituencies following the 1996 reform.

To manage anxiety engendered by the risk that private sector interest groups might employ modes of financial accounting contrary to its priorities, the state felt impelled to establish and directly control the operation of institutional arrangements for accounting standardisation. At the same time, the state conferred privilege on private sector interest groups having the greatest potential for acting in conflicting ways by involving them on the basis of voluntarism in a state-controlled consultative process. The consultation and standardisation process has been essentially technocratic, producing outcomes consistently supportive of or, at any rate, not in conflict with key priorities of the state for accounting standardisation. To palliate the anxieties of groups excluded from the consultative process, the state has repeatedly conceded the inclusion of additional interest groups in the process, legitimating the process through procedure rather than by the content of its outcomes (Jönsson, 1991). The purpose of the procedure as directed by the state has been to implement, propagate and reinforce its vision of Colbertist accounting. Although the operation of the procedure can be regarded as broadly achieving its purpose, the effect of repeatedly extending the set of recognised constituencies admitted to the process has affected its manageability, provoking pressures for reform.

The initial institutional arrangement adopted by the state to achieve its aims with accounting standardisation was established as part of the first attempt to construct and impose a national accounting code. For this task, the state, or more precisely the Vichy Government, established the 1941 *Commission du Plan Comptable* (1941 Comm) with a membership of 32, including 17 from various government agencies (Decree 41–1847, 22/4/1941, modified by Decree 41–4856, 19/11/1941). Its structure and operation exhibited bureaucratic domination, technocratic direction by a statistician, and involvement of private sector interests on the basis of voluntarism. The outcome in the form of the 1942 PCG was clearly intended to support state priorities rather than those of the private sector (Standish, 1990). Since this occurred under atypical conditions of economic duress and limited civil autonomy, the institutional arrangement for accounting standardisation and experience with it could not be confidently taken as a predictor of what might happen under peacetime conditions.

The next stage was ushered in following the decision of the initial post-war French administration to implement a national accounting code. The institutional arrangement established for the purpose was the 1946 *Commission de Normalisation des Comptabilités* (1946 Comm) with 25 members, supplemented by a further 41 persons recorded as participating in its work (Brunet, 1947), summarised in terms of composition and affiliation in Table 1.2. The 1946 Comm was required to propose a national accounting code to the Finance Minister (Decree 48–519, 4/4/1946, Art.2). As the only available model was the 1942 PCG and as the 1946 Comm Secretary was previous secretary of the now-dissolved 1943 *Comité d'Adaptation du Plan Comptable*, i.e. the 1942 PCG (Decree 48–519, 4/4/1946, Art.6), the exercise was clearly intended to legitimate the vision of Colbertist accounting expressed in the 1942 PCG. The 1946 Comm composition and the involvement of external experts (Brunet, 1947) reveal significant aspects for subsequent evolution of the French approach to accounting standardisation. First, the 1946 Comm was constructed and operated as a coalition of interests. Of its 25 members, 23 had an identified organisational affiliation, as did 38 of the 41 external experts. Second, a number of those involved had more than one affiliation, mostly combining senior government and academic positions, or qualification as a public accountant and representative of a specific interest group. Third, the coalition of interests included all government ministries or agencies important at the time in post-war reconstruction, as well as private sector interest organisations and institutions representing the accounting profession, the national

Table 1.2 Membership composition, 1946 Commission de Normalisation des Comptabilités

	MEMBERS	EXPERTS	TOTAL
Public sector - ministries, agencies and istitutions			
CNC officers: President, Vice-President, Secretary	3		3
Government ministries and public institutions:			
Agriculture	1		1
Industrial Production	2	2	4
Labour		2	2
National economy, finance, taxation	4	2	6
Statistics		2	2
Other	1	6	7
Total public sector	11	14	25
Private sector and non-government			
Accounting profession	1	8	9
Economic interest groups:			
Chambers of commerce		2	2
Craft/agriculture	2	3	5
Enterprise chief accountants	1	2	3
National employers	1	1	2
Small and medium enterprises	1	2	3
Quasi-professional bodies		1	1
Professors of accounting/economics	2	4	6
Trade unions	3	2	5
Other experts	3	2	5
Total private sector and non-government	14	27	41
Total	25	41	66

employers' council, small and medium enterprise, arts and crafts, agriculture and the trade union movement.

The importance attached to legitimation of the concept of a national accounting code is indicated by inclusion in the work of the 1946 Comm of nine professors and educational administrators. Of the five accounting professors included, three held influential appointments and made noteworthy contributions to the accounting literature supporting the concept of a national accounting code: A. Brunet (Brunet, 1951), Professor at the *Conservatoire National des Arts et Métiers* (CNAM), as well as high public official and author of the report of the 1946 Comm; J. Fourastié, Professor at the *Ecole Nationale d'Administration* (ENA) (Fourastié, 1943; 1945), and P. Garnier (Garnier, 1947), Professor jointly at the *Ecole des Hautes Etudes Commerciales* (HEC), premier grande école in business studies, and CNAM. Garnier and the two educational administrators all held positions with the CNAM *Institut de Technique Comptable* (INTEC), an organisation of continuing significance for its accounting education programmes based on the PCG, offered throughout France, as well as in various Francophone nations.[7] The concept of accounting as a form of state-ordained national language can be extended by viewing accounting standardisation as part of industrial standardisation, exemplified by involvement in the 1946 Comm of a representative from the *Commission de Normalisation*, responsible for technological standardisation (Maily, 1946). In summary, the 1946 Comm is significant, first, in showing undisputed mastery of the state over the process of drawing up a national accounting code and the involvement of external experts representing wide economic and social interests and, second, for connecting the process and its desired outcomes to state priorities for treating accounting standardisation as an element of language and technical standardisation.

Responsibility for further development and application of the PCG was vested in the *Conseil Supérieur de la Comptabilité* (CSC), replaced in 1957 by the present *Conseil National de la Comptabilité* (CNC). The evolution of CSC/CNC membership structure in terms of public or private sector affiliation is shown in Table 1.3.[8] The years shown in the Table are 1947 when the CSC was constituted, 1950 when it was enlarged, 1957 when it was replaced by the CNC, and 1971, 1992 and 1996 when CNC membership composition was revised. Over that interval, total CSC/CNC membership increased from 22 in 1947 to 103 in 1992, followed by a reduction to 58 in 1996. Within the total membership, public sector membership, rising from 14 in 1947 to 28 in 1992 but falling to 13 in 1996, declined proportionally over the period from 64% to 22%. Private sector membership rose from 8 or 36% in 1947 to 75 or 73% in 1992. Although reduced to 45 in 1996, private sector membership then rose to 78% of total membership.

Table 1.3 reveals important state priorities for accounting standardisation and its process. Overall composition of the 1947 CSC, compared to the 1946 Comm, underlined the intention of the state to proceed from legitimating its concept of Colbertist accounting to implementation, emphasised by its proportion of public sector membership at 64%, higher than for any subsequent period of the CSC/CNC. With 22 members, fewer than the 25 1946 Comm members and significantly fewer than the 32 1941 Comm members, the 1947 CSC might almost have operated as an executive body. Its technocratic composition meant that the state was minimising its anxiety over attitudes toward a national accounting code in the public and private sectors, but disregarding the anxieties of groups excluded

Table 1.3 CSC/CNC membership 1947–1996 by economic sector affiliation

SECTOR	1947	1950	1957	1971	1992	1996
Public:						
No.	14	25	19	28	28	13
%	64	42	29	34	27	22
Private and non-government:						
No.	8	34	47	55	75	45
%	36	58	71	66	73	78
Total						
No.	22	59	66	83	103	58
%	100	100	100	100	100	100

from the standardisation process. The 1947 CSC therefore did not conform to the Versailles syndrome. On general historical grounds, this was not tenable. The 1950 reformed CSC, with membership expanded from 22 to 59 and a wider set of constituencies, reverted to a more characteristic state procedure that has persisted to the present. There was nevertheless significant continuity from earlier arrangements for accounting standardisation, with 27 of the 59 members having held prior appointments. Of the 27, one had been appointed to the three prior bodies (1941 Comm, 1946 Comm and 1947 CSC), two had been members of the 1941 Comm and involved in the 1946 Comm, and eight had been involved in the 1946 Comm and were members of the 1947 CSC. Whilst the sector composition of these 11 multiple appointees exhibits no particular bias (5 public sector; 6 private), state control over membership appointment suggests that renewed appointment would have been confined to those who supported the national accounting code and were useful to its implementation. Finally, in considering channels of state influence, it is to be noted that the CSC/CNC has throughout included a significant number of members with prior public sector career experience or service to the state.[9]

Table 1.4 shows CSC/CNC membership composition classified by designated affiliation or attachment within the public and non-public sectors. With the 1950 CSC expanded from 22 to 59 members, public sector membership nearly doubled, from 14 to 25, but declined from 64% to 42% of overall membership, while non-public sector membership expanded from 8 or 36% to 34 or 58%. The accounting profession, which would ultimately bear the weight of the application of the PCG to the private sector, was now represented by nine members, compared with two in the 1947 CSC. Employer organisations, under a cloud immediately after the war as tainted with war-time collaboration, were readmitted to the process with four representatives. Directors of accounting in companies, with only one representative in the 1947 CSC, reverted to the three representatives of the 1946 Comm. Trade unions, with three 1946 Comm representatives but omitted as a category from the 1947 CSC, were assigned four representatives. In addition, the 1950 CSC included a new membership category with four quasi-professional bodies, such as the *Société de Comptabilité de France*.

The CSC/CNC has not at any stage been vested with regulatory authority, but adapting the argument of Young (1994), it might be said that its deliberative space available for occupation became overcrowded with the 1950 reform and progressively more so up to the 1996 reform. This overcrowding was particularly marked by repeated extension to the range of accredited quasi-professional bodies in the fields of accounting, finance and management, as well as of bodies representing employer interests. From Table 1.4, it can be seen that the 1996 reform sought to redress the unwieldy CNC composition by an almost total elimination of membership representation of quasi-professional bodies. At the same time, it retained significant representation from the two institutions of the

Table 1.4 CNC membership by designated affiliation or attachment 1947–1996

	1947	1950	1957	1971	1992	1996
Government ministries, councils, agencies:						
CNC President/Secretary-General	2	2	2	2	2	1
Finance/Budget	3	4	5	5	6	4
Financial statement collection and analysis				3	3	
Government Commissioner to OEC	1	1	1	1	1	
Industry/Commerce	1	1	2	2	1	
Justice	1	1	1	1	1	1
National Institute of Statistics (INSEE)			1	1	1	1
Securities Commission (COB)				1	1	1
State Audit Office/Control Service		1	1	1	2	2
Statutory commissions	4	10				2
Other	2	9	6	11	10	1
Total government ministries, councils, agencies	14	29	19	28	28	13
Private sector and non-government:						
Accounting profession:						
Statutory auditors (CNCC)				1	9	5
Registered public accountants (OEC)	1	9	9	9	9	5
Total accounting profession	1	9	9	10	18	10
Specified quasi-professional bodies		4	8	14	18	2
Economic interest groups:						
Commerce, industry and trades chambers/tribunals				1	5	12
Enterprise chief accountants		3	7	7	2	4
Employer organisation representatives		4	4	4	7	7
Trade union representatives		4	4	4	5	5
Other					5	
Total non-government economic interest groups		11	15	16	24	28
Other:						
Nominated by CNC President			5	5	5	
Personal standing in the field of accounting	7	6	10	10	10	5
Total other	7	6	15	15	15	5
Total private sector and non-government	8	30	47	55	75	45
Total	22	59[10]	66	83	103	58

accounting profession, the *Ordre des Experts Comptables* (OEC) and *Compagnie Nationale des Commissaires aux Comptes* (CNCC), and increased that of designated economic interest groups. The reform, in other words, more firmly exhibits a corporatist character through concentration on key economic interests and their representation dominated by government ministries, councils and agencies, and state-recognised organisations in the private and non-public sector. Comparison of the 1996 CNC with 1946 Comm membership (Table 1.2), shows a high degree of correspondence of categories. Of the public sector, these are the Ministries for Finance/Economy and Commerce/Industry, as well as the National Institute of Statistics, *Institut National de la Statistique et des Etudes Economiques* (INSEE), to which should be added the Justice Ministry, represented at all stages of the CSC/CNC. The Finance/Economy Ministry has at all times included representation of the Tax Administration, the *Direction Générale des Impôts* (DGI). Of the private and non-government sector, the comparison shows representation in both 1946 and 1996 by the accounting profession; chambers of commerce, agriculture and crafts; the national employer organisation, trade unions; and professors and educators. These categories may be regarded as the essential core of the French institutional arrangement for accounting standardisation, the importance of which was reasserted in the 1996 reform by increasing their proportionate weight in CNC membership.

The membership composition of the CSC/CNC over their combined 50 year history conforms to the concept and practice of solidarity examined in Section 2. Non-government members contribute to the CNC process on the basis of voluntarism, rendered in return for the privilege of inclusion. The PCG has been adopted and applied over wide-ranging areas of French financial affairs under a non-coercive regime, in which legal measures to punish financial entities for non-compliance with its requirements are effectively unknown. The tenor of the CNC process is *dirigiste* and technocratic, with outcomes responding to state priorities rather than commercial forces. This has been seen in its halting and incomplete response to problematic issues raised by securities markets, international pressures for consolidated accounts and, as a particular difficulty of recent years, recognition of widespread and substantial unrealised losses on property values. During the history of the PCG and institutional arrangements for its production, there has been no strong evidence of concern by the state with issues of accounting doctrine comparable to that expressed by the accounting profession. Discussion of basic accounting principles in the PCG has in all versions been exiguous, *eg.* a single page in the 1986 PCG (CNC, 1986, I.5). As observed generally, and as applies to France, a strong and centralised state does not consider accountability an important issue (Jönsson, 1991, p.542).

The way in which state domination of the process operates has been further tested by examining the pattern of involvement of constituencies represented in the key CNC processes of accounting standardisation. As the CNC process following the 1996 reforms has not yet been fully established, observations relate to recent years prior to the reform and concentrate on the composition of its standing commissions, the key specialist units used to develop recommendations and rulings for consideration and adoption by the CNC itself. Reorganisation in 1992 established four standing commissions as follows:

> Consolidated accounts (CONS);
> Financial instruments (FI);
> Management accounting (MA);
> Small and medium enterprises (SME).

The appointment of CNC members and external experts to these commissions is shown in Tables 1.5 and 1.6. Table 1.5 shows appointment of CNC members to

Table 1.5 Appointment of CNC members to standing commissions

	No.	%
Appointment:		
Single	59	57
Multiple	14	14
Total appointment	73	71
No appointment	30	29
Total membership	103	100

standing commissions, with 14% of members holding multiple appointments and 29% without appointment.

Table 1.6 presents an analysis of appointment of CNC members and external experts to standing commissions. In 1992 there were in all 158 appointments, comprising 92 CNC members and 66 non-member external experts. The Table shows multiple appointment combinations, with two CNC members appointed to all four commissions and one member to three commissions Multiple appointments mostly paired management accounting with small and medium enterprises, or consolidated accounts with financial instruments. External experts held single appointments except for two experts appointed to the consolidated accounts and financial instruments commissions.

Table 1.6 Structure of CNC standing commission appointments by membership category

MEMBERSHIP CATEGORY	CONS		FI		MA		SME		TOTAL	
Appointments	No.	%	No.	%	No.	%	No.	%	No.	%
Members:										
All 4 commissions	2	4	2	4	2	7	2	8	8	5
3 commissions	1	2	1	2			1	4	3	2
2 (CONS + FI)	6	12	6	10					12	8
2 (CONS + MA)	1	2			1	4			2	1
2 (FI + MA)			1	2	1	4			2	1
2 (MA + SME)					3	11	3	11	6	4
1 commission	18	37	11	19	12	44	18	69	59	37
Total members	28	57	21	37	19	70	24	92	92	58
External experts:										
2 (CONS + FI)	2	4	2	4					4	3
1 commission	19	39	33	59	8	30	2	8	62	39
Total external experts	21	43	35	63	8	30	2	8	66	42
Total appointments	49	100	56	100	27	100	26	100	158	100

From Table 1.6, members took 58% of appointments, with the proportionate appointment of CNC members to standing commissions varying as follows:

Consolidated accounts (CONS)	57%
Financial instruments (FI)	37%
Management accounting (MA)	70%
Small and medium enterprises (SME)	92%

Of the four commissions, the financial instruments commission had the greatest need for technical expertise, reflecting rapid development of new forms of securitised financing, as well as complex conceptual and technical financial accounting issues. This need has been preponderantly met by external experts.

An obvious source of technical expertise for the CNC is that available from its members who may be regarded as expert in accounting. Table 1.7 shows their appointments, with columns indicating numbers not appointed to a commission (0), appointed to one or two commissions (1, 2, and their total, 1+2) and total number available for appointment. The final column shows the participation rate in commissions of CNC members classified as accounting experts, expressed as a percentage of those available in each category. In total, 12 or 23% of members were not appointed to a commission, 34 or 65% were appointed to one commission and 6 or 12% to two commissions. There were no appointments of accounting experts to more than two commissions. The overall participation rate in commissions was 77% but with considerable variation in participation between categories shown in Table 1.7. The overall rate of 59% for members of the accounting profession was lower than that of any other category of accounting experts or of other members (Standish, 1997, Ch.4). Within the accounting profession group, there was marked disparity between registered public accountants with 75% participation and statutory auditors with 44%, the lowest of

Table 1.7 Standing commission members with accounting expertise

	APPOINTMENTS					
	0	*1*	*2*	*1+2*	*Total*	*%*
Accounting profession:						
OEC	2	6		6	8	75
CNCC	5	3	1	4	9	44
Total accounting profession	7	9	1	10	17	59
Other quasi-professional bodies:	1	5	1	6	7	86
Economic interest groups:						
Employer organisations		1	1	2	2	
Enterprise accountants		4	2	6	6	
Trade unions		2		2	2	
Other		2		2	2	
Total economic interest groups		9	3	12	12	100
Professors of accounting	1	5		5	6	83
Personal standing	3	5		5	8	63
Retired senior CNC or COB officials		1	1	2	2	100
Total appointments:						
No.	12	34	6	40	52	77
%	23	65	12	77	100	

any group of accounting experts or other private sector members.

A comparable analysis is given in Table 1.8 for private sector members other than those with accounting expertise and for public sector members, not including CNC officers. In the case of the 20 non-accounting expert private sector members, four or 20% were not appointed to a commission, 14 or 70% were appointed to one commission and two or 10% to two commissions, with an overall participation rate in commissions of 80%. There were no non-accounting experts appointed to more than two commissions. In the case of the 24 public sector members, seven or 29% were not appointed to a commission, 11 or 46% were appointed to one commission, three or 13% to two commissions, one or 4% to three commissions and the two tax administration (DGI) members were appointed to all four CNC commissions, being the only CNC members with that extent of involvement, giving an overall public sector participation rate in commissions of 71%. Those ministries or agencies judged to have a more direct interest in the CNC and PCG had an overall participation rate of 73% compared with 67% for other agencies.

Table 1.8 Standing commission members without private sector accounting expertise

			APPOINTMENTS					
	0	1	2	3	4	1-4	Total	%
Private sector								
Economic interest groups:								
Commerce, industry/trades chambers	1	4				4	5	
Trade union representative	1						1	
Other		3				3	3	
Total economic interest group	2	7				7	9	78
Specified professional bodies:								
Education		1				1	1	
Financial investment		4				4	4	
Management	2	1	1			2	4	
Total specified professional bodies	2	6	1			7	9	78
Personal standing		1	1			2	2	100
Total private sector								
No.	4	14	2			16	20	80
%	20	70	10			80	100	
Public sector								
Finance (excluding DGI)	1	1				1	2	
Financial statement collection/analysis	1	1	1			2	3	
Industry/commerce		1				1	1	
Justice				1		1	1	
National Institute of Statistics (INSEE)		1				1	1	
Securities Commission (COB)		1				1	1	
State Audit Office	1	1				1	2	
Tax administration (DGI)	1				2	2	3	
Total selected public sector agencies	4	6	1	1	2	10	14	73
Other public sector agencies	3	5	2			7	10	67
Total public sector								
No.	7	11	3	1	2	17	24	71
%	29	46	13	4	8	71	100	

In considering the influence of membership constituencies, the accounting profession is of particular interest, given its comparative advantage in the subject matter of accounting standardisation and closer proximity to commercial accounting. As shown in Table 1.4, it constitutes the largest single constituency group of CNC private sector members and the largest overall group if public sector representatives are not regarded as a single constituency group. The potential influence of the accounting profession group on the CNC process and its outcomes needs to be considered both from the viewpoint of the profession as such and from the viewpoint of its representatives. The ability or need of the profession to exert a coordinated influence is affected by the institutional structure of the French accounting profession, divided along functional lines into its two constituent bodies, the OEC for registered public accountants and the CNCC for statutory auditors. Although the two bodies have largely overlapping memberships, each is constituted under different laws and regulations, each is subject to the supervision of different Ministries, namely Finance and Justice respectively, and each in turn is required to supervise the professional conduct of its members discharging different legal responsibilities. The effect of these differing institutional responsibilities is to limit the possibility of the two arms of the profession maintaining a common viewpoint on all issues regarding CNC process or accounting standardisation.

A further aspect of potential institutional influence by the accounting profession concerns its relationship with the state. In addition to ministerial supervisory arrangements for the two professional bodies, their chief executive officers are ordinarily career civil servants who revert to a government ministry on completion of term of office. In a sense, these bodies can be regarded as part of the overall organisation by the state of a structure and process for oversight of the private sector. These factors ensure that both bodies are well aware of state policy and the general accumulation of values and attitudes of the civil service toward their mission and competence, even if at times differences emerge between priorities of their members and those of the state and its civil servants. The accounting profession has not sought to control the process of accounting standardisation in France, but instead has contributed through the CNC process to development and application of the PCG within the framework established by the state. In summary, the institutions of the French accounting profession have no direct control or influence over accounting standardisation independently of the CNC, nor in any sustained way have they adopted independent public positions on the objectives or process of standardisation.

In moving from consideration of influence by the professional institutions on the CNC process to influence by professional representatives, attention needs to be paid to the context of their involvement. Accounting profession representatives might alternatively be regarded as an economic interest group, having to balance the demands of their professional institutions, individual accounting firms and clients. Given the economic structure of public accounting and auditing firms, in which chargeable hours drive income, there is a direct opportunity cost to members of the profession from involvement in CNC activity, at all times on a voluntaristic basis. These factors could be expected to affect adversely the practical possibility of participation in CNC commissions and arriving at sustainable common ground on issues relating to the CNC process and its outcomes. Data in Table 1.7 showed representatives of the accounting profession having a lower overall rate of appointment to standing commissions than any other major constituent group. This is even more pronounced in the case of statutory auditors. Viewed another way, the 17 CNC accounting profession memberships accounted for 18% of the 96 members other than CNC officers, but their 10 standing commission appointments accounted for only 11% of the 92 appointments held by those 96 members.

The role of accounting profession representatives in the CNC contrasts with that of enterprise chief accountants, who by definition employ accounting skills at high levels of organisational responsibility but are not members of the accounting profession.[11] By contrast with their professional counterparts, enterprise chief accountants are not subject to direct opportunity costs, while involvement in CNC activities may offer valuable opportunities to defend the interests of their enterprise or its industry in accounting policy issues. The high level of involvement in the CNC process of this constituency, habitually drawn from large companies, is shown by the appointment of all 6 CNC members in 1992 to commissions, including two double appointments and one as management accounting commission president. Their authority stems from the experience and situation of their own company and its context, as shown by their pattern of appointment to commissions, with four to the consolidated accounts commission, three to management accounting, one to financial instruments, but none to the small and medium enterprises commission.

Civil servants representing specific government agencies make up the other major group of CNC members. Their diverse responsibilities render improbable a coordinated and constant view toward accounting standardisation operating across all the agencies concerned. Instead, it can be expected that public sector representatives seek to maximise outcomes consistent with the policies and priorities of their particular agency. In doing so, their roles are supported by laws and decrees relevant to that agency which they are bound to uphold. In some respects, the CNC presents a structure in which the generalised interest that members of the accounting profession may have in accounting doctrine is matched against the interests of the state. In this dialectic, the comparative advantage of professional accountants and auditors in understanding accounting doctrine and its application at the level of the enterprise has to contend with a public sector focus on the interests and maintenance of authority of the agencies represented, possibly supported by shared values about the role of the state.

Analysis of the CNC structure and composition, and the role and record of the state in its selection of bodies to be represented, together with their relative representation, confirm that the CNC is structured and operates consistently with the Versailles syndrome. That is to say, the state has conferred representation on a broad range of constituencies within and outside the public sector as a means for binding disparate groups into a consultative process on accounting standardisation. It has exercised its authority by varying the composition of representation significantly over time. The private and non-government sector, anxious to be represented, has repeatedly sought and achieved expanded representation, even at the risk of the cumulative effect diminishing the capacity of the CNC to manage the process. The accounting standardisation process has operated to reinforce the state interests of Colbertist accounting rather than according primacy to market needs for commercial accounting. Consistent with this, professional accountants have had a voice in the CNC process but, at least prior to the 1996 reform, little actual influence on its outcomes.

FRENCH ACCOUNTING STANDARDISATION: A SOCIOHISTORICAL PERSPECTIVE

To examine more closely the operation of the French approach to accounting standardisation and its outcomes, we present a sociohistorical perspective of relationships between the state, accounting profession and enterprises in this regard. Our examination falls into two principal periods, from the Second World War to the first OPEC oil-price shock (1946–1973), generally referred to in France as the 'Thirty Glorious Years', and the period from then until the present, which we refer to as 'Crises of Globalisation'. Each case is further divided into two sub-periods. A summary diagram of relationships and interest groups is shown for each period and sub-period, with principal interest groups of the time highlighted in bold and indirect relationships denoted by dotted lines.

Thirty Glorious Years: National planning and accounting standardisation

The period 1946–1975 in France is seen as one of thirty glorious years of economic, social and political change (Fourastié, 1979). For present purposes, it is appropriate to divide it into two sub-periods, 1946–1957 and 1958–1973. The year 1957, which saw the adoption of the revised PCG and the inauguration of the European Economic Community, may be regarded as marking the end of post-war economic reconstruction.

1946–1957: Post-war reconstruction

From 1946 to 1957, France was absorbed with reconstruction. Its reduced post-war condition was reflected in a rundown infrastructure and skill deficiencies, with accounting skills a prime example. The state alone had the authority and means to undertake sweeping economic and social reconstruction. In taking initiatives in economic affairs, as in accounting standardisation, to deal with the situation, it was accordingly in a sense required to act in its *dirigiste* tradition.

Centralised planning, as the chosen organisational instrument, was to be flexible and indicative, not rigid and authoritarian as in the Soviet bloc. In other words, the state did not wish to coerce but rather persuade through consensus. It sought to show, not impose, the path of development. There would be regulatory and fiscal incentives through tax relief measures, preferential interest rates, public purchasing and grants. Although it is difficult to establish precise links between French national economic planning and accounting standardisation, their concurrent emergence reflected a common parentage in dominant ideas and aspirations present in the post-war political atmosphere (Fourquet, 1980).

National planning arrangements were established in 1946 (Bauchet, 1962) with the Commissariat Général du Plan (CGP), supervised by an Interministerial Committee and operating through its modernisation commissions. Their composition included civil servants but with the majority of members drawn from the professions, trade unions and independent expertise. In assembling diverse viewpoints related to a given economic sector, the objective was to build consensus on the economic development outlook and facilitate implementation of a plan which nevertheless would only be indicative. The same principle applied to the 1946 Commission de Normalisation des Comptabilités (1946 Comm) and the 1947 and 1950 Conseil Supérieur de la Comptabilité (CSC). Trade union representation in the 1946 Comm and enlarged 1950 CSC, as well as the CGP modernisation committees, reflected an ideological stance accepted by the state and articulated in terms of large national themes rather than concern for the microeconomic operation of a capitalist economy. This is made clear from a 1949 conference of the Conseil Economique, another state-established consultative body for bringing together diverse interest groups to reflect on and express opinions regarding national economic policy direction (Lutfalla, 1950). The conference considered the merits of a national accounting code and of proceeding further with application of the 1947 PCG. Votes on three resolutions were taken, classified by interest groups as shown in Table 1.9. The first two expressed opposition to mandatory imposition of the PCG until specific, and possibly unattainable, preconditions were met; the third supported adoption of a general law for application of the 1947 PCG. As can be seen, voting patterns reveal diametrical opposition of opinion between private sector enterprise overwhelmingly opposed to the PCG and trade union representatives in complete support. Trade union members were also included in the agriculture group and the Groupe de l'Union Française, voting unanimously on all resolutions against delay in implementation of the PCG and in support of a law for its application. Between these extremes, the voting position of interest groups can be interpreted largely in terms of the extent to which groups were dependent on state support of one kind or another. The Groupe de la Pensée Française, which might be regarded as representing an intellectual rather than an economic interest, voted unanimously in support of application of the PCG.12

Although private sector enterprise had its day in these 1949 proceedings of the *Conseil Economique*, its views had little or no effect. An important instance of official disregard of private sector views on the concept and application of a national accounting code is found in the 1949 CSC report setting out proposals for an accounting law (Lauzel, 1949, pp.14–16). The extensive report to the *Conseil Economique* on behalf of its *Commission des Finances, du Crédit et de la Fiscalité* (Lutfalla, 1950) cited support by accounting directors of enterprises and employer organisations but did not refer to the views of private sector enterprise chief executives who, as noted above, expressed opposition to the PCG elsewhere in the same report. The report author, Lutfalla, chief executive of a nationalised insurance company, voted with the majority in all three foregoing resolutions and

Table 1.9. Conseil Economique 1949 voting patterns on affirmation of the 1947 PCG

	YES	NO	TOTAL
No mandatory application of the PCG without meeting preconditions			
Agriculture/crafts/cooperatives	14	27	41
Family associations/handicapped persons	3	5	8
French Thought		6	6
French Union	8	5	13
Nationalised enterprises		3	3
Private sector industrial and commercial enterprise	23	1	24
Trade unionists	1	41	42
Total	49	88	137
Opposition to imposition of PCG on private sector enterprise until accounting standardisation satisfies prescribed conditions			
Agriculture/crafts/cooperatives	14	28	42
Family associations		5	5
French Thought		5	5
French Union		5	13
Nationalised enterprises		3	3
Private sector industrial and commercial enterprise	23	1	24
Trade unionists		41	41
Total	45	88	133
Recommend adoption of a general law for putting into effect accounting standardisation based on the 1947 PCG			
Agriculture/crafts/cooperatives	31	8	39
Family associations/handicapped persons	2	7	9
French Thought	6		6
French Union	6		6
Nationalised enterprises	5		5
Private sector industrial and commercial enterprise	1	22	23
Trade unionists	41		41
Total	92	37	129

was subsequently appointed a member of the 1950 CSC. Illustrating the ability of the state to involve opposed interest groups in its accounting standardisation process and to neutralise the effect of their stance, Waendendries, presenter of one of the two resolutions opposing the PCG and member of the group of private sector enterprise chief executives who voted against the PCG (Lutfalla, 1950, pp.128-137), was also appointed to the 1950 CSC.

The intended role for the 1947 PCG as the capstone of accounting standardisation was conceived as a support to national economic accounting, to be achieved on the basis of enterprise financial information in accordance with relevant statistical concepts in the field of aggregation of economic data (Brunet, 1947, pp.9–13). In organisational terms, the linkage between the PCG and the statistical nature of national economic accounting was reinforced by the 1949 appointment of Closon, Director-General, INSEE, as President of the fledgling CSC.[13] Elaboration of a national economic plan and adoption of steps for its achievement presupposed that the state had available an appropriate statistical and accounting technology. Pursuit of this goal led to development of a mode of national accounting intended to measure macroeconomic aggregates of performance against the national economic plan and to inform direction of state intervention in economic affairs. Notwithstanding this policy emphasis, a macroeconomic orientation for accounting standardisation remained limited in the 1947 and 1957 PCG, for two reasons (Brunet, 1947, p.17). First, delays in modernisation of public sector accounting and in orienting it to national accounting weakened the case for requiring private sector accounting to be oriented in the same direction. Second, shortages of educators and resources for professional education and training in accounting constituted a profound obstacle to the production of adequate accounting skills.

State dominance of accounting standardisation during this period occurred in a vacuum created by the political and, in a sense, moral weakness of employers and the accounting profession. The period of liberation from late 1944 was a difficult one for French employers (Ehrmann, 1959). Their new representative organisation, the *Conseil National du Patronat Français* (CNPF), established in 1946, was little consulted on national economic planning and even less on accounting standardisation. The case of the accounting profession was not greatly different, with the *Ordre des Experts Comptables* (OEC), reestablished by Edict 45–2138, 19/9/1945, given no specific authority in that regard either. As a body with a small membership, OEC was at that stage seen but not heard.

In summary, between 1946 and 1957 the state dominated accounting standardisation through a limited number of ministries and agencies. Figure 1.1 summarises the structure of French accounting standardisation in this period and the principal parties involved. The effect was to establish a distinctive French approach to accounting standardisation with four particular characteristics. First, the state determined the institutional structure for standardisation and controlled its operation. Second, standardisation outcomes in the 1947 and 1957 PCG, each with

Figure 1.1 French accounting standardisation process, 1946-1957

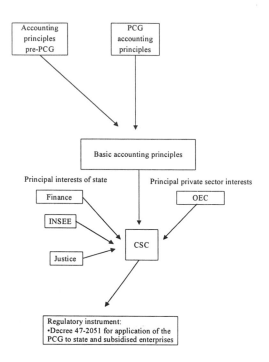

sections on financial and management accounting, were intended to meet the needs of a mix of economic and social actors, both external and internal to the enterprise. Third, the institutional arrangement adopted was intended to involve all parties likely to be concerned with accounting issues and to obtain their agreement on outcomes, thereby conferring a consensual appearance to the process. Fourth, it was not necessary nor intended to adopt coercive measures to put accounting standardisation into operation (CNC, 1965 [PCG 1957], Introduction). Accordingly, the 1947 PCG had no higher legal status than as an attachment to a Ministerial Order, though the state also invoked various regulations to give effect to the PCG.

1958–1973: Modernisation and opening out - reinforcement. of the French approach to accounting standardisation

From the commencement of the Fifth Republic in 1958 to the 1973 oil crisis, the French economy underwent decisive transformation. Gross domestic product growth averaged 5.5% compared with 4.6% in the preceding years of the 1950s. Exports, hitherto neglected, became an essential motor of growth and the manufacturing sector developed strongly relative to the primary and tertiary sectors. By the end of the period, France was a modern nation, achieved as much by political as economic choice. Founding of the European Community, the 1968 Customs Union of its six founding Member States, and the 1973 EC accession of Denmark, Ireland and UK were events and influences further stimulating growth and modernisation. Throughout, the state continued its *dirigiste* stance but adapted its modes of intervention and notably of planning.

For as long as France remained a relatively closed economy, economic prediction and planning were easier. Once it became an open, industrialised economy, these turned out to be more difficult and the national economic plan less satisfactorily conformed to its intended role as guardian against misfortune (Massé, 1967). Moreover, with private enterprise reasserting itself as a decisive element of the economic system, the plan had to meet the test of decision usefulness at the trade and industry sector level and for individual enterprises.

The economic plan changed from being an instrument of *dirigisme* to providing a scenario for future directions. Nevertheless, the *Commissariat Général du Plan* (CGP) and national economic planning remained as a web of diverse interests and an adjunct or even alternative to market forces (Asselain, 1995, p.98), even if the designated economic and social partners took increasing liberty in responding to the principal directions of the plan. The CNPF gave vent to a new wind of economic liberalism with its 1965 publication of a liberal charter in response to Gaullist projects for corporatist association between capital and labour. Nevertheless, the linkage between accounting standardisation and state interests, which might have been expected to weaken, if anything strengthened.

The 1950 CSC of 59 members was replaced by the 1957 CNC, having a slightly expanded membership of 66 (Tables 1.2 and 1.3). Public sector involvement reduced to 19 or 29% and private and non-government sector membership increased to 47 or 71% following increased enterprise accountant representation and additional recognition of quasi-professional bodies and persons of standing. Representation for the accounting profession and various economic interest groups reflected their growing economic significance. Even so, the hold of the state on accounting standardisation remained firm. CNC membership size and spread meant that it operated as an assembly, emphasised by the 1971 expansion of both membership sectors, further diluting effective possibilities of private sector influence on accounting standardisation. In the same period, the state took two major steps to expand the application of the 1957 revised PCG. First, Law 59–1472, 28/12/1959, and associated Decree 62–470, 13/4/1962, set out a procedure for adaptation of the 1957 PCG to meet the needs of particular activity sectors, resulting subsequently in 77 approved sector adaptations (Standish, 1997, pp.157–158 and p.228). Second, Decree 65–968, 28/10/1965, established a firm linkage between enterprise accounts kept for commercial purposes and tax compliance, by prescribing tax declaration schedules in conformity with the PCG and the broad requirement that valuation rules and accounting entries for PCG purposes correspond to the tax code (Standish, 1997, Ch.3.4). This change for the first time inserted the tax administration, the *Direction Générale des Impôts* (DGI), directly into the CNC process, in contrast to its previous non-involvement and reliance on alternative requirements and procedures regarding enterprise tax compliance. Its involvement was matched by a strengthened interest on the part of private enterprise constituencies, especially the CNPF, with private sector preferences and fears related to tax treatment now extended to the PCG as an implied instrument of tax compliance.

Other significant developments were the establishment of the national securities commission, the *Commission des Opérations de Bourse* (COB) and the national institute of statutory auditors, the *Compagnie Nationale des Commissaires aux Comptes* (CNCC), both destined to assume greater future importance in regard to financial reporting by listed companies and their attitudes toward accounting standardisation. Finally, the stakes associated with the CNC process and its outcomes were further heightened with the development of the *Banque de France* agency for monitoring company financial performance on the basis of standardised financial analysis concepts applied to annual accounts prepared in accordance with the PCG (Centrale de bilans, 1980; Ternisien, 1992). The effect of these changes in representation and influence is shown in Figure 1.2.

Crises and Globalisation: Effects of foreign influences on accounting standardisation

The 1973 OPEC oil price shock signalled a new period for the French economy and other advanced capitalist economies, marked by political and economic difficulties and uncertainties. Following Cohen (1996), the period is divided into two sub-periods, 1974–1983 and 1984 to the present.

1974–1983: Economic fluctuations and the apogee of French-style accounting standardisation

Following the OPEC oil price shock, French industrial output fell for the first time since 1945, with a succeeding pattern developed of alternation between recovery and stagnation. Moreover, recovery periods were not as strong as in other leading economies, such as the USA, Germany or Japan. These growth rate fluctuations were accompanied by destabilising factors which proved difficult to master. Inflation was high until 1983, unemployment grew and the franc exchange rate was at times volatile. Faced with these difficulties, national economic planning came to lose any real meaning and the state intervened in a more indiscriminate way. Under President Giscard d'Estaing, 1974–81, and policies of liberalism, national economic planning was pushed to one side.

Figure 1.2 French accounting standardisation process, 1958 - 1973

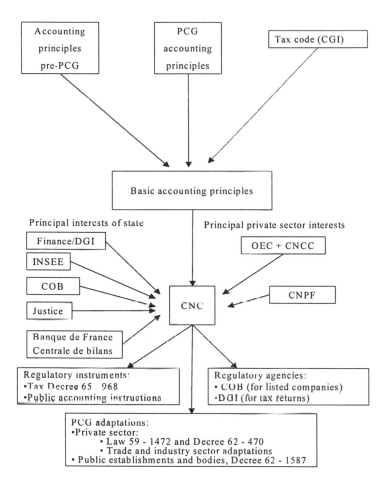

With the 1981 arrival of the socialists in power, the VIIIth National Economic Plan for the period 1981–85 was abandoned and the concept of a plan as a quantified framework for national economic development shelved. With the XIth Plan for 1984–88, objectives were specified only in terms of comparison with economic performance of other industrialised countries. In place of formalised national economic planning, the 1981–82 nationalisation of major company groups by the socialist government forcefully asserted its view and the role of the Colbertist state as entrepreneur (Barreau, 1990), creating a pattern of high-profile intervention in economic affairs without the underpinning of a purposive framework.

With French-style accounting standardisation detached from national economic planning, a new *raison d'être* was needed. This emerged as a consequence of the Fourth Directive for harmonisation of financial reporting requirements in the EC Member States. In France, the Directive was adopted through revision of the 1957 PCG, still in effect, and Law 83–353, 30/4/1983, often referred to as the accounting law (de Kerviler, 1986), to amend accounting requirements of the Commercial Code applicable to registered enterprises (incorporated or otherwise). The accounting law reflected via the Fourth Directive certain influences from the English-speaking world, notably the requirement that annual accounts be true and fair (Pérochon, 1981). In addition, the 1982 PCG reinforced the macroeconomic orientation of preceding versions, with retention of the earlier requirement for classification of charges in the accounts of individual enterprises by nature or origin, and the introduction of a structure to the profit and loss account intended to facilitate calculation of central elements of national accounting, notably value added and gross operating profit or loss. Whereas the newly-imported criterion of true and fair seemed of uncertain significance (de Kerviler and Standish, 1992), the influence of national accounting had increased. This latter development reflected the influence on the CNC of a member group of economic statisticians, experts in national accounting, financial analysts and accounting educators, interested in relating standardised enterprise accounting performance data to macroeconomic considerations (Richard, 1996, p.121).

The emergence of accounting law has to an extent marked a change in spirit of the French approach to accounting standardisation, giving it a coercive character that it did not initially possess. As with national economic planning, the PCG was intended to reflect a general consensus, without the need for a detailed regulatory framework but at the same time responsive to demands from the state. The socioeconomic actors involved in its elaboration would be guarantors for its interpretation and application in good faith, as remarked by the then CNC President (Dupont, 1981). The incorporation of elements of the PCG into regulations and statutory law, themselves unsatisfactorily ranked in order of authority, means that judicial interpretation has entered into questions of legal application of accounting rules. On one view, the 1983 accounting law instituted an embryonic accounting code, to rank with other French legal codes such as the *Code Civil* or *Code de Travail*. The risk from legal codification, however, is of a lack of conceptual and operational adaptability, seen for instance in the difficulty for the legislator in dealing with accounting for financial instruments and developments in international accounting standards.

As regards evolution of the standardisation process in the period, the only significant developments were the superimposition of the Fourth Directive as the ultimate authority for financial reporting by commercial enterprises and the inclusion of accounting principles in the Commercial Code. Otherwise, Figure 1.2 above would need little modification. Standardisation remained largely shielded from external influences, especially given that Member State options in the Fourth

Directive largely enabled France to retain core elements of the PCG. Even the addition of the true and fair override seems in retrospect little more than symbolic, given its uncertain significance in French law.

1984 onwards: Globalisation and putting French-style accounting standardisation to the test

Since 1984, economic liberalism has strengthened, albeit as a highly contested issue. Nationalisation of major enterprises by the socialist government in 1981–82 has been largely reversed by successive rounds of privatisation in 1986–88, 1993–96 and somewhat unexpectedly in 1997 since the return of the socialists to power. In the same period, French securities markets have experienced unprecedented development in traded volume and range of securities. Nevertheless, French-style accounting standardisation and its institutional framework have made increasingly heavy weather of the emerging context of privatisation, deregulation and globalisation. Forceful demands for new or improved financial information associated with national and international securities markets express the concerns of the professional investor. For France, with its tradition of a state-dominated economy, a large small and medium enterprise sector and banks as major providers of risk finance, the accounting standardisation process had previously given scant regard to information needs of securities markets. More fundamentally, the French state had paid little attention to the significance of securities markets as mechanisms for encouraging equity investment in a society famed for its *rentier* approach to saving and investment, with interest-bearing securities regarded as sensible and equity investment as (foolishly) speculative (Zeldin, 1979, 58–62).

Prior to this period, French economic development was financed to a significant extent by the state directly through grants and debt instruments. This has been characterised as capitalism without capital (*capitalisme sans capitaux*), with the French Treasury pursuing a policy of administered investment financing through a constellation of financial intermediaries, many of them state-owned banks and lending funds (Cohen, 1996, 258–259). This policy and practice explain the disinterest of the French state in accountability as understood in globalised international securities markets and conceptions of corporate governance. Given that the state was bypassing securities markets through its financing practices, it had no particular need for consolidated accounts or equity accounting. To the disinterest of the state in consolidated accounts was added private sector antipathy. In France, the historical anxiety of owners of property, whether real or financial, toward the state, borne of unhappy experiences of expropriation and harsh taxation, has been reflected in the premium attached to secrecy of commercial affairs, the very quality that consolidation of accounts and pressures for greater transparency in financial reporting are intended to restrict. In short, prior to the necessary adoption of the Seventh Directive by Law 85–11, 3/1/1985, and the 1986 PCG amendment for the same purpose, the only significant voices in France for production and use of consolidated accounts were the limited number of French companies with securities listed on foreign exchanges and the COB. When the change came, it did so in a compromised fashion, with one set of accounting rules applicable to accounts of the individual enterprise and another for consolidated accounts allowing optional use of specified accounting methods found in international accounting standards but not otherwise permissible in France (Standish, 1997, Chs.3.2 and 5.2.2).

The retarded interest in market-driven financial accounting was unhelpful for French groups needing to obtain finance by issuing securities in foreign markets, discovering in the process that French accounting standards were inadequate in that context given their failure to incorporate conceptual and technical developments in accounting for equity and debt structures, a wider range of asset categories, exceptional components of profits and losses, and cash flows. Market benchmarks have either been US FASB standards for US-listed major French groups or IASC standards, with the latter increasingly promulgated by the French professional member bodies, the OEC and CNCC, as well as by the Big–N firms. In this context, the COB, necessarily concerned at the difficulties posed for French groups by conflicting international accounting standards, has grown in importance as an actor in accounting standardisation, with added leverage from its IOSCO membership. Moreover, in the private sector, attitudes toward international influences have been changing. Although Table 1.1 shows stock exchange principal market listings falling each year since 1991, the mandatory requirement for consolidation accounting has concentrated attention on international methods and practices, as has growing cross-border merger and acquisition investment activity involving French companies and investors.[14]

The changed pattern of influences on accounting standardisation to emerge in this period is shown in Figure 1.3: for the first time, major foreign influences appear as elements of globalisation, namely IOSCO, IASC and Big–N firms. Among public sector interests, INSEE and the *Banque de France Centrale de Bilans* have become less important. In the private sector, the accounting profession and French multinationals have become far more important. Nevertheless, the central interests of state retain full authority for outcomes from accounting standardisation. To the long-standing interest of the Finance Ministry and DGI needs to be added the Justice Ministry, given the increased regulatory specification of French accounting standards. In the case of the DGI, INSEE and *Banque de France Centrale de Bilans*, it can also be said that their role, having achieved their central objectives for accounting standardisation, need be no more than general oversight of its continuing process.

Faced with these new and insistent influences, the French process for accounting standardisation, conceived in a spirit of *dirigisme*, has been found inadequately responsive and struggling to bring sufficient technical capacity to bear on development of standards. The resulting frustrations provoked the first serious questioning since 1946 of the institutional arrangement in place, leading to the 1996 major reform initiated by Decree 96–749, 26/8/1996.

The key elements of this reform are, first, reconstruction of CNC membership and reduction from 103 to 58 members, with elimination of various previously

Figure 1.3 *French accounting standardisation process, 1985 - 1997*

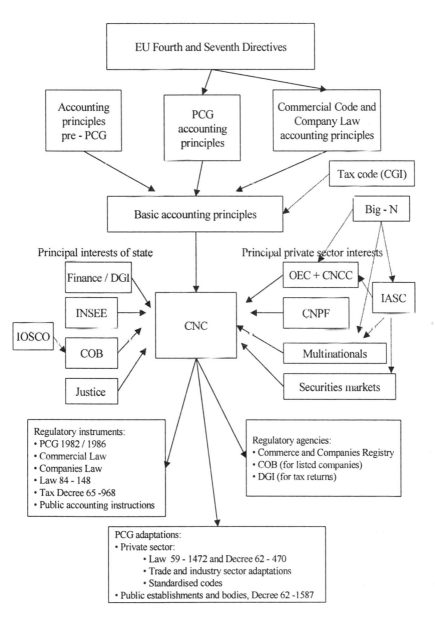

represented public sector agencies and private sector interests, and recognition of previously unrepresented interests; and second, establishment of the Urgent Issues Committee, *Comité d'Urgence* (CU), to expedite consideration of accounting issues. In addition, the government has proposed establishment of the Accounting Regulation Committee, *Comité de Réglementation Comptable* (CRC), to clarify and expedite adoption of accounting standards by regulation. CU and CRC membership composition is shown in Table 1.10.

The reform objective is to render the French accounting standardisation system more effective and to enable it to react more readily to foreign, especially US FASB and IASC, standards. The CNC retains the role of providing recommendations and rulings on accounting issues, with neither CU or CRC having the authority to initiate standardisation. Both the latter have more limited membership than the 1947 CSC and to that extent run counter to the general conformity with the Versailles syndrome of French arrangements for accounting standardisation. Interpretation of the motivation for reform and of the significance of the CU and CRC and their relationship to the CNC can only be conjectural in advance of experience but a number of questions and significant issues arise.

First, the voice of globalisation will be more clearly articulated in the standardisation process in relation to international accounting and auditing standards, and their application to financial reporting for securities markets. This is particularly signified in the person of the CNC President appointed as part of the reform, Barthès de Ruyter, the first non-civil servant in that role, former Big–6 French firm managing partner and former IASC Chairman. Institutionally, these globalisation issues could be expected to receive greater attention by the COB and the accounting profession. Here, though, waters muddy, given that both OEC and CNCC embrace practising firms of all sizes, the smaller of which show little interest in radical change to the PCG and French accounting standardisation outcomes generally and which may find compliance with standards written for international needs burdensome and irrelevant.

Second, the CNC retains a large and diverse membership. The future range of accounting issues for attention has increased, with added responsibilities for accounting applicable to the banking and insurance sector, and to provident and mutual institutions. As resourcing for the CNC and the way in which it attracts and deploys technical staff are unchanged, uncertainty remains about how it will satisfy heightened expectations for its future performance.

Third, though the CU and CRC are intended to expedite the adoption and regulation of accounting standards, both bodies will have a heavy state presence. The CRC composition is remarkable, compared with institutional arrangements for accounting regulation elsewhere. Whilst in practice the Finance, Justice and Budget Ministers will delegate detailed consideration and approval of accounting regulation, the fact of their specification raises, and is meant to raise, the level of state involvement in the process. Representation for the first time of the *Conseil d'Etat* and *Cour de Cassation* underscores increasing legalisation of the process

Table 1.10 Membership, Comité de Réglementation Comptable and Comité d'Urgence

	CRC	CU
State:		
President: Minister for the Economy or representative	1	1
Vice-President: Justice Minister or representative	1	1
Budget Minister or representative	1	1
Member, *Conseil d'Etat*	1	
Councillor, *Cour de Cassation*	1	
COB President or representative	1	1
CNC President	1	1
CNC Vice-President – Director of Public Accounting		1
Total government ministries, councils, agencies	7	6
Private sector and non-government:		
OEC President or representative	1	1
CNCC President or representative	1	1
Enterprise representatives appointed by the Minister for the Economy	3	
Representative, *Cour des Comptes*	1	
Trade union representatives	2	
CNC Vice Presidents:		
Enterprise representatives		2
Mutual associations representative		1
Total private sector and non-government	8	5
Total	15	11

and its outcomes. Contrasting with the apparent formalisation of the process for converting CNC standards into regulation, with the majority of CRC members *ex officio*, is the inclusion of trade union representation. As trade unions are significantly represented in the CNC (Table 1.4), is this merely tokenism or does it portend politicisation of the role of the CRC? Representation of the *Conseil d'Etat, Cour de Cassation, Cour des Comptes*, and trade unions were added by amendments to the original proposed CRC during passage of the legislation. An amendment to include the Governor of the *Banque de France*, or representative, was also proposed but not accepted.[15] These may be both a foretaste and repeat of previous CNC membership expansion as the Versailles syndrome reasserts itself.

The significance and intention of the reforms are difficult to interpret. They have been seen as strengthening the role of the accounting profession and private sector enterprise. The profession, rather to one side in the previous standardisation process that consisted largely of dialogue between a strong state and employer organisations, may have gained new influence from its ability to use the emerging power structures of international accounting standardisation (Jönsson, 1991, p.542). On the other hand, state control over the process and its outcomes has been further strengthened through superimposition of the CRC which the state dominates and which will effectively act as gatekeeper for admission of standards. In addition, inclusion in the reformed CNC composition of representation for the *Commission de Contrôle des Institutions de Prévoyance et des Mutuelles* indicates an intention to extend accounting standardisation and regulation more firmly to the *mutualité* sector, the core of ideas and practice of social solidarity, until now rather on the margins of accounting standardisation.

CONTRADICTIONS, DILEMMAS AND WAYS AHEAD

In this chapter, we have argued that the French approach to accounting standardisation reflects a more general concern by the state, grounded in long historical experience, to establish and manage relationships and institutional arrangements linking interests of the state and the citizenry. It has felt impelled to construct a regime for financial accounting that could serve its needs, initially for statistical surveillance of private enterprise performance and subsequently for financial information compatible with income tax concepts and compliance arrangements. Private sector interests, at a low ebb of effectiveness immediately after the war, accepted these state initiatives with more or less good grace. To palliate their anxieties over where the process might lead and what form its outcomes might take, the state has involved a wide range of interests in an institutional arrangement that exhibits the Versailles syndrome of inclusion but until now little effective influence.

The sociopolitical relationships pertinent to accounting standardisation that had evolved relatively slowly over a 50–year period without major disruptions since the war have more recently been greatly perturbed by globalisation, national deregulation and competition between national and international accounting standards. The nature and evolution of arrangements have been more particularly examined in relation to two major periods from 1946 to the present. Each time span has been associated with a certain configuration of relationships between interests of the state, the accounting profession and the private and non-government sector, expressing the role, composition and functioning of the accounting standardisation process and organisation. During the first major period, the state was dominant, directing the objectives and structure of the process to serve its interests as organiser of the national economic life and tax collector. During the following major period, the effective weight that the state could bring to bear has tended to diminish, whilst that of the accounting profession and enterprises, particularly of French multinationals, has grown, as further confirmed by the 1996 reform.

More recently, manifestations of globalisation have been knocking with increasing insistence at the French door. These are seen, rightly or wrongly, as a direct challenge to deeply held French views about the nature of the state and its relationships with the citizenry and, more particularly in this arena, to the rationale for the French national accounting code. When originally adopted, it appeared a simple and elegant way to deal with pressing problems of social and economic reconstruction. Moreover, it came with an acceptable intellectual provenance (Standish, 1990). But times change and the accounting standardisation process has manifestly been struggling to keep the PCG abreast of needs and events. There is no reason in principle why France should not adopt a standardisation arrangement based more heavily on accounting expertise and with a strong focus on market-driven forces, akin to the US FASB or UK ASB. But this would mean jettisoning many intellectual and emotional attachments and seems unlikely to happen in the foreseeable future.

This analysis is necessarily simplified. It does not fully take into account the diversity of political, social and economic interests affected by accounting standardisation. Neither the state, nor enterprises, nor the accounting profession constitute homogeneous parties of interest. The constituent state agencies have divergent interests. Within the business sector, accounting issues frequently divide large enterprises concerned with international financing and securities markets from the small and medium enterprise sector operating only within a local, national or perhaps European context. The accounting profession itself reveals a number of cleavages: *experts-comptables* and statutory auditors, international (especially Big–N) and indigenous French firms, large and smaller firms, partners of firms and salaried professionals. The analysis does not fully deal with timing differences between economic and social evolution in France and those of changes to the French system of accounting standardisation. Nor have we fully unmasked the strategies and tactics of delay or acceleration applied to those changes by the principal actors, especially the state.

Thus it is possible, contrary to the appearance of the 1996 reform, that the state has not renounced or relaxed its influence over accounting standardisation. Instead, it may have decided rather to influence it in a different manner, participating directly as in the past in CNC activities but indirectly through the CRC where it can exercise a right of veto by declining to transform CNC rulings into regulations, even where strongly favoured by the accounting profession or major enterprises. In short, it would be premature to conclude beyond doubt the termination of an historical period inaugurated in 1673 by the Edict of Colbert and its famous related *Code Savary*, which marked the beginning of state intervention in accounting matters. Nor could it be confidently concluded that the Minister for the Economy, signatory to the 1996 decree for CNC reform and ministerial descendent of Colbert, has brought Colbertist accounting to an end or dismantled the Versailles syndrome as applied to accounting standardisation. Had he done so, we would be speaking not of reform but truly of revolution.

NOTES

[1] International comparisons of levels of public sector employment are difficult due to differences in institutional arrangements and employment conditions. Nevertheless, a 1997 report estimates public administration employment in France at 25% of total employment, compared with 16% in Germany (*Perspectives économiques no.53*, Le Figaro).

[2] As noted by many commentators from Colbert and de Tocqueville onwards (Fukuyama, 1995, Ch.11).

[3] There have been many calls in recent years within France to address these issues, a recent example being recommendations by Paris Europlace, an organisation of leading French companies (*Financial Times*, 25/2/1998, p.2).

[4] The number of PCG prescribed accounts has increased in successive versions. In addition, the 1982 PCG was expanded by the 1986 section to deal with consolidated accounts (Standish, 1997, Ch.2).

[5] Miller, 1990, sees Colbertist accounting as linked to a vast programme of government by inquiry. Whilst this is plausible, he presents no evidence to show that the state directly linked its administrative practices in any way to the accounting requirements of the *Ordonnance*.

[6] Never officially approved or adopted.

[7] Continuing this tradition, a later Director of INTEC produced the leading textbook concerning the 1982 PCG (Pérochon, 1983).

[8] Data sources for Table 1.3 and following tables on CSC/CNC membership are as follows:

[9] 1947: Decree 47–188, 16/1/1947, *Journal Officiel* (JO), 18/1/1947, 753; Ministerial Order, 21/3/1947, JO, 22/3/1947, 2712.

[10] 1950: Decree 50–409, 31/3/1950, JO, 6/4/1947, 3730–1.

[11] 1957: Decree 57–129, 7/2/1957, JO, 8/2/1957, 1575.

[12] 1971: Ministerial Order, 29/11/1971, CNC *Etudes et documents 1958–1974*, 194, 196.

[13] 1992: Ministerial Order, 10/7/1992, CNC *Rapport d'activité 1992*, 101–104.

[14] 1996: Decree 96–749, 26/8/1996, JO, 27/8/1996, 12840–1; Ministerial Order, 26/8/1996, JO, 12857; Ministerial Order, 28/8/1996, JO, 12935; Ministerial Order, 7/10/1996, JO, 15059.

[15] A notable example was the inclusion in the 1947 CSC, but not in the prior 1946 *Commission*, of Caujolle, first President of the OEC at the time of its establishment in 1942 by the Vichy Government.

[16] The difference between Tables 1.3 and 1.4 regarding the 1950 CSC membership and affiliation classification results from 3 non-government members being attached at that time to state bodies.

[17] Membership of OEC and CNCC is restricted in both cases to persons in public practice. There are no recognised professional institutions in France for accountants in commerce and industry.

[18] Including Caujolle, first OEC President in 1942 and 1947 CSC member.

[19] In addressing the occasion to mark the 50th anniversary of the PCG/CNC, Closon referred to the fundamental importance at the time of bringing CNC and INSEE together in this way (CNC, 1997).

[20] As is indicated by coverage of the subject from an international viewpoint in the leading French accounting commentaries, eg. Raffegeau *et al.* (1996).

[21] *Assemblée Nationale*, 15/1/1997, Item no.3049, Amendment no.2.

REFERENCES

Albert, M. (1991). *Capitalisme contre capitalisme*. Paris: Seuil.

Asselain, J-C (1995). *Histoire économique du XXème siècle: la réouverture des économies nationales (1939 aux années 1980)*. Paris: Presses de Sciences Po et Dalloz.

Barreau, J., ed. (1990). *L'Etat Entrepreneur: Nationalisations, gestion du secteur public concurrentiel, construction européenne (1982–1993)*. Paris: L'Harmattan.

Bauchet, P. (1962). *La Planification Française*. Paris: Seuil.

Bendix, R. (1978). *Kings or People: Power and the Mandate to Rule*. Berkeley: University of California Press.

Bérard, V., and Y. Lemarchand (1994). *Le Miroir du Marchand*. Paris: Editions Comptables Malesherbes.

Bernard, Y., and J-C. Colli (1984). *Dictionnaire économique et financier*. Paris: Seuil.

Bourgeois, L. (1896). *La Solidarité*.

Brunet, A. (1947). *Rapport général, présenté au nom de la Commission de Normalisation des Comptabilités*. Paris: Imprimerie Nationale.

Brunet, A. (1951). *La Normalisation comptable au service de l'entreprise, de la science et de la nation*. Paris: Dunod.

Centrale de bilans: Service de l'information (1980). *Les ratios de la Centrale de Bilans de la Banque de France*. Note d'information n° 43.

Cohen, E. (1996). *La Tentation hexagonale: la souveraineté à l'épreuve de la mondialisation*. Paris: Fayard.

Conseil national de la comptabilité (1965). *Plan comptable général* (1957 PCG). Paris: Conseil national de la comptabilité.

Conseil national de la comptabilité (1986). *Plan comptable général*. Paris: Conseil national de la comptabilité.

Dupont, J. (1981). Sens et portée d'une révision, *Analyse financière*, 1 er trimestre, pp. 3–8.

Ehrmann, H. (1959). *La politique du patronat français 1936–1955*. Paris: Armand Colin.

Forrester, V. (1996). *L'Horreur économique*. Paris: Fayard.

Fourastié, J. (1943). *La Comptabilité*. Paris: Presses Universitaires de France.

Fourastié, J. (1945). *Comptabilité générale conforme au Plan comptable général*. Paris: Librairie Générale de Droit et de Jurisprudence.

Fourastié, J. (1979). *Les Trente glorieuses*. Paris: Arthème Fayard.

Fourquet, F. (1980) *Les Comptes de la Puissance*. Paris: Encres.

Fukuyama, F. (1995). *Trust: The Social Virtues and the Creation of Prosperity*. London: Hamish Hamilton.

Garnier, P. (1947). *La Comptabilité: Algèbre du droit & méthode d'observation des sciences économiques*. Paris: Dunod.

Hayward, J. (1961). The official philosophy of the French Third Republic: Léon Bourgeois and Solidarism, *International Review of Social History*, Vol. 6, pp. 22–25.

Hoffman, S. (1974). *Decline or Renewal? France since the 1930s*. New York: Viking Press.

Jönsson S. (1991). Role making for accounting while the state is watching, *Accounting, Organizations and Society*, Vol. 16, Nos. 5/6, pp. 521–546.

Kerviler de, I. (1986). *Droit comptable (Entreprises)*. Paris: Economica.

Kerviler de, I., and P. Standish (1992). French accounting law: origins, development and scope, in M. Bromwich and A. Hopwood eds., *Accounting and the Law*. London: Prentice Hall in association with The Institute of Chartered Accountants in England and Wales, pp.130-158.

Lauzel, P. (1949). *Propositions du Conseil Supérieur de la Comptabilité relatives à un éventuel projet de loi comptable*. Paris: Ministère des Finances et des Affaires Economiques.

Lutfalla, G. (1950). Rapport présenté au nom du Conseil économique, in Conseil économique, *Mise en application du Plan comptable*. Paris: Presses Universitaires de France.

Maily, J. (1946). *La Normalisation*. Paris: Dunod.

Massé, P. (1967). *Le Plan ou l'anti-hasard*. Paris: Gallimard.

Méline, J. (1905). *Le Retour à la terre et la surproduction Industrielle*.

Miller, P. (1990). On the interrelations between accounting and the state, *Accounting, Organizations and Society*, Vol. 15, No. 4, pp. 315–338.

Pérochon, C. (1981). Présentation générale du nouveau plan comptable, *Analyse financière*, 1er trimestre, pp. 9–26.

Pérochon, C. (1983). *Présentation du Plan comptable français*. Paris: Foucher.

Raffegeau, J., Dufils, P., Lopater, C., and Arfoui, F. (1996). *Comptable 1997*. Paris: Editions Francis Lefebvre.

Richard, J. (1996). *Comptabilités et pratiques comptables*. Paris: Dalloz.

Sautel, G. (1982). *Histoire des institutions publiques depuis la Révolution Française*. Paris: Dalloz.

Schama, S. (1989). *Citizens: A Chronicle of the French Revolution*. London: Viking.

Standish, P. (1990). Origins of the Plan Comptable Général: a study in cultural intrusion and reaction, *Accounting and Business Research*, Autumn, pp. 337–351.

Standish, P. (1997). *The French Plan Comptable*. Paris: Ordre des Experts Comptables, in conjunction with The Institute of Chartered Accountants in England and Wales.

Ternisien, M. (1992). *Lire et Interpréter les Comptes de l'Entreprise*. Paris: Dunod.

Tilly, C. (1984). *Big Structures, Large Processes, Huge Comparisons*. New York: Russell Sage.

Young, J. (1994). Outlining regulatory space: agenda issues and the FASB, *Accounting, Organizations and Society*, Vol. 19, No. 1, pp. 83–109.

Zeldin, T. (1979). *France 1848-1945: Ambition and Love*. Oxford: Oxford University Press.

2

THE STATE OF ACCOUNTING
AND THE STATE OF THE STATE

Apostolos Ballas, Dimosthenis Hevas
and David Neal

INTRODUCTION

This chapter focuses on accounting regulation in Greece, identifies key moments in the development of the state and uses these critical moments to illustrate their impact on shaping policy. The history of Greece that we will concentrate on is the history of the modern state and its responses to the challenges that have faced it both internally and externally. However, it will also be necessary to discuss briefly the nature of the state itself, including the issue of national identity and its relation to individual identity within society. The eventual aim is to observe the characteristics of the Greek accounting system in relation not only to the nature of the state but also to the particular historic circumstance surrounding the development of its rules and regulations on accounting.

The fundamental hypothesis of this chapter is that to understand the 'shape' of the accounting regime we must explore the critical relationship between the history of the state and the outcomes of its rule making system, and the regulatory system that aims to put those rules into practice. This follows a line of thinking developed by Benson (1983), which highlights three levels of structure within a policy making process. These are the *surface structure* that consists of the visible rules and visible administrative structures that underpin those rules, an area of extensive descriptive analysis in the research literature. The second level is that of *interests* built into the policy area. This too has received a significant amount of attention from scholars of accounting from many different viewpoints, ranging from positive accounting theory that concentrates on agency problems to sociological analyses of the role of the accounting profession. The third level of structure is the *deep structure* that 'determines within limits the range of variation of surface levels' (Benson, 1983, p.5). These are the rules of structure formation and it is these that we primarily seek to establish for the Greek state before locating its accounting regime.

It must be emphasised that the relationship between these levels is not simply deterministic but involves a complex dialectical process. In pursuing this search for deep structure the aim is to understand both the status and the potential of Greek accounting regulation by understanding the interrelationship between Greek accounting policy and Greek culture and history. As an example we could cite the case of the inherent conflict in Greek accounting policy between tax accounting and financial reporting for external users. The deep structure of this conflict can be examined in terms of the nature of commercial development in Greece, with the predominance of two key groups in the economic structure. The first is the private family company and the second is that of large-scale state involvement in industry and particularly in banking. There is also a cultural emphasis on both *private* and *family* that extends not only to commercial activity but also to politics. This means that no strong emphasis on accountability to stakeholders or to society (as in the UK and Germany respectively) has developed. In fact, even the seemingly inflexible rules of the tax accounting system are open to negotiation (article 70, L. 2238/94) between the private company or individual and the state, with arbitration by experts such as auditors and other accounting practitioners. To understand how such practices have arisen, we must first explore the formation of the Greek state and the origins of the *state-private* relationship.

THE FORMATION OF THE GREEK STATE

The modern Greek State dates from 1821 and the Greek War of Independence. However, one cannot begin to think about Greece without the glories of its ancient civilisation coming to mind. Many of the vital breakthroughs in our understanding of ourselves and the universe in which we live were developed by the ancient Greeks. The height of ancient Greek civilisation was the city-state of Athens in the sixth and fifth centuries BC. The demise of the city state came from within Greece when first

Philip and then Alexander of Macedonia established control over the whole of Greece, and extended the empire as far as Persia and Egypt. This was the height of Greek power but the empire was unwieldy and short-lived. It was eventually swallowed up by the Romans in the seventy years from 215 to 145 BC. However, the Romans left the Greeks a high degree of autonomy and Greek remained the dominant language of the Eastern Mediterranean for the period of the Roman occupation. The demise of the Roman Empire in the West caused Constantine to establish a new centre in Byzantium (later renamed Constantinople) and, after the fall of Rome in 476 AD, this became the dominant power in the southern and eastern Mediterranean for the next thousand years.

In 1453, Greece (or more precisely the majority of the regions that we now call Greece) became part of the Ottoman Empire when Constantinople fell to the Muslim Turks. During this period, the area became something of a rural backwater. While Turkish rule was occasionally heavy-handed and brutal, it was also sporadic and allowed local chiefs considerable autonomy. The preservation of the Greek identity during this period was also partly through the Orthodox Church which was allowed to continue despite some enforced conversions by the Turks. This was combined with the continued use of the Greek language in the trade of the region and the central importance of Greek officials to the Turks, their influence being exhibited more strongly as Turkish rule became more inefficient and decentralised in the later part of the eighteenth century. Of prime importance at the end of the Ottoman era was the development of a Greek merchant shipping fleet which traded throughout the Mediterranean, a tradition that has continued to the present. These merchants were responsible for providing the material base of the intellectual revival that was such a vital factor in the development of a national consciousness (Clogg, 1992).

The Greek War of Independence began as an insurgence against the Ottoman empire inspired by the internal divisions within that empire. Despite a policy of 'peaceful interference', adopted in order to maintain the delicate balance of power in the Balkans, the Great Powers were drawn into the Battle of Navarino, which destroyed the Turkish Navy. This, when combined with the outbreak of the latest of a string of border wars against the Russians in 1828, made some sort of independent Greece an inevitability. The key problem was 'what sort of independence'?

The Great Powers decided that part of the price for the larger land area granted to the new Greece was for it to become a hereditary monarchy, with the monarch chosen from one of the royal houses outside of the Great Powers, but also not a Greek. It was a measure of the new state's dependence that the Greeks were not a party to the treaty that established Otto, a seventeen year old Bavarian prince who had never been to the country and who only spoke German, as King of the Greeks under a guarantee from the protective powers. Although the monarchy was to be a feature of Greek politics for the next one hundred and fifty years, the 'foreign' influence gradually diminished as successive monarchs became integrated into Greek social life. However, the alliance of the royal house to the other royal families of Western Europe was to remain a strong factor in the position of the ruling elite on key issues.

The determination of the internal nature and structure of the Greek state was an important issue during this time. The major players were now in place, namely an imposed monarchy supported by the major external powers of the time; secondly a small liberal intelligentsia influenced by the latest ideas on democracy developed in Britain and France; and thirdly a commercial elite who, not for the last time, were rebuilding their private and family based businesses after the ravages of war. This third group were to some extent outside of the state system, both physically, since many of the centres of commerce remained outside the boundaries of the new state, and by inclination, partly due to the interaction with the new state and its Bavarian influence, but also based in the history of mistrust and distance from bureaucratic structure which they had built up under Ottoman rule.[1] A fourth group were the former bureaucrats of the Ottoman empire and the professional politicians, who brought with them the system of 'Rouspheti' (gifts and favours), which became a feature of Greek politics - the state then, as now, was the major employer and, to many, the basic purpose of politics was to be able to gain access to state coffers so as to "*dispense patronage to their electoral clienteles and their extended families*" (Clogg, 1992, p.55). A fifth group were the independent clans of the mountains who characterise the difficulty of governing such a diverse state as Greece and again illustrate the tension between state and private control. The sixth and last group was external to Greece but were no less important in the shaping of the nation. These were the financiers that held sovereign debt, mainly in London. During the war of independence, Greece had contracted loans mostly on disadvantageous terms and these were extended in 1832 to pay for the army (again a recurrent theme) and the monarchy as well as servicing the original debt. These were to place severe strains on the economy and the ambitions of the Greek state. The influence of these loans and the likely use of taxes to repay them were partially responsible for a business class concentrating on offshore activity, an enduring feature of Greek life.

These groupings and characteristics are the foundations of the Greek state even today. Despite a liberal constitution ceded by Otto in 1847, "*problems arose from the grafting of the forms of western constitutionalism, which had evolved over centuries in societies with a very different historical experience, onto a traditional society, whose values had been critically influenced by the centuries of Ottoman rule and differed significantly from those prevailing in the industrialised societies of western Europe*" (Clogg, 1992, p.53). Even the demise of Otto in 1862, when he was forced to abdicate, left little unchanged since the Great Powers simply replaced him with a Danish prince, who although not the candidate chosen by the Greeks, became George I of the Hellenes. He was to rule for 50 years during which time the now familiar tensions of Greek politics were played out.

The advent of World War One saw Greece take the path of neutrality after bitter internal divisions, particularly between the political leadership and the monarchy. In 1917, however, the Greeks entered the war in Macedonia on the side of the British and French. At the end of the war, Greece was granted occupation rights over parts of Eastern Thrace and Asia Minor. But this did not contain Greek ambition and, due to a combination of opportunity and threat offered by the new Turkish nationalist regime of Mustafa Kemal, or Ataturk, Greece attacked Turkey. What resulted was a decisive defeat for the Greeks who were forced out of Smyrna. The Greeks had to accept mediation with the Turks which led to the Treaty of Lausanne in 1923. Part of this agreement was that minority populations were to be 'exchanged', and Greece was faced with the resettlement of 1.3 million Greeks into an existing population of just 5 million, and with an economy which had been on a war footing for almost ten years.

Partially as a result of the repatriation and the endemic crisis in the Greek economy there was a polarisation in the political arena, which led to a battle over the ensuing years between the forces of left and right, corresponding roughly to supporters and opponents of the king. In 1936, the king declared martial law following a series of violent strikes. This led to five years of a fascist regime that, although modelled on the Axis powers, was a supporter of neither. During World War II, the military were defeated by the Axis forces and Greece became the scene of one of the most brutal resistance campaigns in Europe, while the traditional rulers of Greece (the king and the pre-war generals) languished in Cairo in exile. When the Germans were driven out in 1944 most of the resistance joined a British sponsored interim government in an attempt to reach a peaceful agreement, but the disenfranchising of the left within the interim administration and the refusal of the king to dilute his claims to sovereignty (again with British support) made a civil war likely. In December 1944 this broke out after British troops fired on a demonstration in Athens. This continued as a bitter guerrilla conflict until 1949, but by 1947 the US had taken over the role of the British and begun to implement the Truman Doctrine. They assisted the National Army with massive military aid.

The period that followed saw Greece firmly in the US sphere of influence. However there were only minor economic benefits for Greece as most of the aid received was of a military rather than an economic character. During this period, the major demographic change that had begun after World War I continued, as there was a further migration from the country to the larger cities and a large foreign exodus. The state was dominated by the harmonious cohabitation of the crown, the military and the establishment, who were gelled together by an ideology of cold war anti-communism and an electoral system that guaranteed a rightist majority (Doukas, 1993). Parliament was effectively sidelined by brokered deals that favoured the established interests. By the end of 1964, a centre-left wing election victory reflected a dislike of the status quo. However, the failure of premier Georgos Papandreou to control the army, and the growing fear among the establishment of a left wing takeover, led to a coup in 1967 by the so called 'Colonels.'

The next seven years saw a return to the type of fascism of the late 1930's with all political activity banned and the press censored, and there were also major violations of human rights. The regime was unpopular both inside and outside of Greece. However, by 1974, an atrocity against rioting students in Athens and a disastrous excursion into foreign affairs over Cyprus spelt the end for the Colonels. The army finally mutinied and Konstantinos Karamanlis returned from exile in France to head up an interim administration. Karamanlis was no radical, having been premier in the 1950's, but a swift exit from NATO and a largely rhetorical stand against the US was enough to ensure his centre right coalition (New Democracy) a large majority in free elections at the end of 1974.

Karamanlis can undoubtedly be given much credit for the transition to democracy in Greece. The crown had lost any force it once had, and was abolished by a plebiscite in 1975, and the military was discredited by the Junta. A major plank of Karamanlis' politics was for Greece to become a member of the then EEC. The importance of Community membership in the transition to democracy cannot be understated. In fact, "*it would become clear that compulsory harmonisation of legislation and institutions would facilitate both the transition to, and consolidation of, the Greek democratic system, in so far as it would limit possibilities for significant diversions from the Western European norm*" (Doukas, 1993, p.509). This lack of deviation from Western European norms was to be important for accounting regulation, as we shall see. However the transition to democracy "*did not seriously challenge the traditional (pre 1967) patterns of political behaviour and participation, or the decision-making norms*" (ibid, p.510). Indeed, the norms in question were those established by strong party elites and management, largely bypassing parliament.

The transitional phase had reached its final stages in 1980, when Greece entered the European Community and all the main macro-political issues had been resolved (namely, the army and the constitution). It was tested and found sound by the election of PASOK in 1981, with Andreas Papandreou as premier. That PASOK had changed from the radical movement of 1974 to a pragmatic party of modernisation was one of the major reasons for this victory but in doing so it had adopted many of the characteristics of its rightist rivals. One might argue that by this stage the basic rules of Greek democracy, based on party elites and clientelistic networks, were the same for both parties, the administration being 'colonised' by party faithful. Furthermore, the traditional state-society relationship was not revised, with the state remaining as the main focus for any type of change, including accounting change.[2]

STATE CAPITAL AND PRIVATE CAPITAL

An understanding of the interaction between state and private capital is important for any attempt to 'locate' Greek accounting regulation (Neal, 1997). The development of the Greek economy under Turkish rule had left much of Greece as a rural backwater, but the position of Greece in the Eastern Mediterranean led to the development of important trade centres, and the growth of an indigenous shipping fleet, which served the whole of the area, and which is still a major Greek industry. This industry is, by its nature and by the inclination of its private owners, to some extent 'stateless' and the capital involved is highly mobile. This makes it difficult for the Greek state to exert any significant control over this important area of private capital.

The post-war position was heavily influenced by the country's place in the American sphere of influence. Much of the aid provided by the US to promote its interests in the period through to 1967 was used to bolster the military, but there was some growth in the industrial sector in this period. However, much of this, and certainly most of the growth in heavy industry, took place under state control, which was a significant feature of the Greek economy. This also led to extensive foreign borrowing by the state, which increased the risk of high levels of taxation, and a further reinforcement of the mistrust between state and private sectors.

The state sector is now being unravelled by a privatisation process, which is causing another shift in the balance of power. However, much of the economy is still formed of either small family owned firms or the state sector. The penetration of the economy by foreign owned manufacturers is limited in comparison to other EU members (most operate branches rather than use Greece as a manufacturing base), and, even among the larger Greek firms, many are still privately owned. This has two important influences on accounting practice, namely the reduction of agency problems, at least between factions of private capital, and the relative lack of influence of foreign accounting practices from the source of multinational companies.

As mentioned, the vast majority of Greek companies are small and both family owned and managed. This implies that the separation between management and owners, which is a familiar characteristic of businesses in certain other European countries, does not exist and neither does the need of the owners to control the managers. Consequently, there is a very limited need for financial statements serving the stewardship function of accounting.

Given the size of Greek firms and their management structure, it is not surprising that few firms are quoted in the Athens Stock Exchange (ASE). Many are controlled by one or two major shareholders. The only financial reporting regulations that are specific to the ASE concern the publication of quarterly financial statements by quoted firms and the format of financial data in the prospectuses of firms issuing new shares. In addition, companies quoted on the ASE appear to pay relatively high dividends and this reduces the pressure for quality financial statements. As far as the other source of financing (*i.e.* debt) is concerned, the main criteria used by the Greek banking sector for loan evaluation has been the existence of collateral. Furthermore, since many banks were state-owned, there was a tendency for companies to obtain loans through political intervention. Again, it can be argued that the state-private relationship diminishes the need for corporate financial reports.

THE BOUNDARIES OF THE STATE

The question must now be asked as to how we distinguish the state from society, how the state acts, what type of state the Modern Greek state is, and what impact this has on the development of accounting rules. If national identity and its construction is a difficult and contested area, then state theory is fairly described by Jessop (1990) as a 'conceptual swamp'. Following Jessop, a major part of this problem is in the definition of the state: "*any actual existing state is a more or less distinct ensemble of multi functional institutions and organisations which have at best a partial, provisional and unstable political identity and operational unity, and which involve a complex and overdetermined dynamic"* (ibid, p.339). Thus, differences can legitimately arise concerning which characteristics of the state are treated as primary and definitive and which are treated as secondary and contingent.

One way to look at the state is to examine the links between the state and society and the boundaries of these links. The first link is via the method of representation chosen. Ham and Hill (1993) recognise that characteristics of the state, determined at an earlier stage in the history of each nation state, provide a framework of constitutions, procedures and rules, albeit continuously renegotiable, within which political competition occurs. In doing this, they emphasise institutional arrangements in an environment where such arrangements are fixed, at least in the medium term. However, in the Greek case, these fundamental institutional arrangements have been constantly renegotiated until the quite recent past. One continuity within the many surface changes is that political parties have been key organisations in the transition to a modern state structure, especially since the end of military rule in 1975. The key questions then are: how might we categorise the arrangements through which the political parties gain control of the state and do the political parties represent fixed interests?

An analysis of the Greek state must be made alongside an acknowledgement of the economic and social background in the formation of interest group politics. The relatively fragmented nature of Greek capital, the geographic diversity of the country, and the reliance on the state for industrial infrastructure and employment together with its control of the banking system, means that the state has a far reaching power and that interest groups are only weakly represented, and then by direct association with a political party. The radical autonomy for the state has meant that, unless the apparatus of the state becomes directly involved in an issue, it is unlikely that an interest group will be able to determine any outcome. The environment is one of limited direct private sector influence, with an emphasis on direct political action. This action normally takes the form of party membership in one of the two main parties (Christofilopoulou, 1992). Therefore the influence of professional bodies tends to be indirect, through certain members who hold government responsibility. One reason for the importance of the state has been the relatively underdeveloped nature of the economy, including an underdeveloped capital market. This has led to the position where, as Papas (1993, p.8) argues in his study of financial reporting in Greece, *"economic entities have become accustomed to seek long-term government assistance and protection whenever relative income positions have been threatened by competition or structural change. This propensity has had a strong bearing on the attitudes and behaviour of economic agents in Greece."* Thus, in relation to accounting regulation, and probably in other areas also, we can infer that the Greek state has demonstrated a remarkable degree of autonomy from societal interests. Indeed, there has been a marked separation between role of the *polis* as providing the moral and social cohesion outlined by Aristotle in his description of the city state, and the political practice of the modern state.

NATIONAL IDENTITY

Greece is a relatively new democracy but many of the functions of the state, in terms of institutions, and many of the defining characteristics of political activity in Greece have deep historical roots, as has been established by the above historical analysis. Two other points can also be made. The first is the importance of the state in 'sponsoring' accounting regulation and the second is the importance of outside influences on the development of the Greek tradition in this respect

Tradition, and its invention, can be seen as part of the rhetoric of nationalism. However, while it is relatively straightforward to show a process of construction and a 'politics of interests' to be at the heart of such myths, they do not fully explain why essentialist identities continue to be involved and why they have such a deep hold over politics in certain states (Calhoun, 1995). In drawing conclusions about the power of such identities, we must be aware that this is a contested area. The case of Greek accounting rules is not offered to inform the debate on social theory, but rather some pointers from the social theory debate are used to illustrate some of the constraints on accounting. Indeed, in the context of this discussion, the aim is to distinguish two points. The first is to locate the unique influences from the history of Greece that form part of the elusive concept of a national identity and will therefore lead to a unique configuration of forces acting on accounting regulation. The second is to understand that the nation state can never be seen in isolation, with the process of 'globalisation' being deeply rooted in international interventions (Ebbers and McLeay, 1997).

One of the key points in examining the role of national identities is that such identities are almost always overdetermined and that what is observed can be constructed from a number of different historical stories, each of which may be a theoretically sound account from within its own context. Accordingly, it is possible to outline a history of Greek accounting that centres around the historical agency of a number of powerful individuals. An example of this approach would be an explanation of the Greek General Accounting Plan as gaining entrance to the political agenda at a certain period of time because it served the interests of one such agent (Karamanlis) to push it forward, not for its own sake but as part of an overall strategy to join the European Community, which was itself a part of a broader plan to 'modernise' Greece.

Equally it may be valid to use a Marxist approach that emphasises the class configurations and the importance of economic relations in determining the particular political relations that ensue and also that accounting regulation is a reflection of this determining historical materialist reality. In this context, the development of external reporting may be explained by the needs of international capital as it seeks to constantly gain new markets and uses accounting to control and monitor its input. In the present analysis, emphasis could be placed on the notion that Greek capitalism has been constrained in its development and that the socialisation stage of capital may not have been fully achieved. In this case, there would be little demand for audit and the necessary financial reports to satisfy a socialised capital class. As capital in Greece is mainly a private affair, the only disputes over the distribution of value are between the private capitalist and a large state bureaucracy, hence the importance of tax records.

While a number of such accounts may be valid it is important to be aware each account can give insight, *but* that each is a partial and incomplete theoretical simplification of a complex and still indeterminate 'current state of play'. However, given that accounting regulation is generally located at the nation state level, or at the very least that international influences (such as the IASC and the EU) are 're-interpreted' at the national level, then to understand the deep structure of a particular accounting regulatory regime we must swim in the dangerous waters of identifying national differences. The purpose is to identify how the categorisation of accounting regimes is shaped by our interpretation of national identity. Moreover, we also need to identify the possibilities that exist for such systems whilst noting that, within the realm of possibilities, not everything is still available. The possibility of the Greek state standing back from accounting regulation now seems unlikely but, given certain economic developments (such as an influx of foreign direct investment that require audit services or the development of a large scale market in the trading of Greek public securities), the role of the state may change and new strategic arrangements will need to be made by the state. The project of state formation and national identity formulation is an ever renewing one, and accounting regulation may be seen as a state 'project' that is both informed by the relations within the state and by accepted norms, and which to a greater or lesser extent may change those norms.

Table 2.1 provides an overview of certain regional influences on accounting regulation in Greece. The first of these, the influence of the Ancient Greek tradition on Europe, has undoubtedly led to the partial construction of a Greek 'European' identity. The influence of the Ottoman Empire is also still felt deeply in Greek culture, although it is easy to overdetermine such analysis. Consider the culture of gifts and favours, which is a heritage from this period The State has to become involved in accounting in such circumstances, because it is the State that allows the distribution of political favours. The most direct way that it could do this is in its sponsorship of bookkeeping for tax purposes. In Greece, when other forms of 'constituency' for accounting were underdeveloped, those small numbers of people interested in external reporting had to wait to have any influence on the state system until they received support from a more powerful ally, namely the EU.

The influence of France on Greek development was brief in direct political involvement, but was large in an indirect way. The French legal code, enacted by the newly independent Greek state in 1835, was to have powerful effect. Given that the Greek legal structure was based on the Napoleonic code, it is hardly surprising that the Greek General Accounting Plan should be based on the French Model, with Greek additions and exclusions.

The influence of Britain was also important during the development of modern Greek accounting, in particular in the role that a few 'experts' from Britain played in the creation of the Greek audit profession (Ballas, 1998). Interestingly, due to the nature of the Greek accounting and the structure of the economy at this time (1955), it

Table 2.1 *Regional influences on Greek accounting regulation*

INFLUENCES ON GREEK DEVELOPMENT	MAIN RESIDENT ELEMENT	ACCOUNTING IMPLICATIONS
Ancient Greek	Idea of Greece as 'European'	Membership of European Union – adoption of EU accounting regulation
Ottoman Empire	Clientelist politics, system of 'Rouspheti' and territorial uncertainty	Difficulties concerning accountability and auditing resolved in a private but political domain
France	Commercial Code	Basis for implementation of French accounting plan
Germany	Bureaucratisation of legal process	Prescriptive rules predominate
Britain	Audit	Concentration of audit function and emphasis on state/business relationship
EU	Security of democracy and inflow of regional laws.	Fourth and Seventh Directives adopted into the General Accounting Plan

was decided that public interest arguments, which in Britain 'dictated' an independent rent seeking profession, should in Greece generate a bureaucracy under heavy state protection and sponsorship. The reasons for this are again that the role of the audit was shaped by Greek conditions which, while not unique, were very different from Britain. The absence of major 'public firms' and the emphasis placed on bookkeeping records for tax purposes meant that there was no constituency other than the state to receive audit services. Control was essential for the state, as political favours (and penalties) were to be delivered through the tax system, since tax charges were based on accounting rules.

The deciding influence in the creation of a body of Greek accounting principles was that of the EU. Little direct state interest had been shown in accounting in Greece, with the exception of bookkeeping for tax purposes. A number of ad hoc attempts to create interest, including the translation of Australian General Accounting Rules, which have become subsequently based on a 'conceptual framework' approach to accounting theory, and the French plan (in 1953 and 1954 respectively) had failed. Venieris (1999) states quite categorically that these plans and ad hoc groupings failed because the attention of the politicians was diverted to other projects. This indicates clearly that external reporting is not a tool in the construction of the state, but more likely a product of the condition of the state, and the stage and status of the strategic coupling that the state is involved in with other groups within society. In this case, however, the strategic coupling was with an international body and the absence of an external reporting framework became an international issue.

An external reporting framework was a requirement for entry to the EC. It was not a central requirement but rather a necessary (and possibly tedious) condition for entry. According to Calhoun (1995, p.265-6), "*the international affairs of the presumptively equivalent states are public and addressable in the international public sphere, while their internal, domestic affairs are treated as private*". It may therefore be possible to suggest that the Greek General Accounting Plan was addressed to an international audience while the domestic affairs of taxation and its related bookkeeping remained an exclusively Greek domain. It will be interesting to observe the heightening of the tensions that already exist between these two areas in Greece should the EU expand its activities to the harmonisation of tax regimes.

A CULTURE OF FORMALISM

The Greek state has historically been perceived as something alien, unfair towards its citizens, occasionally oppressive and, at times, as being a mere organ of foreign powers (Clogg, 1992). The distrust between the Greek State and its citizens is pervasive. Clientelisitc relations between the state (especially politicians) and citizens are a defining feature of modern Greece to the extent that, as a recent survey showed, there are hardly any people working for the government who do not owe their jobs to politicians' patronage[3]. Since the modern Greek State has historically been functioning on the principle of patronage, it is hardly surprising that it is not trusted by its citizens. The state is not perceived to protect and advance the public interest but to be looking after sectional interests (Charalambis, 1996). Thus, citizens' behaviour is typically ambivalent: on the one hand they try to gain the favour of the state either for themselves and their families or for their particular sectional groups, while, on the other hand, they try to get the better of the state in their transactions with it (Tsoukalas, 1993). Thus, Greek citizens find themselves in a vicious circle that spirals towards more and more regulation as the state tries to outthink what the citizens will do.

The key to escaping from the vicious circle is trust (Casson, 1995). In societies of high trust, moral sanctions are relied upon to reinforce certain types of behaviour. High trust encourages spontaneous co-operation and reduces the need for state intervention, thus reducing monitoring costs. In such environments, self-regulation of accounting can develop and users of financial statements can accept that they represent a 'true and fair view' of the reporting entities' activities. Conversely, low trust undermines spontaneous co-operation, and increases the need for state intervention to detect dishonest behaviour, thus increasing monitoring costs through the enactment of increasingly more complex rules. In such environments, state regulation of accounting becomes necessary.

Although in a low trust society there is a greater need for state intervention, the state is part of the problem. Casson (1995, p.197) provides a concise explanation for the largely self-defeating nature of state rule-making: "*The problem is that in a low-trust society people not only cannot trust each other, they cannot trust the intervenor either. Indeed, since the intervenor often has more power than anyone else, particularly if he is backed by the coercive power of the state, he is more to be feared than other people. Although there are evils that need correcting, therefore, they cannot be tackled because the solution - namely intervention - is feared more that the problem itself. Fear of intervention means that trust becomes focussed, not on people, but on processes instead. Intervention, when it occurs, is governed by rules: discretionary intervention is disliked because it is believed that discretionary powers are easier to abuse. Rules make it easier to detect when the intervenor cheats.*"

Rules, however, not only increase the cost of monitoring for dishonest behaviour but accentuate the distrust that already exists between the citizen and the state. The spiralling use of rules for the regulation of accounting leads to formalism, defined as an excessive adherence to prescribed forms and the use of forms without regard to inner significance. Both are observed in accounting regulations in a number of countries, including Greece.

The fact that accounting regulation in Greece is highly detailed has been extensively documented (Papas, 1993). What is surprising is that a large majority of companies make an effort to comply, despite the related costs. This is true even in the case of subsidiaries of multinational companies that have to prepare a different set of accounts for the group consolidated statements. Yet, although the 'true and fair view' has been embedded in Greek company law since 1986, to the best of our knowledge it has not been invoked to justify deviations from the regulations. Such disregard of content in order to comply with regulations is also evident.[4] Indeed, formalism in Greek accounting is a defining characteristic. It provides reporting entities with ground rules on what is 'acceptable' in a manner which can be communicated easily without having to document why a specific alternative (disclosure, valuation rules, etc.) is preferred. The existence of a thick rule book allows preparers to claim that 'rules are rules' and close the discussion.

STATE POLITICS AND ACCOUNTING REGULATION

The importance of the role of the state can also be illustrated by the various attempts to create a Greek Accounting Plan, prior to its introduction in 1980 (Ballas, 1994). The first attempt was in 1954 and since then various committees of academics and practitioners have come together with this aim (Venieris, 1999). All failed because of a lack of internal cohesion and also because of a lack of interest by the state in general purpose accounts as opposed to tax 'constructions.' It was only in 1975, when the question of the entry of post-Junta Greece into the European Community was being considered, that the issue of the national accounting plan came onto the mainstream political agenda. The purpose of the plan now became more than a 'local' issue in Greece since it would be necessary to adopt accounting legislation once membership had been obtained to comply with the fourth and seventh directives.

When the original plan was adopted in 1980, it was not compulsory. By 1986, however, the necessary company law arrangements were in place to provide full compliance with the directives and the plan had been made compulsory for all firms. The working of the plan is administered by the National Accounting Council . The role of the state can again be seen here in that the Council is under the auspices of a government ministry and acts as an 'interpreter' of the National Plan, in the sense of giving practical guidance on its application, and as an adviser to the government on accounting issues.[5] Thus, although the state could not resist external pressures to implement accounting regulations, it still dominates any internal debate. This point is further illustrated in the three issues considered below.

Accounting regulation and the fiscal authorities

The influence of taxation on accounting practice is related both to the need to satisfy legal requirements but also to the lack of any other motivation for proper financial reporting. Most businessmen would argue that, if an expense is not allowed for tax purposes, financial reporting rules should not force them to report a lower profit. Tax accounting and its influence on financial reporting raise more than a few issues about proper procedure and what are the priorities of the state in so far as accounting is concerned.[6]

When the first Tax Code in Greece was adopted in 1948, at the instigation of the American Mission to Aid Greece during its Civil War, the government's stated goal for introducing the Code was to combat tax evasion and to increase confidence in the tax system.[7] The argument used was that if accounting books existed, kept by everyone in the same way, citizens would accept that they are paying a fair amount of tax (in the sense that everyone was paying the same proportion of tax related to income). Reality however, is at odds with the official version. The amount of tax revenues that the Greek State needed at the time was trivial at best because the National Army (the government side in the Civil War) and reconstruction efforts were financed by the US government. Furthermore, the government had imposed real estate taxes and import duties. Therefore, the issue was not to levy tax on those not paying their taxes at the time but, in order to avoid politically embarrassing situations with other social groups, to make it appear that taxes will be levied on the nonpayers in the future.[8] Indeed, during certain periods of modern Greek history, broad social classes were given a devil's bargain by the State: 'you pretend to pay taxes, we pretend that you have the right to vote' – a version of 'no taxation without representation'.

The changing fiscal situation of the past twenty-five years, however, has meant that the state has had to extend the collection of taxes. As discussed earlier, despite the introduction of more detailed rules, the application of the regulations is by no means clearer and still reflects the ongoing relationship between the needs of the state and private capital, namely that political considerations are predominant.

Accounting regulation and the audit profession

According to Ballas (1998), public accountants as a profession first appeared in Greece as a result of the Economic Cooperation Agreement (ECA) between Greece and the USA in 1948. In 1955, the Greek audit institute, the 'Body of Sworn-in Auditors' (Soma Orkoton Logiston, for short SOL), came into existence. A major part of the discussion on the development of SOL centred around whether they should or should not be civil servants. The Greek state was primarily motivated by its own needs and other interested parties, including the accountants and their potential clients, were too weak to resist this even if they had wanted to.

Thus, traditional studies of Greek accounting attach a low significance to the Greek profession. However, if one looks at the composition of relevant committees more closely and takes into account that even the simplest transaction can be an act of patronage and not necessarily one of reciprocal obligation then the influence of the profession can be seen to take effect through political action.[9] For example, the vast majority of the members of the committee that prepared the Greek Accounting Plan were members of SOL or persons who had completed at least part of SOL training (and thus had at least accepted some of the SOL principles).

Further evidence can be gathered from the study of the National Accounting Council's workings. Membership, as prescribed in law, does not grant any special rights to the profession. However, very quickly after it was constituted, all decision making authority was delegated to its Chairman and its Secretary General. Both were formerly members of SOL before the latter was disbanded in 1991. Indeed, one was the spokesman for a faction in SOL that believed that part of the auditors' job was to dispense justice in the manner of a judge. This would have placed auditors in an even stronger position as arbiters between the state and the private company, with political considerations again being the dominant force.

Accounting regulation and academia

Traditionally in Greek politics, the power of university faculty is very high. This can be explained by the prestige attached to education, especially higher education, in Greek society (Tsoukalas, 1986). It is reflected in the positioning of academics in the public sector in a manner that cannot be attributed to their specific discipline or expertise. Until recently, however, this was not the case with Accounting faculty.[10] Thus, for example, no university faculty were members of the committee entrusted to prepare the Accounting Plan. A committee of six academics acted as review board when the plan was complete and before it was submitted to Parliament. However, there is no evidence that they had any influence on the Plan.

The Accounting faculty also had limited influence in the development of the Tax Code. For example, for the last revision of the Code, the Government invited the opinions of leading Greek accounting academics. Indeed, one was a member of the committee that prepared the new Tax Data Code. However, in spite of this and although the government had promised that the committee's opinion would be taken into account, the end product bears little relationship to its proposals.

A possible explanation for the low influence of accounting academics in accounting legislation (at least, in comparison to certain other countries) is the behaviour of the Ministry of Finance bureaucracy that has its own priorities, and the lack of political influence of professional groupings as opposed to party apparatus (Christofilopoulou, 1992).

CONCLUSIONS

The particular occurrence of accounting regulation that we observe in Greece can be seen in many ways to be unique to its social, historic and economic development. The approach adopted here to Greek history has been similar to that employed by Miller (1986) in the analysis of French National Accounting, namely to make a broad sweep through the roots of the nation state in a bid to understand the essential nature of the current political and cultural relations that exist in Greece today and to therefore locate accounting regulation within that context.

The first factor to note is that the 'deep structure' (Benson, 1983) both contributes to and limits the development of Greek accounting. The Greek National Accounting Plan was developed from the French plan, but has some local touches that change the purpose of the accounting significantly. The rigidity of the French plan was imposed to assist in the collection of macroeconomic data in a period when the economy was more planned than it is now. Although the French plan has been modified over time, the roots of accounting in France are still firmly embedded in its original purpose. In Greece, the same style of Plan was adopted but for very different reasons, with the rigidity of the plan being required for fiscal purposes not for planning purposes. The style is therefore the same but the objective is different, both plans expressing the needs of the state at the time of their introduction, the Greek version also containing some particular requirements as an expression of national identity.

The second point to draw from Greek history is the predominant role of the state[11] and how this has developed. The state system in Greece is both new and old at the same time. It is new in that modern Greek democracy dates only from 1974 and many fundamental cornerstones of this political system have only been developed since that time. It may not be surprising that accounting regulation had to wait for space in the face of such fundamental reform. It is old in that Greek politics still works more by direct political action (lobbying), as articulated by Aristotle, rather than through indirect agencies as does the model provided by the UK and the USA. The historical anomaly is that it was these two powers that reinforced in Greece this choice of centralisation in the accounting domain with their support for the creation of a state-controlled audit function.

The final point to note in locating accounting regulation in history is the limits that the historical root places on both categorisation of the accounting regime and its future direction. Categorisation and classification of accounting systems has been a fertile ground for scholars in recent years (for a review of this literature, see Nobes and Parker, 1998, ch.4) but in the classification of regimes there is inevitably simplification. In Nobes and Parker (1998), Greece is not noted in any of the classification systems but, by implication from the analysis, it would be included in plan-based systems. However, as we have shown above, although the surface characteristics of Greek accounting may place it in this category, a significant difference is obscured by doing so. Indeed, the further away from the initial inspiration of the French Plan in time, the greater the divergence between the two plans because of the progressive influence of Greek national identity. That is, whereas there is an inherent assumption in classification systems of increased standardisation, for this case we could argue that divergence is more likely.

NOTES

[1] The traditions of privacy and independence are deep seated and are still observed in the adversarial nature of the current system that pitches state control against business independence.

[2] Although many of the new appointees to government were young and professionally trained, their influence came not from their membership of a professional body but from their position within the party (see Christofilopoulou, 1992). This had important ramifications for the development of accounting standards.

[3] This survey was commissioned by the Ministry of the Interior and reproduced in most Greek newspapers. For a discussion see *To Vema*, March 30, 1997.

[4] A good example is accounting for fixed asset investments under L. 1078/71. That law required companies to record as of the beginning of accounting life of new machinery, the year they were installed in the company's location. Furthermore, if a specific piece of equipment had been imported, companies had to show the permission from the Bank of Greece to export foreign exchange. However, if equipment was bought on credit, the Bank of Greece permission was given in the period the machinery was paid off. Since in no accounting period did the company both install the equipment and export the payment the asset never became operational, and therefore local tax offices refused to accept that the asset should benefit from investment incentives. Administrative Courts of First Instance agreed with them. The issue was solved with further regulation.

[5] This leads to a rather 'technicist' agenda, with few large scale disputes being raised by ESYL, when compared for example to the ASB in Britain which sponsors a review of the fundamental principles of accounting in areas such as valuation and measurement

[6] The influence of tax accounting is so strong that it has caused deviations from the Fourth Directive. For example, an interesting 'peculiarity' of Greek financial statements is that income tax is not reported among the expenses, as articles 23 to 26 of the Fourth Directive require, but in the Statement of Retained Earnings. This is in conformance with Greek Tax Law that does not allow income tax to be a deductible item. Another explanation is that this separation of the tax number from the income statement facilitates the audit of tax calculations that are influenced by how profits are distributed.

[7] The American influence in accounting developments in Greece, with particular reference to the accounting profession, is extensively explored in Ballas (1998).

[8] This is also consistent with the derogations and exemptions that could be found in the small print.

[9] In many ways, this comes to the heart of the issue which is the question of the outcomes of accounting regulation in Greece being a part of the whole development of the Greek state.

[10] This can perhaps be explained by the fact that accounting educators in Greece were usually educated abroad and in their writings did not take into account political priorities of the time. Rather, Professors like Tsimaras, Chrisokeris, Chrisokhou etc. tried to introduce to Greek accounting practice concepts that were generally accepted abroad, but not 'suitable' for the political economy of Greece.

[11] Aristotle, in his work *The Politics*, describes different types of democracy, one of which may be not too far from the reality of many modern states. The current state of politics in Greece may be described fairly

as 'paternalistic' or 'clientelist' in the same way that Aristotle described the 'democracy' of the ideal city state, not as pure rule by a democratic assembly, but as a 'polity' which was the 'mean' between oligarchy and democracy.

REFERENCES

Ballas, A.A. (1994). Accounting in Greece, *The European Accounting Review*, Vol.3, No.1, pp.107-21.

Ballas, A.A. (1998). The creation of the audit profession in Greece, *Accounting, Organizations and Society*, Vol.23, No.8, pp.715-36.

Benson, J.K. (1983). Interorganisational networks and policy sectors, in D. Rogers and D. Whetten (eds.) *Interorganisational Coordination*. Iowa: University of Iowa Press, pp.3-31.

Calhoun, C.J. (1995). *Critical Social Theory: Culture, History, and the Challenge of Difference*. Oxford: Blackwell.

Casson, M. (1995). *Entrepreneurship and Business Culture: Studies in the Economics of Trust*. Aldershot: Edward Elgar.

Charalambis, D. (1996). *The Relationship of the Private and Public in the Greek Political System*. Athens: Sakis Karagiorgis Foundation.

Christofilopoulou, P. (1992). Professionalism and public policy making in Greece, *Public Administration*, Vol.70, No.1, pp.99-118.

Clogg, R. (1992). *A Concise History of Greece*. Cambridge: Cambridge University Press.

Doukas, G. (1993). Party elites and democratisation in Greece, *Parliamentary Affairs*, Vol.46, pp.506-16.

Ebbers, G., and McLeay, S.J. (1997). Accounting and 'Volksgeist' - territorial claims on accounting regulation, *The Journal of Management and Governance*, Vol.1, No.1, pp.67-84.

Ham, C., and Hill, M. (1993). *The Policy Process in the Modern Capitalist State*. Hemel Hempstead: Harvester Wheatsheaf.

Jessop, B. (1990). *State Theory: Putting the Capitalist State in its Place*. Cambridge: Polity.

Miller, P. (1986). Accounting for progress - national accounting and planning in France: a review essay, *Accounting Organisations and Society*, Vol.11, No.1, pp.83-104.

Neal, D. (1997). Locating accounting regulation in Greece, in J. Flower and C. Lefebvre (eds.) *Comparative Studies in Accounting Regulation in Europe*. Leuven: Acco, pp.127-57.

Nobes, C., and Parker, R. (1998). *Comparative International Accounting*. Hemel Hempstead: Prentice-Hall.

Papas , A.A. (1993). *European Financial Reporting - Greece*. London: Routledge.

Tsoukalas, C. (1993). Free riders in wonderland: on the Greeks in Greece, *Greek Review of Political Science*, pp.9-52 (in Greek).

Tsoukalas, C. (1987). *State, Society and Labor in Postwar Greece*. Athens: Themelio (in Greek).

Venieris, G. (1999). Greece, in McLeay, S.J., *Accounting Regulation in Europe*. London: MacMillan, pp.147-76

3

REGULATING ACCOUNTING WITHIN THE POLITICAL AND LEGAL SYSTEM

Roberto Di Pietra, Stuart McLeay
and Angelo Riccaboni

INTRODUCTION

This chapter provides an analysis of the process of accounting regulation in Italy, where corporate governance is greatly influenced by a legislature operating in its traditional interventionist form. The rules governing accounting in Italy are the product of the wider political system, rather than of a specialized institution charged with the task of overseeing accounting developments.

In this respect, although prior research in this area helps us to understand certain of the processes underlying accounting regulation, the difficulty associated with approaching accounting regulation through the workings of a government agency or a private standard setting body becomes immediately evident when we consider the situation in Italy.

In fact, the process of accounting regulation in Italy does not depend on the existence of a delegated agency or on self regulation, nor does it even rely to any great extent on there being a set of acceptable accounting standards. Instead, it is the law that is paramount. Explaining this mode of regulation and comparing it with alternative approaches is the main aim of this chapter.

THE POLITICS OF ACCOUNTING REGULATION

On the subject of accounting regulation, only a limited set of universally accepted concepts has been formulated. While numerous studies merit attention for the concepts and approaches they present, few of these appear to be generally applicable in the universal sense to which we aspire here. Indeed, the research that led to the formulation of such concepts was for a considerable period carried out by reference to systems of accounting regulation belonging to fairly similar social and economic situations. When this was not the case, comparisons proved to be influenced by an underlying ethnocentric approach, as demonstrated by Wallace and Gernon in their review of comparative research in accounting (1991). In fact, only in rare cases has the truly comparative nature of the phenomena in question been addressed. In this field, as in others, it appears to be important to formulate a more encompassing research strategy which locates different instances within their global context, explaining their characteristics as a function of their varying relationships to the regulatory project as a whole .

Most of the characterizations normally found in the research literature achieve total relevance only when associated with a particular political and legislative context, and their application to situations different from those in which the terms were formulated is often ineffective. Such is the case with 'standards' and 'standard setting bodies', the inherent semantic content of these terms representing the existence of a particular context that is not necessarily to be found in all cases. In spite of these reservations, research on accounting regulation provides an insight into a range of relevant matters, including:

- theories capable of explaining the events that contribute to the development of accounting regulations (Watts and Zimmerman, 1978; Bromwich, 1985; Horngren, 1985; Robson, 1993);
- ways of enforcing such regulations and the role of the institutions that represent those with a vested interest (Benston, 1980; Jönsson, 1991; Mitchell and Sikka, 1993); and
- lobbying of regulatory bodies and the political activity involved in defining their agenda (Walker and Robinson, 1993 & 1994; Klumpes, 1994).

In this latter context, the meaning attributed to political activity in accounting regulation normally refers to a series of decisions, actions and processes during and after the preparation of an accounting standard. In a comparative context, this approach can be limiting since it assumes that the existence of a standard setting agency to oversee the process is of fundamental importance (Di Pietra, 1997). More precisely, it might be taken for granted that every system of accounting regulation foresees the existence of such a body either invested with authority by the legislature or resulting from market forces. Such circumstances may well exist in many countries but certainly not in all. Moreover, the fact that there may exist regulatory systems without the organized authority of a standard setting body does not necessarily mean that political activity is absent in the development of the local rules and regulations surrounding financial reporting. This is clearly demonstrated by the Italian case, as illustrated below.

ACCOUNTING REGULATION IN ITALY

The first official mention of financial reporting in Italian law may be traced back to the Commercial Code of 1865, when company directors were barred from voting to approve their company's annual accounts. However, it was actually the 1882 revision of the Commercial Code that supplied Italy with its first official regulations obliging companies to actually prepare financial statements. Later, financial reporting was governed by the 1942 Civil Code, which was supplemented by fiscal regulations that exerted a significant influence on financial reporting in Italy. A fundamental change in the regulatory process occurred in 1974 with the establishment of the Italian Stock Exchange and Companies Commission (*Commissione Nazionale per le Società e la Borsa*). A regulatory agency, CONSOB was empowered from the outset to require audited annual accounts from companies quoted on the stock exchange. However, the number of companies affected by this was not large (Riccaboni and Ghirri, 1995).

In fact, until the European accounting directives were enacted in Italy in 1991, the annual accounts (*Bilancio*) of most Italian companies were made up solely of a balance sheet (*Stato patrimoniale*) and a profit and loss account (*Conto dei profitti e delle perdite*), in accordance with the codified law of 1942. [1] [2] Implementation of the European Company Law Directives brought about a wide-reaching change in the accounting regulations through extensive revision of the Civil Code.[3] At the same time, a joint board of the professional accounting bodies (which had been in existence for some years with a view to establishing an authoritative set of accounting principles) set about revising its earlier recommendations in order to achieve conformity with the new provisions of the Civil Code. The principles of the CSPC (*Commissione per la Statuizione dei Principi Contabili*) have never been officially recognized as law, although some limited acknowledgement of their existence has been forthcoming from CONSOB along with default recognition of International Accounting Standards. In general, however, as described below, the regulation of accounting in Italy continues to live up to its traditional image of rigid legal prescription by the state combined with a certain flexibility of interpretation (Zan, 1994; Di Toro and Ianniello, 1996).

Laws and decrees

In Italy, the state exercises its authority through a number of regulatory instruments, not only parliamentary laws (*legge*) but also legislative decrees (*decreti legislativi*) and law decrees (*decreti legge*) prepared by the Government within the limits of the Constitution. Law decrees are issued by the President of the Republic, in the form of presidential decrees (*Decreti del Presidente della Repubblica* - DPR). The use of these different legislative instruments in accounting is apparent in Table 3.1, which gives an overview of the present situation.

1. Parliamentary laws (Legge)

Parliamentary laws are enacted following the approval of each of the two houses of Parliament, the Chamber of Deputies (*Camera dei Deputati*) and the Senate (*Senato*). Usually, any proposal of law is first discussed in a parliamentary committee which is nominated by the President of the Chamber or by the President of the Senate and which takes into consideration the composition of the Parliament. After the committee has completed its work, the bill is discussed by the Parliament and, if approved, becomes (with eventual modifications) a law of the Italian Republic.

When dealing with specialized matters such as accounting regulations, the parliamentary committee will delegate the preparation of a draft law to a sub-committee of experts, such as leading academics in commercial law or accounting. However, other experts in lawmaking are present on these commissions, and the tendency has been for accounting regulations to be drawn up primarily by lawyers rather than by accountants. This was the case in the Uniconti Commission of 1942 which attempted to draft an accounting plan for Italian companies, and the D'Alessandro Commission of 1986 which was responsible for the revision of the Civil Code when implementing the Fourth and Seventh European Directives.

2. Legislative decrees (Decreti legislativi)

Legislative decrees are prepared by the government and issued in the form of a decree signed by the President and then published in the Official Gazette, coming into effect fifteen days thereafter. A legislative decree arises when the Parliament delegates powers to the government through a delegating law (*legge delega*) which places the necessary restrictions on the scope of the eventual legislation and defines its timetable. This was the case, for example, when Law 69 of 26 March 1990 delegated responsibility for the incorporation of the Fourth and Seventh Directives into Italian law, which was enacted through legislative decree Lgs D 127 of April 1991. In fact, in this case, the D'Alessandro Commission had already been at work for some years prior to the issue of the delegating law, having

Table 3.1 *Accounting legislation in Italy*

YEAR	DATE	TYPE OF LAW	N°	LEGAL OBJECTIVES AND CONTENT
1969	29 December	DPR	1127	Enactment of the First EC Directive
1974	8 April	LD	95	Creation of CONSOB; disclosure requirements of listed companies
1974	7 June	L	216	Following LD 95/1974; powers delegated to CONSOB
1975	31 March	DPR	136	Following L 216/1974; audit and accounts of listed companies
1978	14 December	DPR	14	Layout of annual accounts of insurance companies
1980	4 February	MD	-	Layout of annual accounts of service companies controlled by regional authorities
1983	19 February	L	72	Revaluation of assets and equity (Legge Visentini)
1985	4 June	L	181	Interim accounts of quoted companies
1986	10 February	DPR	30	Enactment of Second EC Directive
1988	4 November	L	481	Provisions by banks against foreign loans
1990	26 March	L	69	Delegation of legal authority to the Government to enact EC Directives
1990	27 April	LD	90	Income determination for tax purposes
1991	9 April	Lgs D	127	Enactment of Fourth and Seventh EC Directives
1991	8 October	MD	-	Layout of annual accounts of electricity companies
1992	27 January	Lgs D	87	Enactment of EC Directive 86/635 concerning the annual accounts of banks and financial institutions
1992	24 June	MD	-	Guidance on preparation of annual accounts following Lgs D 87/1992
1992	21 October	MD	-	Changes in the layout of the income statement, including separate disclosure of interest on specific loans
1992	30 December	Lgs D	526	Enactment of EC Directive 90/604 concerning the translation of annual accounts into ECU (Art. 2435 Civil Code) and abridged financial statements (Art. 2435b)
1994	2 May	Lgs D	315	Enactment of EC Directive 92/101 concerning purchase of controlling company shares (Art. 2357 and 2357b of the Civil Code)
1994	29 June	LD	416	Regulations concerning fiscal income
1994	8 August	L	503	Law ratifying LD 416/1994, whilst removing the requirement for a fiscal appendix (items 24 and 25 of income statement)
1995	7 January	LD	1	Mandatory elimination of fiscal items from group accounts (reversal of relevant legislation in L 503/1994)
1995	9 March	LD	64	Option to base group accounts on amounts used for tax purposes
1995	26 April	MD	-	Layout of annual accounts of service companies controlled by regional authorities
1995	27 October	LD	442	Annual accounts of publishing companies
1996	29 December	LD	554	Revision of LD 442/1995
1997	8 October	Lgs D	358	Company reorganizations and taxation
1998	24 February	Lgs D	58	Consolidated Finance Act
1998	24 June	Lgs D	213	Accounting for exchange differences

Note. *L = Law, Lgs D = Legislative decree, MD = Ministerial decree, LD = Delegated legislation, DPR = Presidential decree* originally been established as a Working Group by the Ministry of Justice. A first draft of the proposed legislation was issued in 1986, and a second in 1988, both accompanied by Commission reports. Following the *legge delega*, a third draft and report of February 8, 1991 was sent to the President of the Chamber of Deputies to be examined by a number of Parliamentary Commissions. After a few minor changes, Lgs D 127 was approved.

3. Law decrees (Decreti legge)

A law decree is intended for urgent and exceptional matters only, and is issued with a decree signed by the President of the Republic and countersigned by the President of the Government. It is then published in the Official Gazette and comes into effect on the day of publication. A law decree must be sent to the Parliament for enactment into law on the day that it is issued and confirmed in law within sixty days. For instance, the removal of the requirement for a fiscal appendix reconciling accounting profits and taxable profits as part of the annual accounts package was legislated upon in this way (LD 416 of 29 June 1994 and L 503 of 8 August 1994). If a decree fails to become law within sixty days of publication in the *Gazzetta Ufficiale*, its effects are null and void starting from the day of issue.

Art. 77 of the Italian Constitution states that the government may use law decrees in cases of exceptional urgency only. However, due to the traditional slowness of Parliament in legislating, the use of a law decree having immediate effect has been turned into a pragmatic expedient. Unfortunately, this procedure can limit the opportunity for public scrutiny, although it is worth noting that recent changes have made their reiteration - when not converted into law - far less easy.

4. Presidential decrees (Decreti del Presidente della Repubblica)

In addition to their use in ratifying legislative decrees and law decrees, Presidential decrees are also issued on specific points of law as an adjunct to enabling legislation. For instance, the law giving powers to the stock exchange commission CONSOB (Law 216 of 7 June 1974, which ratified a previous law decree LD 95 of 8 April 1974) also authorized the government to lay down specific rules on auditing and accounting. These specific pieces of legislation were then covered by subsequent Presidential decrees (DPRs 136 and 137 of 31 March 1975). Presidential decrees such as these are issued with the signature of the appropriate Minister and with the ratification of the President of the Republic. There are many examples in the field of tax regulation where, under the signature of the Minister of Finance, taxation changes have become law with a Presidential decree (e.g. DPR 42 of 4 February 1988).

5. Ministerial decrees (Decreti ministeriali)

Inevitably, delegated legislation has increased the power of the government, which is particularly evident in the field of business law. Indeed, the legislative powers of ministers are exercised through a further type of legislative instrument known as a Ministerial decree. Such decrees may either concern administrative matters (*atti amministrativi*) or contain ministerial orders (*regolamenti ministeriali*). In the latter case, if the law delegated the appropriate powers, a minister may issue supplementary regulations and, in cases where specific problems have arisen, official interpretations of laws and decrees which have already been enacted. Ministerial decrees have less authority than law, being categorized as secondary legislation. Nevertheless, they play an important role in accounting regulation.

Interpretations and rulings

Because of the rigidity of the lawmaking process, there are a number of ways in which official interpretations of the law can be given. As shown in Table 3.2, these include circulars and decrees prepared at the Ministerial level which provide legal clarification. Both the Ministry of Finance and the Ministry of Justice issue legally binding orders in this respect. Rulings resulting from court hearings include those of the *Corte di Cassazione*, the Constitutional Court, and Tribunals held on a regional basis.

Capital market regulations

As mentioned earlier, CONSOB regulates the activities of the capital market and, together with the Bank of Italy, ensures the functioning of a market in stocks and shares. These activities are carried out under the supervision of the Minister of the Treasury, with periodic accountability to Parliament. The regulatory power of CONSOB is particularly relevant to the preparation of annual accounts through its actions in overseeing the listing of securities issued by companies. For instance, CONSOB exercised its powers to request annual consolidated statements from listed companies even before the enactment of the Seventh Directive. The Bank of Italy's main concern is with financial institutions, but it is nevertheless an important conduit for accounting regulation in that sphere.

CONSOB releases circulars (*circolare*) and formal decisions (*delibera*) as well as other announcements (*comunicazione*) which tend to be in the form of responses to particular queries. These are published in the monthly bulletin of the Bank of Italy (*Bollettino mensile della Banca d'Italia*) and, if circulars or decisions are mandatory, they are also published in the Official Gazette (*Gazzetta Ufficiale della Repubblica Italiana*). The Bank of Italy coordinates its regulation

Table 3.2 Legal interpretations and judicial rulings

YEAR	DATE	DOCUMENT	CONTENT
Clarification of accounting law by government departments			
Ministry of Finance			
1994	27 May	Circular 73/E	Income statement and notes to the accounts
1994	September	Committee report	Principles of clarity and truthfulness (Italian please)
1995	15 February	Ministerial decree	Anticipated depreciation allowed for tax purposes without being recorded in the income statement
1996	3 May	Circular 108/E	Leasing companies
Ministry of Justice			
1993	19 March	Note 1624/13/1/UI	Application of LD 127 to partnerships
1994	14 June	Circular 13/94	Statutory auditors
Rulings on accounting law by Italian courts			
1970	7 September	Corte di Cassazione (Judgment 1281)	Proof of debt (the annual accounts, as any other accounting record, represent proof of a debt)
1978	4 September	Tribunale di Milano	Anticipated depreciation (not to be recorded in the annual accounts)
1984	12 January	Tribunale di Milano	Anticipated depreciation (may be recorded in the annual accounts if the principle of clarity is respected by providing detailed information in the Management Report)
1985	27 February	Corte di Cassazione (Judgment 1699)	Inventories (Last In, First Out)
1986	18 March	Corte di Cassazione (Judgment 1839)	Fiscal and civil valuation criteria
1986	3 July	Corte di Cassazione (Judgment 4382)	Mergers (revaluation of assets)
1988	5 May	Tribunale di Genova	Reinvested profit (annual accounts prepared in accordance with fiscal law are valid, if this is required in order to take advantage of tax benefits and if adequate information is given in the Management Report)
1991	22 October	Corte di Cassazione (Judgment 11202)	Anticipated depreciation
1993	11 March	Corte di Cassazione (Judgment 2959)	Principle of clarity
1993	3 November	Commissione Tributaria Centrale (Decision 3015)	Mergers (accounting for deficits)
1994	21 March	Tribunale di Torino	Negligence of auditing firms
1994	18 June	Tribunale di Sondrio	Subsidiary companies
1998	22 April	Corte di Cassazione (Judgment 4095)	Sale and leaseback

of disclosure by financial institutions with CONSOB, sometimes requiring agreement (*d'intesa*) as in the case of brokers and other times requiring only consultation, as in the case of pension funds. Each official decision (*provvedimento*) of the Bank of Italy in this respect is also published in the Official Gazette. A list of the most relevant accounting regulations issued by CONSOB and by the Bank of Italy is shown in Table 3.3.

Table 3.3 *Accounting regulations issued by CONSOB and the Banca d'Italia*

YEAR	DATE	DOCUMENT	CONTENT
CONSOB			
1982	8 April	Delibera 1079	Reference to accounting principles issued by the CSPC
1987	8 April	Delibera 2837	Interim reporting by listed companies
1993	31 March	Comunicazione 93002423	Differences between Civil Code regulations and CSPC recommendations (re. Delibera 1079/1982)
1994	23 February	Comunicazione 94001437	Information disclosed by holding companies (re. Lgs D 127)
1994	12 April	Comunicazione 94003771	Auditors and the treatment of anticipated depreciation (under art. 67 TUIR as modified by LD 139/1994)
1994	30 June	Delibera 8195	Interim reporting by listed companies
1994	1 August	Delibera 9389	Interim reporting by listed companies
1995	20 June	Comunicazione 95005249	Consolidated accounts
1997	20 February	Communicazione 97001573	Reference to International Accounting Standards
1997	20 February	Communicazione 97001574	Company control
1998	24 February	Communicazione 98015375	Annual accounts: related party transactions
1998	15 April	Communicazione 98027756	Pre-merger transactions
1998	19 October	Communicazione 98081334	Company reporting: extraordinary operations
Banca d'Italia			
1992	2 July	Provvedimento	The preparation of annual accounts and consolidated accounts by banks and financial institutions
1992	15 July	Provvedimento	The layout and rules of preparation of the accounts of financial institutions
1993	1 February	Provvedimento	Changes to Regolamento of 2 July 1991
1995	16 January	Provvedimento	Income statement layout

The ambiguous status of accounting principles

In 1989, through its resolution n° 1079, CONSOB recommended the application of 'Correct Accounting Principles' (*Corretti Principi Contabili*) and thereby gave some acknowledgement to the accounting profession's own accounting principles board, the *Commissione per la Statuizione dei Principi Contabili*, whose guidelines were the only valid source in Italy. More explicitly, the stock exchange commission stated that, in cases where such principles were found to be inadequate, reference should be made to International Accounting Standards on the condition that these did not conflict with local legal provisions. Indeed, the resolution in question states clearly that 'when accounting principles drawn up by the CSPC are incomplete or non-existent, those of the IASC are to be applied as long as they do not conflict with laws in force'.[4]

However, in spite of CONSOB's tacit recognition of the CSPC insofar as the accounts of quoted companies are concerned, the CSPC has never received official recognition in law. Indeed, the only occasions on which the legislature explicitly delegated the formulation of accounting regulations were in 1975 to CONSOB with reference to the listing of companies and later, by legislative decree (Lgs. D. 87 of 27 January 1992) and subsequent ministerial decree (24 June 1992), to the Bank of Italy with regard to financial institutions. But nevertheless, the indirect recognition given by CONSOB has spread, and is also reflected in the Consolidated Laws on Income Tax (*Testo Unico delle Imposte sui Redditi* - TUIR), which again refer to "Correct Accounting Principles".

The process of developing and updating this body of accounting rules is in the hands of the *Dottori commercialisti* and the *Ragionieri*, whose respective national administrative bodies are the *Consiglio Nazionale dei Dottori Commercialisti* (the CNDC) and the *Consiglio Nazionale dei Ragionieri* (the CNR).[5] When it was set up in 1975, the members of the CSPC were nominated solely by the CNDC but subsequently the CNR was provided with one third of the seats. For some time now, the commission has been composed of a President and an equal number of eleven representatives nominated by the CNDC and CNR respectively for a period of three years (Zappalà, 1982).[6] The recommendations issued to date by the CSPC can be seen in Table 3.4.

Immediately following its inception, the CSPC's statements were drawn up to express the point of view of the Italian accounting profession only (Tomasin, 1982). Now, although there is no set procedure, each issue that reaches the agenda of the CSPC is assigned to a working group of approximately 10 people, or to a single draftsman, the draft document normally being distributed for comment to the stock exchange commission (CONSOB), an association representing industry and commerce (*Associazione fra le Società Italiane per Azioni* - ASSONIME), another association representing auditors (*Associazione Italiana Revisori Contabili* - ASSIREVI), the Italian Banking Association (*Associazione Bancaria Italiana* - ABI) and certain other interested parties. A copy is also sent to the Ministry of Finance for an informal response, and eventually a revised document is published.

Table 3.4 Recommendations issued by the CSPC

N°	TITLE OF CSPC RECOMMENDATION	YEAR
1	Annual accounts – aims and requirements	1975
2	Composition and layout of annual accounts of commercial and industrial enterprises	1977
2-bis	Integration and explanation of statement 2	1982
3	Inventories	1978
4	Basic principles of accounting for property, plants and equipment	1979
5	Cash and bank overdrafts	1980
6	Receivables	1980
7	Payables and other liabilities	1981
8	Securities, investment and consolidated annual accounts	1983
9	Translation of operations in a foreign currency into national currency	1988
10	Long-term contracts	1991
11	Annual accounts – aims and requirements (update of n° 1)	1994
12	Composition and layout of annual accounts of commercial and industrial enterprises (update of n° 2)	1994
13	Inventories (update of n° 3)	1994
14	Cash and bank overdrafts (update of n° 5)	1994
15	Receivables (update of n° 6)	1996
16	Property, plant and equipment (update of n° 4)	1996
17	Consolidated annual accounts (update of n° 8)	1996
18	Accruals and deferred items	1996
19	Provisions for risks and charges – Employee severance indemnities – Payables (update of n° 7)	1996
20	Securities and investments (update of n° 8)	1996
21	The equity method (update of n° 8)	1996
22	Memorandum accounts	1997
23	Work in progress	1997
24	Intangible assets	1998
25	Accounting for taxes on income	1998
26	Accounting for transactions and balances in foreign currencies	1999
27	Introduction of the Euro as a reporting currency	1999

The role of ASSONIME and ASSIREVI has gone beyond that of acting merely as representatives in the consultative process preceding the publication of CSPC documents. As mentioned already, ASSONIME represents the interests of Italian limited liability companies. and assists such companies in interpreting the law, particularly through its *Circolari*. For instance, ASSONIME's Statement n° 139/94 provided a timely commentary on Law 503/94 which abolished the fiscal appendix (see below). ASSONIME publishes a newsletter that provides technical guidance on the problems faced by Italian companies in interpreting business law, whilst ASSIREVI (the association comprising audit firms registered by CONSOB, 23 at present) publishes its own commentaries dealing with both auditing standards and accounting principles. Details of the relevant interpretative documents issued by these two associations are given in Table 3.5.[7]

Table 3.5 Influential interpretations of Italian accounting regulations

YEAR	DOCUMENT	CONTENT
ASSONIME Circulars		
1982	Circolare 96	Accounting principles and the preparation of annual accounts
1994	Circolare 1	Application of Lgs. D. 127 to financial holding companies
1994	Circolare 34	Layout of annual accounts of industrial holding companies
1994	Circolare 42	Preparation of annual accounts
1994	Circolare 139	Changes to the rules on business income and to the Civil Code regulation on annual accounts
1995	Circolare 53	Income tax and taxation on net equity
1996	Circolare 50	Annual accounts of leasing companies
ASSIREVI Research Documents		
1993	Documento di ricerca 26	Differences between Civil Code regulations and CSPC recommendations
1994	Documento di ricerca 35	Accounting treatment of anticipated depreciation

LAWMAKING AND POLITICS IN ACCOUNTING

When rules are set down by the legislature, the normal processes of lawmaking intervene. Thus, when the Ministry of Justice created a Working Group to draft the law enacting the Fourth and Seventh Directives, it was quickly transformed into a full Ministerial Commission (the D'Alessandro Commission, named after its chairman, a Professor of Mercantile law), mainly composed of jurists. To begin with, the 20 members of the Commission comprised eight judges, nine professors of law, one certified accountant, one professor of accounting and one official from the Ministry of the Treasury. Subsequently, the membership was expanded and there were several changes in the composition of the Commission, as seen in Table 3.6.

The two Directives introduced a number of new legal concepts that have undoubtedly had a strong influence on the regulations governing financial reporting in Italy (Riccaboni and Di Pietra, 1996). For instance, the concept of *rappresentazione veritiera e corretta* ('true and fair view') has superceded the expression *chiarezza e precisione* ('clarity and accuracy') which was previously used in Italian law.

The legal drafting problems surrounding the implementation of the Directives were not straightforward. For instance, in the enabling decree (Lgs D 127 of 9 April 1991), articles 1-20 amended the Civil Code with respect to the provisions of the Fourth Directive whilst articles 21-46 set out a new law concerning groups of companies, no reference being made to the Civil Code in the latter case. The

Table 3.6 *Membership of the D'Alessandro Commission*

	ORIGINAL MEMBERSHIP (1983)	NEW MEMBERS (1983-1992)
Judges	8	12
Professors of law	9	7
Professors of accounting	1	2
Dottori Commercialisti	1	1
Official of the Ministry of the Treasury	1	-
Official of the Ministry for State Holdings	-	3
Officials from other ministries	-	2
IRI (State holding company)	-	1
ENI (State holding company)	-	1
Lawyers and notaries	-	3
Representative of the Banca d'Italia	-	3
CONSOB (Stock exchange commission)	-	4
Prime Minister's office	-	2
ASSIREVI (Association of audit firms)	-	2
Ragionieri Commercialisti	-	1
TOTAL	20	44

Note. The new members include not only additional members but also those replacing retiring members.

development of Article 2435 provides a good illustration of the piecemeal evolution of codified law. Article 2435 of the Code was redefined by Lgs. D 127/1991, the title being reworded to *'Pubblicazione del bilancio e dell'elenco dei soci e dei titolari di diritti sulle azioni'* in art. 4 of L 310 of 12 August 1993. A second paragraph was added by art. 3 of Lgs. D 526 of 30 December 1992. A third and last paragraph was added by art. 4 of L 310 of 12 August 1993. Finally, art. 7-bis of LD 357 of 10 June 1994 (converted into law as L 489 of 8 August 1994) extended the first paragraph.

The revision of the Civil Code dealt with changes in the preparation of annual accounts, balance sheet layout, income statement layout, valuation criteria, the notes to the accounts and the management report, as shown in Table 3.7.

The link between the Civil Code and more detailed legislation is also illustrated by the way in which asset revaluation is regulated in Italy. The Civil Code has established that the revaluation of assets is allowed only in extraordinary cases. As inflation cannot be considered an extraordinary event, revaluations due to inflation are allowed only under specific conditions regulated by law, where a relevant decree will stipulate the categories of assets involved, the procedures to be adopted, the changes to be made to the financial statements, and the fiscal effects.

Over the years, laws allowing the revaluation of assets have been issued in 1975, 1983, 1990 and 1991. The first of these (Law 576 of December 2, 1975) provided for a voluntary and tax-free monetary revaluation of tangible assets, the value of the assets and their relative depreciation being adjusted on the balance

Table 3.7 *Articles of the Italian Civil Code relating to annual accounts*

N°	CONTENT OF EACH ARTICLE OF THE CIVIL CODE
2423	Redazione del bilancio – Preparation of annual accounts
2423-bis	Principi di redazione del bilancio – Preparation principles
2423-ter	Struttura dello stato patrimoniale e del conto economico – Balance sheet and income statement layout
2424	Contenuto dello stato patrimoniale – Balance sheet content
2424-bis	Disposizioni relative a singole voci dello stato patrimoniale – Regulations governing balance sheet items
2425	Contenuto del conto economico – Income statement content
2425-bis	Iscrizione di ricavi, proventi, costi e oneri – Recording of revenues, other incomes, costs and other charges
2426	Criteri di valutazione – Evaluation criteria
2427	Contenuto della nota integrativa – Contents of the notes to the accounts
2428	Relazione sulla gestione – Management report
2435	Pubblicazione del bilancio e dell'elenco dei soci e dei titolari di diritti sulle azioni – Publication of the annual accounts and of the list of shareholders and owners of equity rights
2435-bis	Bilancio in forma abbreviata – Abridged version of the annual accounts

sheet and the revaluation surplus being transferred to a revaluation reserve as part of the shareholders' equity. Under this law, any distribution from the revaluation surplus was subject to taxation. The second (Law 72 of March 19, 1983) introduced 'indirect' revaluation which was subject to a maximum revaluation limit. The revaluation surplus had to be allocated to a special revaluation surplus account, and distribution was again permitted subject to taxation. Law 408 of December 29, 1990 was intended to achieve fiscal objectives through a voluntary but taxable revaluation of certain categories of assets. However, with a tax rate of 16% on real estate surplus and 20% on other depreciable assets, this opportunity was not taken by many firms. Finally, Law 413 of December 30, 1991 made revaluation compulsory on certain assets such as real estate and development land, a tax equal to 16% of the revaluation being levied, with various provisions for offsetting.

This interplay between fiscal regulations and legislation has resulted in some far-reaching contradictions in law, particularly over the tax treatment of depreciation where companies have tended to report fiscal depreciation in their published financial statements (Olivieri, 1994; Viganò, 1994). Another conflict between fiscal regulations and accounting law concerns the introduction and subsequent abolition of a requirement to publish as part of the income statement a reconciliation relating to tax charges, known as the *appendice fiscale* (the fiscal appendix).

Since Lgs D 127 stated that the evaluation criteria to be applied in drawing up an income statement were to be those laid down in the Civil Code, whilst art. 75 of TUIR stated that costs, in order to be fiscally deductible, must be charged to the

Table 3.8 Revaluation laws and fiscal regulations influencing accounting

YEAR	DATE	LAW/DECREE	N°
Revaluation laws			
1952	11 February	L	74
1975	2 December	L	576
1983	19 March	L	72
1990	29 December	L	408
1991	30 December	L	413
Fiscal regulations			
1986	22 December	DPR	917
1988	4 February	DPR	42
1990	27 April	LD	90
1991	30 December	L	413
1995	23 December	LD	542
1996	23 December	L	662
1996	31 December	LD	669

income statement, there was an inherent conflict of laws. As a result, Lgs D 127 required a reconciliation to be shown on the front of the income statement, whereby 'Value adjustments made exclusively as a consequence of tax policies' (item 24) and 'Provisions relating to tax benefits' (item 25) showed the effect of tax-allowable amounts of items such as accelerated depreciation. Thus, the 'Result for the year' (item 23) would be stated in accordance with the Civil Code criteria whilst 'Net income or loss' (item 26) would be in accordance with fiscal requirements.

Guidance on accounting treatment was offered both by the Ministry of Finance and CONSOB, and the legitimacy of this kind of legal compromise had been raised in the past in a court case before the Tribunal of Milan, and the high court (*Corte di Cassazione*) had found in 1985 that a company may disclose tax-based figures if it would be against its interest not to do so.[8]

Following the introduction of Lgs D 127, however, there was a vigorous debate on the technical issues of anticipated depreciation and deferred taxation (Ruggieri, 1993; Viganò, 1994; Rizzardi, 1995) and the more pragmatic matter of applying the regulations (Felizani, 1994; Spoletti, 1994; Dezzani, 1994, 1995; Previti Flesca, 1995). Indeed, an apparent benefit of the fiscal appendix was seen to be the effect of increasing financial disclosure (Piccoli, 1995). On the other hand, companies also took the opportunity to account for the maximum amount permitted by the fiscal authorities even where this was not justified, and it has also gave rise to a variety of treatments of balance sheet items and on deferred taxation in particular (Mio, 1996).

At this time, the political interest in accounting matters moved from the committee rooms to the floor of the Chamber of Deputies. During the short lived right wing Berlusconi government in 1994, the requirement of a fiscal appendix was abolished. This was brought into effect through L 503 of 8 August 1994, when the earlier law decree concerned with routine fiscal arrangements, LD 416 of 29 June 1994, was finally converted into law.[9]

The parliamentary debate that took place with respect to the draft converting LD 416 into law included criticism of the growing complexity of accounting requirements by a member of the left coalition Gruppo Progressisti Federativi (On. Agostini) and concern over its relationship to fiscal evasion by the member of the extreme right Alleanza Nazionale, who introduced an amendment from the government side (On. Barra).[10] On this occasion, the opposition voted with the government to remove the fiscal appendix, with the change in the law occurring as a result of last minute amendments introduced during the session of the Parliamentary Finance Committee.[11]

The opportunistic changes to LD 416 were in complete contrast to the lengthy procedures that had required the fiscal appendix in the first place. This led to questioning in the Press of the appropriateness of direct Parliamentary intervention in accounting matters (Caramel, 1994; Piazza, 1994) as well as further reflection on the usefulness of the fiscal appendix (Adamo, 1994; Monfregola, 1994; Fusa, 1994; Moroni, 1994; Albertinazzi, 1995; Guerini, 1995; Artiaco, 1995).

DISCUSSION

In many areas of policy making, the traditional forms of regulation have comprised either corporatist self regulatory arrangements or the assignment of regulatory functions to departments of government under the direct control of the political executive. To a varying extent, these approaches are being displaced by statutory regulation administered by expert agencies (Majone, 1991, 1996). In Italy, however, control of the regulatory process in accounting remains firmly with the lawmakers and their political superiors, in spite of the existence of public agencies and professional institutes with particular interests in the accounting domain.

Table 3.9 provides a summary of the different modes of regulation mentioned above. The first, regulation through parliament and government ties together the risk of regulatory failure with political accountability, eventually in the form of accountability to the electorate. However, as the Italian case shows, a complex framework of legislation is required in order to manage the regulatory detail, and this is prone to short term political interference. Statutory agencies, on the other hand, are likely to be independent of direct political control, particularly as the delegation of significant policy making powers is consistent with a perceived need on behalf of governments to commit themselves to longer term regulatory strategies whilst maintaining political credibility in the shorter term.[12] By implication, such agencies are not accountable to the electorate, and control tends to rest therefore on the strictness of procedural requirements and the transparency of decision making. In the third case, that of self regulation, although this can lead

Table 3.9 *Modes of regulation*

FORM	CHARACTERISTICS OF DIFFERENT MODES OF REGULATION
Regulatory bureaucracy	Hierarchical control with direct oversight by the legislature
	Laws, decrees and orders subject to democratic accountability
	Political interference creates a risk of regulatory failure
Delegated regulation	Powers exercised by a public agency on the basis of a legislative mandate
	Statutory regulations issued by expert and independent agencies
	Prone to lobbying by the regulated interests, bargaining over compliance
Self regulation	Affirmation of neo-corporatist collaboration
	Less formalized rules with more flexible enforcement
	Operated for the benefit of the regulated, with a risk of market failure

to less formalized rules, their design for the benefit of the regulated parties themselves and the tendency towards more flexible enforcement means that it runs the risk of market failure.

In addition to the issues of political accountability that differentiate alternative modes of regulation, two other factors appear to be driving some of the changes in regulatory structure that have been observed elsewhere: cost considerations and the effects of globalization. In the first case, the administrative costs of self regulation are normally internalized in the activity that is subject to regulation, while the cost of a public agency or bureaucracy would typically be borne by the taxpayer. Hence, a move towards self regulation might be expected. Second, growing economic interdependence has the effect of weakening the domestic impact of regulations whilst strengthening their impact externally, thus reducing the need for local coercion and increasing the need for international credibility.

In the area of accounting, the Financial Accounting Standards Board in the USA provides a model of delegated regulation, with minimal legislative oversight (Young, 1994). In Europe, the Accounting Standards Board in the U.K., the recently-formed *Comité de Régularisation Comptable* in France and *The Deutsche Standardisierungsrat* in Germany represent a move in the FASBs direction, although the ASB maintains more of the characteristics of a self regulating professional standard setting body whilst the CRC and DS are shaped by the state dirigisme and bureaucratic centralization which preceded them. In each of these cases, however, the regulatory strategy is to internalize the political process within an accountable agency, albeit with varying levels of political control. This is not the case in Italy, where political activity is highly visible and the traditional regulatory model is still adopted across much of society. In the realm of accounting, neither the transformation towards self regulation through an authorized professional standard setting body nor the delegation of regulation to a specialized public agency have occurred.

NOTES

[1] The term *Bilancio* could easily be translated incorrectly as Balance Sheet. In fact, there has been some confusion in Italian over these two terms, even amongst the legislators who drew up the Italian Civil Code of 1942.

[2] For further details, see Coda (1983), Bruni (1984), Catturi (1992), Cattaneo and Manzonetto (1993), and Colucci and Riccomagno (1997).

[3] For further details concerning the Fourth Directive, see Bertini (1980) and Fanni (1980); concerning the Seventh Directive, see Brunetti (1985), Canziani (1985) and Provasoli (1988).

[4] In addition to this default recognition of IASs contained in the CONSOB's statement, more specific acknowledgement is to be found in another CONSOB resolution (n° 4088 of 1989) which stipulated that IAS 8 should be followed when dealing with extraordinary items, prior period items and changes in accounting policies.

[5] Regulation of the Italian accounting and auditing profession dates back a number of centuries (Alexander and Latini, 1992; Took, 1995). The *Collegio dei Ragionieri* was established in Venice in 1581 following a decree issued by the Venetian Council of Doges and, by the eighteenth century, the *ragionieri* had organised themselves into local colleges in a number of Italian cities. Eventually, this led to legal recognition, albeit under the influence of the French Civil Code during the period of Napoleonic domination in the early 1800s. In Bologna, for example, a local government ordinance of 1813 created the forerunner of the present *Accademia Nazionale di Ragioneria*. However, the first national recognition of the profession of *Ragioniere* by the unified Italian State appeared in Law n° 327 of 1906 which gave the *ragioniere* the right to act as a public accountant. The first mention in law of the more highly qualified commerce graduate (*Dottore commercialista*) is to be found in a Royal Decree of 1929. Both qualifications are now fully recognised in laws since the *Dottore commercialista* was given legal status by Presidential decree n° 1067 in 1953 and the *Ragioniere* by decree n° 1068.

[6] It may be noted that the administration of the CSPC's activities is still carried out by the CNDC, whilst the CNR is responsible for the administration of the equivalent Auditing Commission (*Commissione per la Statuizione dei Principi di Revisione* - CSPR).

[7] Another organisation that also offers interpretation of accounting law is the Milan-based *Associazione di Dottori Commercialisti* (ADC), which offers guidance on certain accounting issues, through its so-called Rules of Conduct (*Norme di Comportamento*).

[8] *Corte di Cassazione*, I *Sezione civile*, n° 1966/1985

[9] LD 416 was in fact one of the law decrees issued by the previous left-wing Ciampi government. Although concerned with routine fiscal arrangements with respect to business income (*disposizioni fiscali in materia di reddito d'impresa*), the decree had met regular opposition, having been issued first in December 1993 as LD 554, again in February 1994 as LD 139 and finally in April 1994 as LD 261.

[10] Stenographic record of parliamentary proceedings (Atti Parlamentari, decreto legge n° 416, 29 June 1994).

[11] At present, Italian companies must give details of any consequences of the fiscal appendix as a note, an interesting outcome in that it raises the profile of the notes to the accounts.

[12] On the subject of regulation theories, see Peltzman (1976), Wood and Waterman (1991), Milgrom and Roberts (1992) and Majone (1996).

REFERENCES

Adamo, S. (1994). L'eliminazione dell'appendice fiscale: riflessi sull'attendibilità del bilancio d'esercizio, *Rivista dei Dottori Commercialisti*, No.4, pp.809-36.

Albertinazzi, G. (1995). Prime considerazioni sull'abrogazione dell'appendice fiscale dal CE, *Rivista dei Dottori Commercialisti*, No.1, pp.125-50.

Alexander, D., and Latini, R. (1995). Italy, in D. Alexander and S. Archer (eds.) *The European Accounting Guide*. London: Academic Press, pp.317-64.

Artiaco, M. (1995). I limiti informativi del bilancio di esercizio secondo il D. Lgs. 127/91, *Rivista Italiana di Ragioneria e di Economia Aziendale*, No.2, pp.86-100.

Benston, G.J. (1980). The establishment and enforcement of accounting standards: methods, benefits and costs, *Accounting and Business Research*, Vol.11, No.41, pp. 51-61.

Bertini, U. (1980). *Il progetto di SpA Europea e la IV direttiva: la contabilità delle imprese e la IV Direttiva CEE*. Milano: Etas.

Bromwich, M. (1985). *The Economics of Accounting Standard Setting*. Hemel Hempstead: Prentice-Hall.

Brunetti, G. (1985). *Il bilancio consolidato - VII direttiva comunitaria e principi contabili*. Padova: CEDAM.

Bruni, G. (1984). *I principi contabili generalmente accettati: l'impresa - economia - controllo – bilancio*. Milano: Giuffré.

Canziani, A. (1985). *La disciplina dei bilanci di gruppo alla luce della VII direttiva comunitaria: il bilancio consolidato - VII direttiva e principi contabili*. Padova: CEDAM.

Caramel, R. (1994). Senza appendice attendibilità del bilancio di esercizio, *Il Sole 24 Ore*, 3 August, p.17.

Cattaneo, M., and Manzonetto, P. (1993). *Il bilancio di esercizio, profili teorici e istituzionali negli anni '90*. Milano: Etas.

Catturi, G. (1992). *La redazione del bilancio di esercizio*. Padova: CEDAM.

Coda, V. (1983). Trasparenza dei bilanci di esercizio e principi contabili, *Rivista dei Dottori Commercialisti*, No.2, pp.183-97.

Colucci, E., and Riccomagno, F. (1997). *Il bilancio di esercizio e il bilancio consolidato dopo l'attuazione delle Direttive comunitarie*. Padova: CEDAM.

Dezzani, F. (1994). Il fisco si gioca in appendice, *Il Sole 24 Ore*, 23 March, p.18.

Dezzani, F. (1995). Ammortamenti anticipati anche soltanto nel 760, *Il Sole 24 Ore*, 3 March, p.16.

Di Pietra, R. (1997). Accounting regulation models in Italy, France and Spain, in J. Flower and C. Lefebvre (eds.) *Comparative Studies in Accounting Regulation in Europe*, Leuven: Acco, pp. 249-86.

Di Toro, P., and Ianniello, G. (1996). *La politica di redazione del bilancio di esercizio*. Padova: CEDAM.

Fanni, M. (1980). *Introduzione alla contabilità delle imprese e la IV Direttiva CEE*. Milano: Etas.

Feliziani, C. (1994). Appendice fiscale al bilancio, *Il Fisco*, No.12, pp.50-61.

Fusa, E. (1994). Codice e fisco sui bilanci ancora in cerca di armonia, *Il Sole 24 Ore*, 30 September, p.16.

Guerini, R. (1995). Stato patrimoniale e conto economico: aspetti controversi tratti dalle esperienze della prima adozione dle D. Lgs. 127/91, in *Rivista dei Dottori Commercialiasti*, No.5, pp.1143-72.

Horngren, C.T. (1985). Institutional alternatives for regulating financial reporting, *Journal of Comparative Business and Capital Market Law*, Vol.7, pp. 267-289.

Jönsson, S. (1991). Role making for accounting while the state is watching, *Accounting, Organizations and Society*, Vol.16, No.5/6, pp.521-546.

Klumpes, P.J. (1994). The politics of rule development: a case study of Australian pension fund accounting rule-making, *Abacus*, Vol.30, pp.140-159.

Majone, G., La Spina A. (1991). Lo Stato regolatore, *Rivista Trimestrale di Scienza dell'Amministrazione*, No.3, pp. 3 - 61.

Majone, G., (1996). A European regulatory state?, in J.J. Richardson (ed.) *European Union - Power and Policy-Making*. London: Routledge, pp. 266 - 277.

Majone, G., (1996). *Regulating Europe*, London: Routledge.

Milgrom, P. and Roberts, J. (1992). *Economics, Organizations and Management*, (1992), Englewood Cliffs: Prentice-Hall.

Mio, C. (1996). I bilanci delle società quotate dopo il D. Lgs. 127/91, *Rivista dei Dottori Commercialisti*, No.2, pp.1173-216.

Mitchell, A., and Sikka, P. (1993). Accounting for change: institutions of accountancy, *Critical Perspectives on Accounting*, Vol.4, March, pp.29-52.

Monfregola, C. (1994). Rimane aperta la questione degli ammortamenti anticipati, *Il Sole 24 Ore*, 15 September, p.15.

Moroni, S. (1994). Così il conto economico ritorna promiscuo, *Il Sole 24 Ore*, 22 July, p.16.

Olivieri, L. (1994). Bilancio e TUIR: le concordanze possibili, *Amministrazione e Finanza*, No.9, pp.54-61.

Peltzman, S. (1976). Towards a general theory of regulation, *Journal of Law and Economics*, Vol.19, August, pp.211-240.

Piazza, M. (1994). Addio all'appendice fiscale, *Il Sole 24 Ore*, 22 July, p.16 and 'Una normativa allineata alle disposizioni UE', *Il Sole 24 Ore*, 5 August, p.18.

Piccoli, A. (1995). L'appendice fiscale: una storia infinita, *Rivista dei Dottori Commercialisti*, No.3, pp.521-30.

Previti Flesca, G. (1995). I concetti delle voci 24 e 25 del conto economico e le loro contropartite patrimoniali, secondo il D. Lgs. 127/91 e la 503/94, *Rivista Italiana di Ragioneria e di Economia Aziendale*, No.5, pp.73-95.

Provasoli, A. (1988). *La valutazione delle partecipazioni e il bilancio consolidato: il bilancio consolidato - VII Direttiva comunitaria e principi contabili*. Padova: CEDAM.

Riccaboni, A., and Di Pietra, R. (1996). Il processo di armonizzazione contabile in Italia dopo il recepimento della IV Direttiva CEE, *Rivista dei Dottori Commercialisti*, No.4.

Riccaboni, A., and Ghirri, R. (1995). *European Financial Reporting: Italy*. London: Routledge.

Rizzardi, C. (1995). Sugli ammortamenti anticipati fisco rispettoso dei bilanci, *Il Sole 24 Ore*, 4 March, p.20.

Robson, K. (1993). Accounting policy making and "interest": accounting for research and development, *Critical Perspectives on Accounting*, No.3, pp.1-27.

Ruggieri, M. (1993). Osservazioni sul reddito di esercizio e reddito fiscale, *Rivista Italiana di Ragioneria e di Economia Aziendale*, No.6, pp.289-300.

Spoletti, F. (1994). Nuovo conto economico tra normativa civilistica e tributaria: ultime considerazioni sull'appendice fiscale, *Rivista dei Dottori Commercialisti*, No.3, pp.501-27.

Tomasin, G. (1982). I principi contabili in Italia, *Rivista dei Dottori Commercialisti*, No.1, pp.1-17.

Took, L. (1995). The history of financial reporting in Italy, in Walton P. (ed.), *European Financial Reporting: A History*, Academic Press, London, pp.157-68.

Viganò, A. (1994). Ammortamenti anticipati ed imposte differite, *Rivista dei Dottori Commercialisti*, No.2, pp.237-52.

Walker, R., and Robinson, P. (1993). A critical assessment of the literature on political activity and accounting regulation, *Research in Accounting Regulation*, Vol.7, pp.3-40.

Walker, R., and Robinson, P. (1994). Competing regulatory agencies with conflicting agendas: setting standards for cash flow reporting in Australia, *Abacus*, Vol.30, No.2, pp.119-39.

Wallace, R.S.O., and Gernon, H. (1991). Frameworks for international comparative financial accounting, *Journal of Accounting Literature*, Vol.10, pp.209-64.

Watts, R., and Zimmerman, J. (1978). Towards a positive theory of the determination of accounting standards, *Accounting Review*, Vol.54, No.2, pp.112-134.

Wood, D.B., and Waterman, R.W. (1991). The dynamics of political control of the bureaucracy, *American Political Science Review*, Vol.85, No.3, pp.801-828.

Young, J.J. (1994). Outlining regulatory space: agenda issue and the FASB, *Accounting, Organizations and Society*, Vol.19, No.19, pp.83-109.

Zan, L. (1994). Toward a history of accounting histories: perspectives from the Italian tradition, *European Accounting Review*, Vol.3, No.2, pp.255-307.

Zappalà, M. (1982). Il lavoro della Commissione per la statuizione dei principi contabili del Consiglio Nazionale dei Dottori Commercialisti, *Rivista dei Dottori Commercialisti*, No.1, pp.18-25.

4

THE 'PUBLIC INTEREST' IN THE CONTEXT OF ACCOUNTING REGULATION

Robert Day

INTRODUCTION

This chapter provides an analysis of the context within which accounting standard setters appear to operate. For this purpose, regulatory agency theory and practice has been utilised. The justifications for classifying accounting standard setting bodies as regulatory agencies are twofold and based on both structure and function. Regulation is defined as 'A rule prescribed for the management of some matter or the regulating of conduct' (Oxford English Dictionary, 1989). In the UK context, the regulation of conduct could be applied to accounting standards. The recognition of accounting standards in company law and the presence of a quasi-enforcement mechanism in the shape of the Review Panel reflects the status of these rules.[1] The classification of standard setting bodies as agencies admits a wide number of possible organisational forms with the term being applied to organisations carrying out a governmental type of function while remaining independent from any branch of government (Shafritz, 1985; Chandler and Plano, 1988). Alternatively, agencies may be described as *"organisations that involve voluntary and private enterprise resources but which nevertheless receive public funding and undertake tasks crucial to public policy"* (Stoker, 1990, p.127).

THE MEANING OF 'PUBLIC INTEREST'

References to 'the public interest' are to be found in a number of different contexts. Often it is used as a justification of action or an underpinning of beliefs. Its frequent use in political speeches and editorials illustrates the point. In law, politics and economics and other fields, it is often used almost as a holy grail, something so universally desirable that it does not warrant definition or interpretation. Perhaps the lack of specificity is caused by the fact that *"intellectual efforts to define the public interest have universally failed"* (Meltsner and Shrag, 1974, p.1), or perhaps public interest has been used strategically so often that it lacks any clarity or credence and its true meaning is obscured. This was put more strongly by Bailey in stating that *"There is perhaps no better example in all language of the utility of myth than the phrase 'the public interest"* (Bailey, 1962, p.97).

The nature of public interest may change over time. An example of this can be found in classic economic thought which tended to equate the market system with public interest, whereas the identification of imperfections in such a system have introduced a varying degree of government interference as being a necessary condition for satisfying such interest (Gill, 1980).

The law recognises the importance of public interest above certain obligations (Cripps, 1987) and this perspective has been referred to as seeking to vindicate causes other than the property or financial interests of their advocates (Robinson and Dunkley, 1995). Even stronger is the assertion that the purpose of law is to serve the public interest (Michael, 1986), but this implies almost a protective role in that 'public interest' means something in which the public, the community at large, has some pecuniary interest, or some interest by which their legal rights or liabilities are affected. Oliver (1991) considers that the exercise of state power under a liberal-democratic political system can be justified in these terms and uses the expression *"stewardship of the public interest"* (p.23) as a description of governmental functions.[2]

Political philosophers over time have implied the public interest as an end; from Plato's concern with the moral development of citizens as the purpose of the city state to Hobbes' emphasis on order through powerful leadership, Locke's protection of natural rights and the utilitarian assertion of the greatest good for the greatest number. More recently, Noll (1971) defined 'public interest' as the policies that the government would follow if it gave equal weight to the welfare of each member. Government therefore has a role if not an obligation to represent the public interest. Indeed it is what government is all about according to Robinson and Dunkley (1995). Public interest, in its broadest sense, is akin to the concept of good government; even adherence to the utilitarian calculus promoting the greatest good must be based on subjective views as to costs and benefits.

Despite the difficulties surrounding a definition, the utilitarian approach would appear nevertheless to provide the most specific understanding of the term. In view of the various contexts within which public interest is mobilised, if a greater emphasis were placed on providing definition, then perhaps seeing the concept operationalised in the light of a specific issue could provide a better critical understanding, but one that might be limited to that specific environment.

There is, however, another way in which public interest may be viewed, and that is as a process rather than an end. If we agree that the pluralistic political system is a fair one, the public interest can only be defined as the outcome of a political process in which various private and group interests compete (Meltsner and Shrag, 1974). Indeed, this leads to the ideal of 'public interest' resulting from a type of consensus-seeking process whereby preferences are examined impartially in seeking as tolerable and comprehensive a compromise among those interests as is possible.

THE PURPOSE OF REGULATION

Despite the fact that the use of regulatory agencies to carry out a variety of functions dates back to the nineteenth century, it is their proliferation in this century that has attracted the interest of both academics and critics. Studies of regulation range from specific studies in such areas as financial services (Moran, 1988; Large, 1993), hospitals (Noll, 1971, 1974) and labour (Moe, 1985), to more general studies often advocating deregulation (Noll and Owen, 1983). Although many of these investigations relate to the pricing of services, this is not usually the sole responsibility of the regulatory agency concerned. The quality of the service supplied and the dissemination of information may also be within the remit of the regulatory agency, but these functions can only be carried out and monitored if product and performance standards exist, as illustrated later in this chapter. In this arena, the public interest often represents some form of balance between consumers and producers.

Regulatory agencies have a clientele to serve (Self, 1977, 1985), which is normally the group that will be protected by their regulations. The traditional view of regulatory agencies was that they protected society by positioning themselves between unethical businessmen and corrupt politicians (Noll, 1971). Lemak's (1985) ideal model of a regulatory agency, based on the notion of fairness, describes procedures to restrain unethical behaviour in the private sector for, according to Stigler (1971), regulation is instituted primarily for the protection and benefit of the public at large, or some large sub-class of the public.[3] Miles and

Bhambri's (1983) 'regulatory activists' see their tasks, as members of the regulatory body, as representing the public interest. These and many other works all tend to emphasise the interests of society as a whole. However, in the context of regulation, Noll, (1971) introduces a third dimension by discussing the balance between employees and owners of regulated firms and the purchasers of the services provided. Noll and Owen (1983) talk of advancing the interests of members of society in their roles as consumers, but doing so in a manner that promotes economic efficiency.[4] Lemak (1985) synthesises public interest into the word 'fairness', meaning the balance between a reasonable return on investment for the producer and the receipt of quality products and services at fair prices for the consumers. All of these definitions appear to incorporate concepts of both equity and economic efficiency, but may also tend to imply conflict insofar as matters of equity are concerned.

REGULATION IN ACTION

Regulatory bodies, as the interface between producers and consumers, usually make statements of philosophy or position. The following section looks at examples from four UK regulatory bodies.

The former Monopolies and Mergers Commission (MMC), in its introduction to reports, often stated the rationale for investigating the particular matter. In its report on discounts to retailers in 1981, for instance, the introduction stated that: *"The Secretary of State in exercise of his powers under section 78(1) of the Fair Trading Act 1973 hereby requires the Monopolies and Mergers Commission to submit to him a report on the general effect on the public interest of the following practice.... "* (MMC, 1981, p.1). The conclusion to this report was again in the same terms: *"We conclude that the general effect of the practice on the public interest over recent years has not been harmful"* (9.23). Generally, the Commission would appear to lean towards consumers in its reports, although such orientation is usually as a result of promoting competition which may imply that firms must make reasonable returns in order to remain in the particular markets.

The 1993 Annual Report of Ofwat states that, within the general function of acting in a manner best calculated to ensure that water and sewage companies can properly carry out and finance their functions, the Director General has a duty to: (i) protect customers; (ii) promote economy and efficiency; and (iii) facilitate competition. It is not simply price that is regulated by Ofwat. The Report talks of ... *"the right quality service at the right price. There must also be scope for the companies to make progress on improving water quality and the aquatic environment"* (Ofwat, 1993). The orientation of Ofwat is not totally towards consumers. The primary duties of this regulatory body is to carry out functions properly and ensuring that: *"companies can finance their functions, in particular by securing a reasonable rate of return on their capital. Lenders and shareholders should be in a position where they can expect to receive a return sufficient, but no more than sufficient, to induce them to make loans and hold shares, if the company operates efficiently"* (Ofwat, 1997).

Ofgas, on the other hand, would appear to have more of a consumer orientation and illustrates this by reference to strategic issues relating to the price and standards of service and procedural issues relating to such matters as consultation and complaints procedures. This is further confirmed by the fact that Ofgas see that its *"principal job is to ensure British Gas does not take unfair advantage of its monopoly powers"* (Ofgas, 1997).

Finally, regulation is sometimes distributative, as illustrated by Oftel (the UK's Office of Telecommunications) whose guide states that the Director General *"must promote the interests of consumers, effective competition, efficiency by those providing services.... In carrying out this function, the Director General has to achieve the best balance as he sees it of these objectives"* (Oftel, 1993).

Generally, it is felt that the introduction of better competition within any of the markets covered by the above examples will work in the interest of consumers, although there would appear to be an appreciation of the fact that firms must make adequate returns in order to ensure better competition and consumer benefits. This would appear to be in accordance with much of the regulatory theory discussed in the previous section whereby a balance may be made between consumer interests and economic efficiency.

ACCOUNTING REGULATION

The public interest aspect of accounting regulation can also be examined in terms of both producers and consumers, the former being the preparers of financial statements and the latter being the users. The regulation of accounting by the promulgation of accounting standards is a mechanism whereby the consumers of information may be assured of the quality of that information. Since the introduction of the limited liability form of company under the 1855 Companies Act, regulation has been in place to protect these consumers, at that time thought to be only investors and creditors. With the development of the stakeholder view of the firm, more users groups are now recognised.[5] It can be argued that the consumers of accounting information need the same protection as the consumers of other commodities. However, as in other spheres of regulation, public interest is also considered to incorporate efficiency. This would appear to have been acknowledged by the ASB (1991) in its Qualitative Characteristics Statement, by recognising a cost-benefit trade-off in the production of information.

The earlier discussions in this chapter would indicate that agencies may serve the public interest in one of two ways: firstly, by the agency providing a definition of public interest against which pronouncements may be compared; alternatively, if the definition is process-based, and provided appropriate procedures are adopted by the agency, then public interest may be satisfied through adherence to the process.

The term 'public interest' was in fact incorporated in the original 1970 Constitution of the ASC, *i.e., "The Committee's objects shall be to define accounting concepts, to narrow differences of financial accounting and reporting treatment and to codify generally accepted best practice in the public interest."* However, no definition was given of what was meant by this. The terminology was changed to 'general interests' in the ASC's 1982 Constitution. Indeed, in a written answer to a parliamentary question on 13th December 1989, John Redwood (the Parliamentary Under Secretary of State at the Department of Trade and Industry) quoted directly from the 1982 constitution: *"...shall not regard themselves as delegates of sectional interests but shall be guided by the need to act in the general interests of the community and of the accountancy profession as a whole"* (Hansard, Vol.163).

The lack of definition by the ASC of the term 'public interest' was partly compensated by the Corporate Report (1975), a document which emphasised users and the responsibility to them by preparers: *"Our basic approach has been that corporate reports should seek to satisfy, as far as possible, the information needs of users. We believe there is an implicit responsibility to report incumbent on every economic entity whose size or format renders it significant. This responsibility arises from the custodial role played in the community by economic entities."* (ASSC, 1975, s1.12). Unfortunately, the Corporate Report did not address the potential problems of conflicting information needs, whereby disclosure benefiting one user group might harm the interests of another group, nor did it appear to recognise that public interest is formed from an array of different interests. In any case, the Corporate Report was never officially accepted as the objectives of, nor as an official policy document of, the ASSC.

In the United States, the situation is similar to that expressed in the earlier quote from Hansard: *"...the standard setters are expected to represent the entire constituency as a whole and not be representatives of a specific constituency group"* (Belkaoui, 1985). The wider public interest definition is also found in the United States where the mission statement of the Financial Accounting Standards Board (FASB, 1978) states: *"The mission of the FASB is to establish and improve standards of financial accounting and reporting for the guidance and education of the public, including issuers, auditors and users of financial information."*

Both UK and US accounting standard setters imply that regulation should be for the benefit of stakeholders, but fall short of giving a definition linked to public interest, perhaps on the grounds that, as with 'true and fair', the context may change over time. Conceptual framework projects have all produced a similar range of stakeholders, thus acknowledging some version of public interest, but have failed to deal with the resolution of inter-group conflicts either by ignoring the possibility or by satisfying the group with the largest demands on the assumption that this will satisfy all others. In its Statement of Principles, the ASB (1991) overcame the problem of differing (but not competing) interests by concentrating on one group: *"As investors are providers of risk capital to the enterprise, the provision of financial statements that meet their needs will also meet most of the needs of other users that financial statements can satisfy. Awarding primacy to investors does not imply that other users are to be ignored. The information prepared for investors is useful as a frame of reference for other users, against which they can evaluate more specific information that they may obtain in their dealings with the enterprise.*" (ASB, 1991, para. 12). It is difficult to see this either as a definition of 'public interest' or as a statement of the way such interest might be satisfied.

THE REGULATORY PROCESS

If consumers and producers jointly define public interest, then in accounting terms the interests of both the preparers and the users of accounts need to be considered in the regulatory process. There would appear to be two ways in which a regulatory agency could satisfy this requirement. Firstly, the composition and the voting powers of the members of the regulatory agency must reflect their constituents. Secondly, inputs to the regulatory process must be made by both preparers and users. This section examines how far this may have been fulfilled.

Membership

Details of membership in the early days of the ASSC and ASC are not easy to obtain. Individuals are often identifiable only from papers and minutes of meetings held in the ASC archives. The 1982 Constitution of the ASC provided for the reservation of up to five places out of twenty on the committee for users. Taylor and Turley (1986) identified four user members of the ASC from their organisational backgrounds. Whereas the ASB's 1991 Exposure Draft on Objectives of Financial Statements, like the Corporate Report (ASSC, 1975), identified seven user groups, the membership of the ASB would only appear to contain one user (although one group, the government, may be said to be represented through its observer status).

Although some writers consider that the background of agency staff only represents one of a broad range of factors affecting agency behaviour (Moe, 1985), Reagan (1987) provides evidence that professional norms do contain value elements as well as reflecting technical ability. On the other hand, Grant and Marsh (1977) consider the 'common background' argument somewhat dubious on the grounds that this facilitates contact rather than creating influence. These apparent contradictions are in some ways reconciled by Lemak (1985), who talks of the interaction of the regulators and the regulated as a form of agency capture, as it is not simply the sharing of norms that leads to influence but also the contacts, both social and institutional (through professional associations), which bring about influence.

From the analysis of the background of members of accounting regulatory bodies in Table 6.1, it would appear that there is a high degree of commonality both in professional training and backgrounds. This analysis of the members of the ASC between 1978 and 1987 shows some changes in the background of members following the new ASC constitution of 1982. Up until that date, all members of the ASC were also members of CCAB bodies, reflecting the allocation of seats between the professional associations (with the ICAEW having the right to appoint 12 out of 23 members). From 1982 to 1987, two members of the ASC were not members of CCAB bodies. Despite the 1982 Constitution providing for up to five of the 20 places being reserved for users of financial accounts, there did not appear to be a significant shift from members in industry and practice to representatives of other organisations during this period.

Table 4.1 *Analysis of ASC members, 1978-1987.*

DATE	ASC MEMBERS	CCAB MEMBERS	ICAEW MEMBERS	INDUSTRY/ PRACTICE	OTHERS
30.11.78	23	23	12	18	5
30.11.79	22	22	12	17	5
30.11.80	22	22	11	16	6
30.11.81	22	22	11	16	6
23.03.82	23	23	12	16	6
30.11.82	20	18	9	15	5
30.11.83	20	18	8	14	6
01.09.84	20	18	8	15	5
01.09.85	20	18	8	15	5
01.09.86	20	18	8	15	5
01.09.87	21	19	9	14	6*

Note. *including 2 members with no apparent industrial/professional connections.*

Those members in practice tended to be partners in larger firms of accountants, while the industry members held senior positions in major companies in the UK. The last column includes those who appear to be neither preparers nor auditors of financial statements: representatives of local authorities, nationalised industries, Lloyds and the Stock Exchange, together with academics.[6] The latter had been members of the ASSC/ASC since 1969, and, from that date until 1990, there had been four such members (Edey, Bromwich, Gray and Nobes). Indeed, the ASC issued a working paper in July 1988 on the establishment of closer links with the academic community. By 1990, there were some nine academics serving as members of or advisers to the ASC and its working parties (ASC, 1/76/2).[7]

The formation of the Accounting Standards Board in 1990 saw the introduction of a full-time Chairman and Technical Director. Up to 1997, there had been no changes in these office holders. By contrast, of the original seven (part-time) members of the Board appointed in 1990, none still were members in 1997. The members in professional practice between both these years were either partners or others holding senior positions, and the industrial members were all of Director level within large public companies.

In the US, insofar as FASB is concerned, in 1987 for example, the seven member Board of FASB contained six CPA's (Certified Public Accountants), four of whom had practising experience with some of the largest international accounting firms, while the others consisted of an ex treasurer of IBM, a director of auditing and accounting with a regional public accounting firm and one academic. Although it is a requirement of FASB that all Board Members sever their relationships with previous employers, six of the members had undergone the same training and had probably acted more as preparers than users of financial statements. By 1995, the composition had changed to only five CPA's, the other two members coming from academia and the securities industry. Nevertheless, the majority voting system could mean dominance by those with a background in big industry and large accounting firms.

The appointment system

Not only may the identity of accounting regulators be significant, but also their method of appointment, *i.e.*, they are appointed by those they are seeking to regulate or by those on whose behalf they will be acting. In the United States, Reagan (1987) describes how attempts have been made to make regulatory commissions more accountable through strengthening the President's power to appoint and remove the chairmen of these commissions. The result of this has led to a reduction rather than an increase in the independence of commissions in the opinion of Welborn (1977): *"through the position of chairman, the regulatory agencies stand in relatively close association with the executive branch in various important respects, rather than being truly independent of it"* (p. 141). This is somewhat in opposition to the theories of agency capture by the regulated industry (see, for example: Lemak, 1985; Thompson and Jones, 1982; Mitnik, 1980), although the two views can be reconciled by the fact that the appointment to a specialist agency may have to draw on the only source of available technical expertise, *i.e.*, the industry being regulated. This is the justification given by Reagan (1987) for so many regulators having a background inside the industry. An alternative analysis might be provided by ascertaining whether regulators are appointed on the basis of their close association with governmental thinking or their perceived independence.

The appointment of all Board members of FASB, a non-governmental agency, rests with the Financial Accounting Foundation (FAF).[8] Miller and Redding (1988) consider it theoretically possible that a Board member might modify a position on an issue to ensure re-appointment, although they claim that there is no evidence that this has ever occurred. They identify the greatest threat to independence arising if a particular group (preparers) were to gain control of the FAF Board of

Trustees, although they talk of this in terms of it being highly improbable. Belkaoui (1985), however, illustrates the control over the US standard setting process by the 'big eight'. This occurs through the control by the 'big eight' of the AICPA whose Board of Directors have exclusive authority to elect and remove the members of the FAF Board of Trustees. If, therefore, the major accountancy firms are considered as preparers rather than users, the hypothetical case described by Miller and Redding (1988) represents reality.

The officers of the ASSC, a committee of the ICAEW, were appointed by the Institute's President. Amendments of its constitution in 1970/71 and 1975/76 brought in other CCAB bodies, each with a fixed number of places. Each of the members was appointed by their own professional body. The revision of the ASSC constitution in 1976 stated in Paragraph 2c) that *"The Chairman and Vice-Chairman would be appointed by the Chairman of CCAB on the recommendation of ASSC...."*. Howlin and Skerratt (1992) describe how, under the new ASC constitution of 1982, a Nominations Committee was set up consisting of a representative of each of the CCAB bodies and the ASC chairman. This balance of representation appears to be evidenced by a letter from W Hyde (who had ceased to be a member of the ASC in 1979) to the President of CCAB dated 5.8.82, stating: *"In formulating our recommended list of members we have taken careful note of the need to ensure appropriate representation, balance, continuity and rotation and to provide for these for the future..."* (ASC 5/3/5). This was presumably written in his capacity as ICMA representative on the Nominations Committee.

The Nominations Committee lapsed between 1982 and 1989 with appointments being made by CCAB office-holders, consulting with the ASC chairman where appropriate (Howlin and Skerratt, 1992). In fact, the 1983 Constitution of the ASC contained the provision in paragraph 12 that the power of appointment of members was vested in the CCAB. In 1986, the ASC revisited its 1981 document 'Setting Accounting Standards' and noted that CCAB bodies had retained effective control of membership matters with only one non-accountant and only three users on the Committee (ASC 1/41/2). The dominance of CCAB members indicated above is not surprising given this structure.

The formation of the ASB has shifted power away from the accounting profession. As an incorporated company, the ASB's procedural arrangements are stated in its Articles of Association. Paragraph 34 (b) and (c) grants powers of appointment, reappointment and removal from office to the Appointments Committee whose powers also extend to the office of Chairman, Vice Chairman and Technical Director. Paragraph 1 of the Articles defines the Appointments Committee as *"...the board of directors as constituted from time to time of The Financial Reporting Council Limited and any 3 other members of the Council of The Financial Reporting Council Limited whom the directors of the Financial Reporting Council Limited may nominate for this purpose from time to time"*.

According to the FRC Memorandum and Articles of Association, the Board of Directors of the Financial Reporting Council cannot exceed four in number (paragraph 23a) and the power of appointment and removal, including that of the chairman, rests with the Secretary of State for Trade and Industry and the Governor of the Bank of England (paragraph 23b) or their duly authorised representatives.[9] Guidelines are, however, given to the two appointees concerning the desired qualification of directors, including (i) membership of the CCAB or with experience relevant to the interests of the accountancy profession; (ii) membership of the Council of the International Stock Exchange or with experience relevant to the carrying on of financial activities; (iii) membership of the governing body of the Confederation of British Industry or with experience relevant to the interests of industry and commerce (paragraph 23c).

The Council of the FRC may have up to 30 members who are appointed by the directors of FRC Ltd. Apart from the directors themselves, there are four reserved places: one government representative appointed by the Secretary of State for Trade and Industry, one representative of the Bank of England appointed by the Governor, plus the Chairmen of the ASB and of the Review Panel, both acting ex-officio. The additional members should be members of the accountancy profession in either the public or private sector and users in order to secure "...*a proper balance between the interests of persons engaged in the preparation of accounts and those engaged in reporting on accounts and of the public*" (FRC Mem and Arts paragraph 4[1][f][2]).

The function of the Council, as given by the Memorandum and Articles of Association, is to: "... *determine the general policy of the Company in relation to the attainment of its objects, and to formulate the general nature of the guidance and advice to be given from time to time by the Company to such companies or other bodies as it may establish or support for that purpose*" (para 42 [1]).

Wilson (1980), In his study of the behaviour of regulatory agencies, identifies in the case of governmental agencies three types of agency member, or employee. The first type, 'politicians', does not apply directly in the case of accounting regulation. The second type, 'careerists', who are described as "*employees who identify their careers and rewards with the agency*" (Wilson, 1980, p.374) did not exist in the ASC because the mainly voluntary nature of the work precluded such a structure, and it is probably too early in the life of the ASB to identify any careerists. For the FASB, the term of office of Board members is limited to two terms of five years. Project managers, however, may remain longer with FASB and can be promoted to that position. Additionally, industry fellows are appointed for two year periods, usually on secondment from Big Eight firms (Miller and Redding, 1988).

'Professionals' are the third type, seeking either a stepping stone to a better career or remaining with the agency for the maintenance of their professional esteem. Reagan (1987) considers that a significant input to regulatory behaviour is the 'revolving-door' tendency for regulators who come from the regulated industries to see things from the industry viewpoint, and to have a strong incentive to please the leaders of the industry they are regulating, in the hope of moving into good private sector positions. The analysis of members of the ASC in this chapter illustrates that a majority held senior private sector positions while working as standard setters, and it would seem unlikely that actions taken when acting as regulators would have damaged their private sector employers (or clients). Although the writer could find no analysis, it would, in the case of FASB, not be unreasonable to assume that Board members on expiry of their term of office returned to the profession, possibly with enhanced reputations. This is more accentuated in the case of practice fellows who are usually seconded from the large firms and, as Miller and Redding (1988, p.46) explain, *"This dominance is not planned, but merely reflects the facts that a larger firm is more capable of absorbing the loss of the fellow's services for two years and of using the special knowledge that he or she gains at the FASB. Virtually all fellows have been promoted to partner after their service, and some have continued to work with the Board as representatives or spokespersons for their firms."*

Inputs

The second way in which the public interest could be reflected in the work of an agency is through inputs to the regulatory process. These inputs exist in the form of comment letters received on Exposure Drafts. Although these may only recognise part of the process, nevertheless such letters represent one of the few indicators of this process. Despite calls for openness, as in the preliminary Watts Report of 1990, the process of standard setting is still carried out behind closed doors in the UK, in contrast to FASB who open Board meetings to the public.

Given the limited openness of comment letters, it is sometimes difficult to distinguish between preparers and users in such letters. Indeed, Beresford (1993) cites a number of examples of preparers presenting themselves to FASB as users.[10] The examples quoted in the following section represent only three UK Exposure Drafts issued by the ASC, but in the opinion of the writer, these tend to reflect the general composition of Exposure Draft respondents.

In the case of ED 16, insofar as foreign exchange provisions were concerned, only two respondents (Delta Group and Thompson Organisation) could be interpreted as acknowledging the needs of users, the former recognising user difficulties, and the latter mentioning difficulties of comparability, which may be assumed to be a user-orientated comment. Nevertheless, as all companies have a statutory obligation to prepare financial statements, it may be assumed that these comments also are preparer-orientated. Of the representative bodies, only the British Property Federation and the Committee of London Clearing Banks replied and both of these replies may have been from a preparer point of view.

In the case of ED 21, more companies seemed to acknowledge user needs. Out of the 45 company respondents, nine mention users or comparability. Of the 7 representative bodies (accounting bodies and the DTI having been excluded from the total), two (The Association of Investment Trust Companies and the Committee of London Clearing Banks) demonstrate their preparer orientation by requesting exemption from the standard in their comment letters.

ED 27 received a similar number of responses from companies (46), but more (13) from representative bodies. Seven of these companies acknowledge the needs of users in some way through mention of shareholder information, comparability or understandability. Insofar as the representative bodies are concerned, only two appear to represent users. One of these, the Society of Investment Analysts, would appear to be a user by definition, and the other, The British Insurance Association, states its interest both as a preparer and as a user for institutional investment purposes.

Generally, it has been assumed in the above analysis that the accounting profession tends to be more orientated towards preparers than users in that they are either preparing financial statements or auditing those statements prepared by clients (although on occasions they could be acting as interpreters of information). Even where replies are received from users, Perks and Georgiou (1992) writing of FRS 1, believe that *"...the Board is influenced more by the interests of producers than by the information requirements of users . An analysis of the responses to the draft standard shows that, amongst users of financial statements, most favoured the direct method; amongst producers of financial statements the overwhelming majority strongly objected to the direct method being required and argued that a choice between the two methods should be allowed. Similarly, the large-scale exemptions for small companies, appear to result from pressure from producers against the proposals in the exposure draft"* (p. 39).

Not only does there appear to be the problem of user inputs not being given sufficient weight in the process of standard setting, but the lack of interest by users could compromise the achievement of a public interest orientation of standards. A former Chairman of the Financial Accounting Standards Board, is of the opinion that a standard which pleases the largest number of respondents to Exposure Drafts may not be consistent with the mission of the FASB (Beresford, 1975). He accounts for the low level of user participation by suggesting that users are not as well equipped or organised as other groups, thus causing an imbalance in decision-making: *"Users are experts in what information would be most useful to them and why and the relative benefits of the Board's proposals in making capital allocation decisions. While other constituents and the Board, can only speculate about what would be most beneficial to users, only the users really know"* (Beresford, 1993, p.73).

CONCLUSIONS

The general function of a regulatory agency is seen as serving the public interest, and most general definitions of this term suggest a balance between the interests of both consumers (users) and producers (preparers). However, the term 'public interest' does not appear to have been defined even when used explicity by the ASC or the IASC or implicitly by the ASB or FASB. If accounting, like many other fields, contains conflicting goals, the solution may only be the achievement of some form of interpersonal utility orderings to achieve a non-dictatorial social welfare ordering (Boadway and Bruce, 1984). At present, some solutions would appear to deny the existence of conflicting aims through emphasising just one user group, shareholders, whose requirements it considers sufficient to cover all other groups.

Insofar as public interest solutions may arise as a result of the regulatory process, two problems have been identified. Firstly, the membership of the regulatory bodies does not appear to be representative of the body it might be assumed to serve, as it appears that users are not now, nor have been in the past, well represented on standard setting bodies. Secondly, it is seen that users appear to have very little input into the regulatory process, which, if they do have differing information requirements, would imply that any process which ignores the idea of balancing demands or achieving a social consensus is unlikely to produce public interest solutions.

NOTES

[1] It is not only since the advent of the ASB that the status of accounting standards has been seen in this light. In 1978, the Chairman of ASC, Mr Tom Watts, stated that «...we must be clear that we are a body which is setting a kind of law and the only way we can do that ... is by consent or persuasion».

[2] Smith and Hague (1973, p.26) describe how, under democratic theory, «power emanates from the people and is to be exercised in trust for the people».

[3] Zander (1968) discusses the monopoly of the legal profession in the context of the public interest.

[4] Perhaps the disclosure to shareholders of useful information which did not harm the reporting enterprise might be a suitable analogy.

[5] The user lists' from the ASSC (1975), FASB (1978) and ASB (1991) all recognise similar groups.

[6] For example, the 30.11.82 membership list included members of the University of Reading, the British Railways Board, the Stock Exchange, the Government Accountancy Service and Somerset County Council.

[7] These references (ASC X/X/X) refer to file numbers in the ASC archive held at the John Rylands Library, University of Manchester.

[8] The Financial Accounting Foundation acts in many ways like the FRC in the UK and as well as having the power of appointments, they are also responsible for funding and overseeing the work of FASB.

[9] This is basically the same institutional arrangement that exists for the Securities and Investment Board (SIB). Other regulatory bodies such as the Health and Safety Commission have members appointed by the Secretary of State for Employment after consultation with representative bodies.

[10] In the UK, the members of the Committee of London Clearing Banks describe themselves as both users and preparers in a comment letter dated 30.6.84 (ASC 1/7/4).

REFERENCES

Accounting Standards Board (1991). *Statement of Principles Chapters 1 and 2. The Objective of Financial Statements and the Qualitative Characteristics of Financial Information*. London: ASB.

Accounting Standards Steering Committee (1975). *The Corporate Report*. London: ASSC.

Bailey, S.K. (1962). The Public Interest: Some Operational Dilemmas, in C.J. Friedman (ed.) *The Public Interest*. New York: Atherton.

Belkaoui, A. (1985). *Public Policy and the Practice and Problems of Accounting*. Westport, Connecticut: Quorum.

Beresford, D.R. (1993). Frustrations of a standard setter, *Accounting Horizons*, December, pp.70-6.

Beresford, D.R. (1995). How should the FASB be judged?, *Accounting Horizons*, June, pp.56-61.

Boadway, R.W., and Bruce, N. (1984). *Welfare Economics*. Oxford: Basil Blackwell.

Chandler, R.C., and Plano, J.C. (1988). *Public Administration Dictionary*. Santa Barbara: ABC Clio.

Cripps, Y. (1987). *The Legal Implications of Disclosure in the Public Interest*. Oxford: ESC Publishing.

Financial Accounting Standards Board (1978). *Statement of Financial Accounting Concepts 1 (SFAC 1). Objectives of Financial Reporting*. Stamford: Financial Accounting Standards Board.

Gill, R.T. (1980). *Economics and the Public Interest*. Santa Monica, California: Goodyear Publishing.

Grant, W., and Marsh, M. (1977). *The Confederation of British Industry*. London: Prentice Hall International.

Howlin, E., and Skerratt, L. (1992). A brief history of the Accounting Standards Committee, in *Handbook for the Accounting Standards Committee Archive*. Manchester: John Rylands Library.

Large, A. (1993). *Financial Services Regulation: Making the Two Tier System Work*. London: SIB.

Lemak, D.J. (1985). Whatever happened to the C.A.B.? in G.A. Daneke and D.J. Lemak (eds.) *Regulatory Reform Reconsidered*. Boulder, Colorado: Westview Press, pp.3-19

Meltsner, M., and Shrag, P.G. (1974). *Public Interest Advocacy: Materials for Clinical Legal Education*. Boston: Little Brown and Co.

Michael, J. (1986). Information law, policy and the public interest, in M. Ferguson (ed.) *New Communication Technologies and the Public Interest*. London: Sage, pp.102-21

Miles, R.H., and Bhambri, A. (1983). *The Regulatory Executives*. California: Sage Publications.

Miller, P.B.W., and Redding, R.J. (1988). *The FASB, The People, The Process, The Politics*. 2nd ed., Illinois: Irwin.

Mitnik, B.M. (1980). *The Political Economy of Regulation*. New York :Columbia University Press.

Moe, T. M., 1985. Control and feedback in economic regulation: the case of the N.L.R.B., *American Political Science Review*. Vol.79, December, pp.1094-116

Monopolies and Mergers Commission (1981). *Discounts to Retailers*. London: HMSO.

Moran, M. (1988). Politics and law in financial regulation, in C. Graham and I. Prosser (eds.) *Waiving the Rules*. Milton Keynes: Open University Press, pp.56-72

Noll, R. G. (1971). *Reforming Regulation: An Evaluation of the Ash Council Proposals*. Washington D C: The Brookings Institute.

Noll, R.G. (1974). The consequences of public utility regulation of hospitals, in *Controls on Health Care*. Washington DC: National Academy of Sciences, pp.25-48

Noll, R.G., and Owen, B.M. (1983). *The Political Economy of De-regulation: Interest Groups in the Regulatory Process*. Washington DC: American Enterprise Institute for Public Policy Research.

Ofgas (1997). *Guide to Ofgas*. http://www.ofgas.gov.uk

Oftel (1993). *A Guide to the Office of Telecommunications*.

Ofwat (1997). *Summary of the Director General's Annual Report 1996*.

Oliver, D. 1991. *Government in the United Kingdom: The Search for Accountability, Effectiveness and Citizenship*. Milton Keynes: Open University Press.

Oxford English Dictionary (1989). Oxford: University Press.

Perks, R.W., and Georgiou, C. (1992). Financial Reporting Standard 1: a fresh start?, *Management Accounting*, February, p.39.

Reagan, M.C. (1987). *Regulation - The Politics of Policy*. Boston: Little Brown.

Robinson, D., and Dunkley, J. (1995). *Public Interest Perspectives in Environmental Law*. Colorado Springs, Colorado: John Wiley and Sons.

Self, P. (1977). *Administrative Theories and Politics*. London: Allen and Unwin.

Self, P. (1985). *Political Theories of Modern Government*. London: Allen and Unwin.

Shafritz, J. M. (1985). *Dictionary of Public Administration*. New York: Facts on File Publications.

Smith, B. L. R., and Hague, D. C. (1973). *Dilemma of Accountability*. Macmillan: London.

Stigler, G.J. (1971). The theory of economic regulation, *Bell Journal of Economics and Management Science*. Vol.2, Spring, pp.3-21.

Stoker, C. (1990). Government beyond Whitehall, in P. Dunleavy, A. Gamble and C. Peele (eds.) *Developments in British Politics*. Basingstoke: Macmillan, pp.126-49

Taylor, P., and Turley, S. (1986). *The Regulation of Accounting*. Oxford: Blackwell.

Thompson, F., and Jones, L.R. (1982). *Regulatory Policy and Practices*. New York: Praeger Publishers.

Welborn, D.M. (1977). *The Governance of Federal Regulatory Agencies*. Knoxville, Tennessee: University of Tennessee Press.

Wilson, J.Q. (1980). *The Politics of Regulation*. New York: Basic Books.

Zander, M. (1968). *Lawyers and the Public Interest*. London: Weidenfeld and Nicolson.

5

PARTICIPATION AND NON-PARTICIPATION IN THE STANDARD SETTING PROCESS

Doreen Gilfedder and Ciaran Ó hÓgartaigh

INTRODUCTION

The Accounting Standards Board ('the ASB') was established in the UK in 1990. Among its objectives is the improvement of standards of financial accounting and reporting for the benefit of users, preparers and auditors of financial information (ASB, 1991). The Board sets out *inter alia* to "*determine what should be incorporated in accounting standards based on research, public consultation and careful deliberation about the usefulness of the resulting information*" (ASB, 1991, p.2) and through "*feedback from both the regulated and the consumer*" (Financial Reporting Council, 1997, p.56). It aims to meet this objective by issuing accounting standards after "*extensive consultation*" (Financial Reporting Council, 1992, p.7). This chapter examines the characteristics of those who formally involve themselves in the standard setting process of the ASB by making submissions regarding its proposals for accounting standards. In doing so, the chapter contributes to a view of the public consultation that shapes accounting standards.

CONCEPTS OF POWER AND ACCOUNTING STANDARD SETTING

There are broadly two contrasting views on the nature of accounting standard setting: the technical view and the political view. The former *"sees the problem of choice as essentially one of identifying 'best' accounting practice . . . which can be solved by the development and application of technical rules or concepts of accounting"* (Taylor and Turley, 1986, p.68). The political view, on the other hand, argues that the best alternative is relative (Kam, 1990) and often depends on the way that proposed standards affect personal interests (Mautz, 1974). Under the political view, policy decisions represent choices between conflicting interests that might be better served by different practices. Hence, the setting of accounting standards is a political activity. The consequences of such activity involve resource allocation and redistribution of wealth between the stakeholders of the reporting entity.

Political choices might not, however, be neutral. Any analysis of political choices must also consider issues of power (Cooper and Sherer, 1984) because, even in ostensibly democratic societies, certain groups may wield disproportionate amounts of power and influence. Similarly, rule makers may unduly favour particular groups (Underdown and Taylor, 1986, p.17).

This chapter explores the exercise of power in the ASB's standard setting process in the context of what Lukes (1974) terms the one-dimensional view of power. The one-dimensional view is *"a focus on behaviour in the making of decisions on issues over which there is an observable conflict of (subjective) interests, seen as express policy preferences, revealed by political participation"* (Lukes, 1974, p.15). This view of power is primarily based on the writings of Dahl (1961, 1976), Polsby (1963, 1968), Merelman (1968) and Wolfinger (1971) and traditionally forms the basis of studies of the regulatory process in accounting. Accounting research based on a one-dimensional view of power typically concerns the distribution of such power. The pluralistic model of power suggests a broad distribution, whereas élitist models posit more narrow distributions. The ASB suggests that its model of consultation is a pluralist one, a process designed to *"seek and consider carefully all points of view"* (Financial Reporting Council, 1994, p.16). Research in other standard setting contexts, however, indicates that such processes are élitist.

Submissions on discussion memoranda and exposure drafts are the most observable form of lobbying and these have formed the main basis for previous lobbying research. Twenty such studies have been published since 1980 (Walker and Robinson, 1993). Such research generally examines the frequency of responses to proposed accounting standards.

It is evident from Weetman, Davie and Collins (1996), who provide a useful summary of prior research in this area, that corporate respondents (preparers of financial statements) are the most numerous and that responses from users of financial statements are generally uncommon. For instance, with regard to the Financial Accounting Standards Board ('the FASB') in the USA, more than 50 per cent of all written responses come from preparers of financial statements, while less than 10 per cent come from users (Miller, 1985). An analysis of submissions to the FASB on 30 randomly selected Statements of Financial Accounting Standards by Mezias and Chung (1989) found that preparers of financial statements write more letters of comment than *all* other groups combined. Tandy and Wilburn (1992) found that 57.9 per cent of all submissions received on the FASB's first 100 statements came from the preparer group. Academic participation was 2.5 per cent while submissions directly representing users of financial statements amounted to only 1.8 per cent.

This paucity of user responses in the written submissions to standard setting bodies has also been observed not only in the US but also in Australia and the UK by, for example, Hope and Gray (1982), Sutton (1984), Walker (1987), Tutticci, Dunstan and Holmes (1994) and Ó hÓgartaigh and Reilly (1997). Armstrong (1977) and Beresford (1991) note that the user community have been minimal contributors to the process. Analysts do not expect to be influential in the lobbying process since they believe that "*the preparers of accounts hold the key to consensus*" (Weetman *et. al.,* 1996, p.74). Ó hÓgartaigh and Reilly (1997) indicate that analysts and institutional investors perceive themselves as users of financial statements rather than of accounting standards and therefore remain removed from the process of standard setting. While these studies offer an insight into participation in the standard setting process in other jurisdictions or in specific instances, none has analysed in a comprehensive manner participation in the ASB's standard setting process since its inception. The next section reports the findings of such an analysis.

PARTICIPATION IN THE ASB'S STANDARD SETTING PROCESS

The first element of this research attempts to ascertain which interest groups participate in the standard setting process of the ASB. The research comprises an empirical analysis of the written submissions prepared in response to Discussion Papers ('DPs') and Financial Reporting Exposure Drafts ('FREDs') published by the ASB.

This aspect of the research examines the number of submissions made to the ASB since its inception to the public hearings on goodwill in October 1995. Submissions on amendments to ASB standards proposed in FREDs 2, 5 and 9 are excluded. Thus 1,519 submissions on 21 of the ASB's projects are recorded. The research focuses on one dimension of lobbying: formal written submissions on discussion papers and exposure drafts. It thereby excludes from the analysis other methods of participation. This approach is consistent with that of other studies such as Weetman *et al.* (1996), Schalow (1995) and Francis (1987). However, written submissions to accounting standards boards may represent a relatively late and insignificant part of the overall political process. Earlier stages include contests over the composition of the standards boards themselves and the overall structure of regulatory arrangements (Walker and Robinson, 1993). Nonetheless, written submissions are a visible form of lobbying which contribute to a perception of the standard setting process as a whole.

To ascertain the participation of each interest group in the standard setting process, submissions are classified into 11 categories, according to the nature of their interest in financial reporting. The classification was carried out by both authors independently of each other. In assessing the affiliation of respondents, consideration was given to any explicit statement which identified the capacity in which the submission was made and also to the general tone of the submission. There may also be overlap between a respondent's role. Many respondents may be users (for example, for credit or investment decisions) as well as preparers of financial statements. They are classified in this study according to the group to which they primarily belong.

A summary of results is presented in Table 4.1. Preparers of financial statements, accountancy firms and their representatives are the most active respondents. The results support the perception that, by comparison with preparers and auditors, few users of financial statements present their views. Preparers and their representatives accounted for 48 per cent of total responses, accountancy

Table 5.1 *Constituent involvement in the ASB's standard setting process*

GROUP	NUMBER OF RESPONSES	%
Preparers of financial statements	617	41%
Representative bodies which represent preparers	112	7%
Accountancy firms	319	21%
Accountancy bodies*	146	10%
Mixed preparer/accountancy	3	-
Mixed preparer/user	39	3%
Users of financial statements	124	8%
Academia	52	3%
Government	10	1%
Law	20	1%
Individuals/affiliation not clear	77	5%
TOTAL	1,519	100%

Note * *Those categorised as 'accountancy bodies' include their faculty (such as the Faculty of Taxation of the Institute of Chartered Accountants in England and Wales) and district societies (for example, the London Society of Chartered Accountants) as well as the accountancy bodies themselves.*

firms and professional associations 31 per cent, while users of financial statements only submitted 8 per cent of responses. It may be argued that users of financial statements, and financial analysts in particular, are represented by their representative associations such as the Institute of Investment Management and Research which submitted responses to 16 of the 21 documents concerned. However, preparers are also represented by, for example, the Confederation of British Industry and the Hundred Group, yet still respond in relatively large numbers to the ASB's proposals.

Those users that did submit responses tended to be suppliers of capital. User respondents comprised investment companies, pension funds, venture capitalists, banks, building societies, industrial development boards and tax authorities. There were no responses from trade unions, consumer associations or other public representative bodies.

It might be expected that the majority of *individuals* would comprise financial statement users. However, only two individual respondents specifically identified themselves as users (these are included in the user group) while 13 individuals were identified as accountants.

Most corporate respondents appeared to participate in the ASB's standard setting process on a selective basis. For example, only 13 of the corporate respondents lobbied on more than 10 of the ASB's proposals. This is consistent with the results of research in the US by Brown (1981) which found that only 27 respondents commented on more than seven of the nine FASB projects analysed.

CHARACTERISTICS OF PREPARER PARTICIPATION

The high degree of preparer involvement in the ASB's consultation process leads to further analysis of the characteristics of those who felt moved to become involved in the standard setting process. This section examines preparer participation in more detail.

The perceived incentives for preparers of financial statements to engage in lobbying activity are great given the economic consequences of accounting standards. Preparers of financial statements are more likely to lobby than users because they may well have more to lose than users have (Bryant and Mahaney, 1981; Sutton, 1984). Users are likely to hold well diversified asset portfolios, the informational effects associated with financial disclosure being restricted accordingly. On the other hand, lack of diversification may render the preparer more sensitive to adverse economic consequences associated with a proposed, the cost of switching investments being less for a large undiversified investor than it would be for a company to change its line of business.

Accounting standards can impact on a company's bookkeeping and regulatory costs. They may also lead to increased taxes and wage claims, a reduction in subsidies granted or an increased scrutiny by monopolies and mergers commissions. Mansfield (1962) also states that increased visibility and size may result in increased competition arising from new entrants attracted by the accounting profit of the industry.

Lukes (1986) also argues that resources - strength, wealth or organisational backing - confer power. This leads to the hypothesis that power resides with those with the will and resources to devote effort to the process. Numerous empirical studies such as, for example, Watts and Zimmerman (1978, 1986, 1990), Hagerman and Zmijewski (1979), Bowen, Lacey and Noreen (1981) and Zmijewski and Hagerman (1981) support the hypothesis that lobbying corporations are, on average, larger than non-lobbying corporations. Sutton (1984) uses a theoretical framework to conclude that large producers are more likely to lobby than small producers. This framework is based on the suggestion by Downs (1957) that size determines the cost of lobbying relative to its benefits. Both Francis (1987) and Saemann (1995) conclude that firm size was a significant factor in the decision of firms to lobby on the FASB's Preliminary Views on 'Employers' Accounting for Pensions and Other Post Employment Benefits'. Morris (1986) and Gavens, Carnegie and Gibson (1989) found similar results for Australian companies.

With regard to the UK, the present study seeks to ascertain the relevance of company size to participation in the ASB's standard setting process. It comprises an analysis of the size of the corporate respondents in an attempt to determine if lobbying firms tend to be larger than their non-lobbying counterparts. Company turnover is used to measure firm size. This is the approach adopted by Francis (1987), Saemann (1995) and Schalow (1995). Rank by turnover is also used. The analysis is based on financial information obtained from Dun & Bradstreet's Corporate Financial Performance: Britain's top 50,000 Companies (Dun & Bradstreet, 1992, 1993, 1994) for the years 1991 to 1994 inclusive. Therefore, a firm is included in the study if it was UK incorporated, formed part of the top

Table 5.2 ASB statements included in study of preparer involvement

ASB STATEMENT	ISSUE DATE
Statement of Principles – Chapters 1 and 2	July 1991
FRED 1	December 1991
Statement of Principles – Chapter 6	December 1991
DP – Accounting for Capital Instruments	December 1991
Operating and Financial Review (OFR)	April 1992
FRED 3	December 1992
FRED 4	February 1993
DP - Role of Valuation in Financial Reporting	March 1993
DP - Fair Values in Acquisition Accounting	April 1993
FRED 6	May 1993
DP – Goodwill	December 1993
FRED 7	December 1993
FRED 8	March 1994
Review of FRS 1	June 1994
DP – Associates and Joint Ventures	July 1994

1,000 UK companies compiled by Dun and Bradstreet, and submitted at least one written response which became part of the public record to an ASB discussion paper or exposure draft issued between 1991 and 1994 (as this is the period for which the Dun & Bradstreet financial information is used). These ASB documents are listed in Table 4.2: they are a subset of the ASB projects noted earlier. ASB proposals issued after 1994 are excluded as the period of this element of the study is 1991 to 1994. Submissions on amendments to ASB standards proposed in FREDs 2 and 5 are also excluded.

A total of 108 firms fulfilled all three conditions. An average of each company's turnover and rank by turnover for three financial years covering the time period 1991 to 1994 (Dun and Bradstreet, 1992, 1993, 1994) was calculated. Similar turnover and ranking figures were obtained for the remaining 892 non-lobbying firms (Dun and Bradstreet, 1992, 1993, 1994).

The 108 companies that lobbied the ASB were compared with the top 1,000 companies that did not. The results are displayed in Table 4.3. As can be seen from

Table 5.3 Median turnover and rank of lobbyists and non-lobbyists, 1991 - 1994

	LOBBYING FIRMS	OTHER TOP 1,000 FIRMS
Median turnover	£1,597,140,000	£400,680,000
Median rank	144	538

Table 4.3, the median turnover of firms that lobbied the ASB was approximately £1.6 billion compared to £401 million for non-lobbyists. The median rank of the lobbying firms was 144 compared to 538 for the non-lobbying firms.

These results are consistent with the proposition that lobbying firms tend to be larger than non-lobbying firms. They are not, however, consistent with the notion of extensive consultation mentioned earlier. The next section concludes by exploring these findings further.

CONCLUSIONS

This chapter presents evidence confirming that, in the UK as in the USA, users of financial statements do not participate to a great extent in the accounting standard setting process. Their presence has been overshadowed by the preparers of financial statements who, together with their representatives, account for almost half of all formal submissions reviewed in this study. The study also provides further evidence that lobbying corporations in the UK tend to be larger than non-lobbying corporations, indicating that the ASB's standard setting process is élitist rather than pluralist.

These findings raise doubts as to whether the consultation process in the UK is as widespread as intended (see Financial Reporting Council, 1992, 1994). They also suggest that one of the Dearing Report's primary criticisms of the Accounting Standards Committee (which the ASB replaced) could similarly be said of the ASB: "*structurally, the present arrangements have not provided the ideal vehicle for involving preparers, users and others from outside the profession creatively*" in the standard setting process (Dearing, 1988, p.11).

While this study focuses on the frequency of written submissions, the origins of such submissions, being visible, contribute to a perception that the standard setting body defines its public narrowly and that its standard setting process is one which relies on a consensus of preparers. Lukes (1974, p.38), in a broader context, argues that "*the sheer weight of institutions*" does not necessarily rely on who prevails in decision making but on who participates in decision making. The high level of preparer participation in the standard setting process suggests that the standard setting body may be receiving only a particular view of its proposals for accounting standards, a view that is tempered by the nature of its respondents. It may, for instance, be hearing more about the cost of implementation of accounting standards to preparers than about their benefits to users of financial statements.

The objective of fashioning standards for the benefit of users, preparers and auditors of financial information through public consultation may be circumscribed in the light of the limited 'public' which obtains access to a regulator's deliberations. Indeed, the standard setting structure may be more a discourse of the powerful than an 'extensive' public consultation.

REFERENCES

Accounting Standards Board (1991). *Statement of Aims*. London: ASB.

Armstrong, M.A. (1977). The politics of establishing accounting standards, *Journal of Accountancy*, Vol.146, February, pp.76-9.

Beresford, D.R. (1991). Standard-setting process in trouble (again), *Accounting Horizons*, June, pp.94-6.

Brown, P. R. (1981). A descriptive analysis of select input bases of the FASB, *Journal of Accounting Research*, Vol.19, No.1, Spring, pp.232-46.

Bryant, M., and Mahaney, M.C. (1981). The politics of standard setting, *Management Accounting*, Vol.62, No.9, March, pp.26-33.

Cooper, D., and Sherer, M.J. (1984). The value of corporate accounting reports: arguments for a political economy of accounting. *Accounting, Organizations and Society*, Vol.9, No.3/4, pp.207-32.

Dahl, R.A. (1961). *Who Governs? Democracy and Power in an American City*. New Haven: Yale University Press.

Dahl, R. A. (1976). *Modern Political Analysis*. New Jersey: Prentice-Hall.

Downs, A. (1957). *An Economic Theory of Democracy*. New York: Harper & Row.

Dearing, R. (1988). *The Making of Accounting Standards*. London: Institute of Chartered Accountants in England and Wales.

Dun and Bradstreet International (1992). *Corporate Financial Performance - Britain's Top 50,000 Companies*. Bucks: Dun & Bradstreet Limited.

Dun and Bradstreet International (1993). *Corporate Financial Performance - Britain's Top 50,000 Companies*. Bucks: Dun & Bradstreet Limited.

Dun and Bradstreet International (1994). *Corporate Financial Performance - Britain's Top 50,000 Companies*. Bucks: Dun & Bradstreet Limited.

Financial Reporting Council (1992). *The State of Financial Reporting: Second Annual Review*. London: The Financial Reporting Council Limited.

Financial Reporting Council (1994). *The State of Financial Reporting: Annual Review 1994*. London: The Financial Reporting Council Limited.

Financial Reporting Council (1997). *Financial Reporting Council: Progress Report 1997*. London: The Financial Reporting Council Limited.

Francis, J.R. (1987). Lobbying against proposed accounting standards: the case of employers'pension accounting, *Journal of Accounting and Public Policy*, Vol.6, No.1, Spring, pp.35-57.

Gavens, J.J., Carnegie, G.D, and Gibson, R.W. (1989). Company participation in the Australian accounting standards setting process, *Accounting and Finance*, November, pp.47-58.

Hagerman, R., and Zmijewski, M. (1979). Some economic determinants of accounting policy choice, *Journal of Accounting and Economics*, Vol.1, August, pp.141-61.

Hope, T., and Gray, R. (1982). Power and policy making: the development of an R&D standard, *Journal of Business Finance and Accounting*, Vol.9, No.4, April, pp.531-58.

Kam, V. (1990). *Accounting Theory*, 2nd. Ed. New York: Wiley.

Lukes, S. (1974). *Power: A Radical View*. London: Macmillan.

Lukes, S. (1986). *Power*. Oxford: Blackwell.

Mansfield, E. (1962). Entry, Gibrat's law, innovation and the growth of firms, *The American Economic Review*, Vol.52, August, pp.479-92.

Mautz, R.K. (1974). The other accounting standards board, *The Journal of Accountancy*, February, pp.56-60.

Mezias, S.J., and Chung, H. (1989). *Due Process and Participation at the FASB*. Morristown, NJ: Financial Executives Research Foundation.

Merelman, R.M. (1968). On the neo-élitist critique of community power, *American Political Science Review*, Vol.62, pp.451-60.

Miller, M. (1985). Too much preparer dominance in standards setting, *The Chartered Accountant in Australia*, Vol.56, No.5, November, pp.28-30.

Morris, R.D. (1986). Lobbying on proposed accounting standards, *The Chartered Accountant in Australia*, Vol.56, No.8, March,

Ó hÓgartaigh, C., and Reilly, E. (1997). Perceptions of performance: the reactions of analysts and institutional investors to FRS 3, *The Irish Accounting Review*, Vol.4, Spring, pp.124-43.

Polsby, N.W. (1963). *Community Power and Political Theory*. New Haven and London: Yale University Press.

Polsby, N.W. (1968). Community: the study of community power, *International Encyclopaedia of the Social Sciences*, Vol.3, New York: Macmillan and Free Press.

Saemann, G.P. (1995). The accounting standard setting due process, corporate consensus, and FASB responsiveness: Employers' Accounting for Pensions, *Journal of Accounting, Auditing and Finance*, Vol.10, No.3, Summer, pp.555-64.

Schalow, C.M. (1995). Participation choice: the exposure draft for postretirement benefits other than pensions, *Accounting Horizons*, Vol.9, No.1, March, pp.24-41.

Sutton, T.G. (1984). Lobbying of accounting standard setting bodies in the UK and the USA: a Downsian analysis, *Accounting, Organizations and Society*, Vol.9, No.1, pp.81-95.

Tandy, P.R., and Wilburn, N.L. (1992). Constituent participation in standard setting: the FASB's first 100 statements, *Accounting Horizons*, Vol.6, No.2, June, pp.47-58.

Taylor, P., and Turley, S. (1986). *The Regulation of Accounting*. Oxford: Blackwell.

Tutticci, I., Dunstan, K., and Holmes, S. (1994). Respondent lobbying in the Australian accounting standard setting process: ED49 - a case study, *Accounting, Auditing and Accountability Journal*, Vol.7, No.2, pp.86-104.

Underdown, B., and Taylor, P. (1986). *Accounting Theory & Policy Making*. London: Heinemann.

Walker, R.G. (1987). Australia's ASRB. A case study of political activity and regulatory 'capture', *Accounting and Business Research*, Vol.17, No.67, Summer, pp.269-86.

Walker, R.G., and Robinson, S.P. (1993). A critical assessment of the literature on political activity and accounting regulation, *Research in Accounting Regulation*, Vol.7, pp.3-40.

Watts, R.L. (1977). Corporate financial statements, a product of the market and political processes, *Australian Journal of Management*, Vol.2, pp.53-75.

Watts, R.L., and Zimmerman, J.L. (1978). Towards a positive theory of the determination of accounting standards, *The Accounting Review*, Vol.53, No.1, January, pp.112-34.

Watts, R.L., and Zimmerman, J.L. (1986). *Positive Accounting Theory*. Englewood Cliffs, New Jersey: Prentice-Hall.

Watts, R.L., and Zimmerman, J.L. (1990). Positive accounting theory, a ten year perspective, *The Accounting Review*, Vol.65, pp.131-156.

Weetman, P., Collins, W., and Davie, E.S. (1994). *Operating and Financial Review: Views of Analysts and Institutional Investors*, Edinburgh: The Institute of Chartered Accountants of Scotland.

Weetman, P., Davie, E.S., and Collins, W. (1996). Lobbying on accounting issues: preparer/user imbalance in the case of the Operating and Financial Review, *Accounting, Auditing and Accountability Journal*, Vol.9, No.1, pp.59-76.

Wolfinger, R.E. (1971). Nondecisions and the study of local politics, *American Political Science Review*, Vol.65, pp.1063-80.

Zmijewski, M., and Hagerman, R. (1981). An income strategy approach to the positive theory of accounting standard-setting/choice, *Journal of Accounting and Economics*, Vol.3, August, pp.129-49.

6

RELATED PARTY TRANSACTIONS: A CASE STUDY OF STANDARD SETTING IN THE UK

Juliet Cottingham and Roger Hussey

INTRODUCTION

The regulation of financial accounting and reporting is dependent in many countries on the requirements of accounting standards. The topic of standard setting has attracted the attention of many researchers and there have been two main approaches to their investigations. One has been an *institutional analysis approach* which focuses on the nature and role of the standard setting body. The other has been a *submissions analysis approach* which examines the responses to proclamations issued by the standard setters. A minority of studies have attempted to capture the full reality of the standard setting process (Walker and Robinson, 1994; Rahman, Ng and Tower, 1994) and these have added greatly to our understanding of the dynamics and power relationships. This chapter contributes to this limited literature by examining the development, over 15 years, of a standard on related party transactions in the UK.

Related party transactions occur as part of the normal activities a company conducts and refers to those transactions that occur between entities where a relationship of control or significant influence exists. There is, however, an issue that the requisite conditions of independence and competitive, free market dealings may not exist (Foster, 1975). The consequences of this may be that as transactions are *"arranged to obtain certain results desired by the related parties, the resulting accounting measures may not represent what they usually would be expected to represent"* (Financial Accounting Standards Board, 1982, par. 15). Although the results may be innocently misleading, there is the peril that fraud maybe taking place.

In the UK a standard was issued in 1995 shortly after a major financial scandal, the Robert Maxwell affair, where it is alleged that both the MGN Group and Maxwell Communications suffered seriously as a result of a number of undisclosed related party transactions. It would be easy to conclude from this that there was a direct link between the fraud and the issue of a standard but the regulators first considered related party transactions in 1981 and an Exposure Draft was issued on the topic in 1989 (Accounting Standards Committee, 1989). The question arises, therefore, on the reasons for the delay in issuing the standard and whether the major fraud was, in any way, a catalyst.

This chapter examines the relationship of various events within the standard setting process. The data for the research have been drawn from examination of the Accounting Standards Committee archives dealing with related party transactions, and interviews with both those who served on the working party at that time and auditors. This has been further supported by participant observation at working party meetings of the Institute of Chartered Accountants in England and Wales responsible for submitting comments on FRED 8 (Accounting Standards Board, 1994) and an analysis of responses to the exposure draft.

The methodology adopted for the research is grounded theory, which was originally conceived by Glaser and Strauss (1967). Grounded theory *"is a qualitative research method that uses a systematic set of procedures to develop an inductively derived grounded theory about a phenomenon"* (Strauss and Corbin, 1990, p. 24). It is accepted that the methodology is a potentially valuable part of the qualitative interpretative field research tradition and can provide an important contribution to the dimensions of knowledge of accounting research (Parker and Roffey, 1996).

In the following section the main studies on standard setting and related party transactions are examined. The methodology section offers a brief explanation of grounded theory methodology, the reasons for its choice in the present study and the procedures adopted. The main section of the chapter analyses and explains the development of the standard.

THE RESEARCH BACKGROUND

Studies on the nature and role of standard setting bodies have drawn from professional logic, neo-classical economies, cognitive psychology, political lobbying and power analysis (Booth and Cocks, 1990). Applied institutional theory has been used to explain why the Financial Accounting Standards Board (FASB) in the USA has been able to exert considerable influence on the practice of accounting (Fogarty, 1992) and evidence has been provided to demonstrate that the process is not dominated by the big firms but is a mixed power system (Hussein and Ketz, 1991).

Previous investigations have often, either implicitly or explicitly, viewed the standard setting process commencing with a crisis or issue (Rahman, 1992; Klumpes, 1994) and the regulators adopting and maintaining a reactive posture. This is not to deny that the process is dynamic and, indeed, a cyclical model of regulation has been used both in the UK (Nobes, 1991, 1992) and in a refined version in Australia (Gordon and Morris, 1996). Many researchers have relied for their evidence on an analysis of the responses to proclamations by the standard setters. They have revealed that corporations are the most active participants (Brown, 1981; Tandy and Wilburn, 1992) and, it is claimed, that the FASB have been responsive to corporate concerns (Brown and Feroz, 1992), possibly due to the big firms of accountants not forming a controlling coalition (Moody and Flesher, 1986).

Despite the value of these studies there is the criticism that "*A simple tallying of comment letters is not likely to capture the extent of participation by firms in lobbying, particularly once other channels for lobbying are opened*" (Lindahl, 1987, p.65). It is also essential to recognise "*that a substantial amount of discussion precedes the exposure drafts of accounting standards*" (Rahman, Ng and Tower, 1994, p.100). For these reasons it is important to attempt to identify non-documented influences of various parties and "*interviews with the individual members of the policy body would be necessary to complement and expand upon the documentary evidence of stated position*" (Hope and Gray, 1982, p.553).

A few researchers have addressed these problems and have captured the series of events and negotiations which take place. There are two investigations which are germane to the present study, both in the nature of the research activity and the concentration on the development of a single standard. Walker and Robinson (1994) have examined the process of generating a standard on related party transactions in Australia and Rahman, Ng and Tower (1994) on accounting for investment properties in New Zealand. Although conducted in different regulatory contexts, both of these studies have proved invaluable guides to the conduct of the present research and the interpretation of the findings.

Related party transactions

The topic of accounting for related party transactions has also been of academic interest to researchers and practitioners. Davies *et al.* (1991) have outlined the following three major ways in which the financial position and operating results can be affected by related party transactions:

- Transactions may be entered into which would not have occurred had there been no related party. For example, a parent company may purchase a large proportion of stock from one of its subsidiaries which would, otherwise, have been unable to sell the stock.
- Transactions may occur under different terms had the parties not been related. For example, a parent company may impose special terms under which a subsidiary leases equipment to another subsidiary which may be very different to current market rates.
- Transactions with third parties may be affected by the existence of a relationship. For example, two enterprises in the same line of business may be controlled by a common party which has the ability to increase the volume of business done by each.

In the above examples the situation is placed in a parent/subsidiary relationship and any consequences reflected in financial statements may be misleading, but totally innocent. Not all relationships are so evident and transactions may be undertaken with the intention to deceive. Experience has shown that business structure and operating policies have sometimes been deliberately designed to obscure a related party (American Institute of Certified Public Accountants, 1975). In this way it is possible for undisclosed special benefits to accrue to one or more of the parties (Mason, 1979).

Among the methods of achieving fraud is the siphoning off of assets through transactions with affiliated companies, kickbacks and irregular transactions between officers and outside parties (Kapnick, 1975). Some of the more notorious cases include Continental Vending (United States v Simon) 1968; Westec 1965; US Financial 1972; Pergamon Press 1969; and Lowson Group 1972.

In 1981 the Accounting Standards Committee (ASC), the body then responsible for accounting standard setting in the UK, addressed the subject of related party transactions, but did not issue Exposure Draft (ED) 46 *Disclosure of Related Party Transactions*, until April 1989. This received criticism from preparers and users and was accorded low priority by that Committee. The Maxwell affair appears to have focused opinions and after a five year intermission, the Accounting Standards Board (ASB), the successor body to the ASC, replaced ED 46 with their own exposure draft on the disclosure of related party transactions: FRED 8 (1994). This attempted to rectify some of the perceived problems inherent in ED 46, addressed some of the issues which needed to be considered, clarified other areas where doubt or queries were made by commentators of ED 46 and served as the basis for the subsequent standard, FRS 8 (ASB, 1995). It is in the context of these events that the analysis in this chapter is unfolded.

METHODOLOGY

There has been recent encouragement for the wider adoption of grounded theory methodology in accounting research (Parker and Roffey, 1996). The number of studies using grounded theory has grown steadily since the original treatise [for example: Conrad, 1978; Turner, 1981 and 1983; Segev, 1988; and Compton *et al.*, 1991] and it has attracted a number of management researchers, particularly in Scandinavia (Gummesson 1991). Its use in accounting research, other than as a subsidiary methodology in a study, has been somewhat limited and it has been argued that few grounded theory generating studies have as yet emerged in the published accounting and management research literature (Parker and Roffey, 1996).

Examples of studies in the accounting literature which are available include an analysis of corporate reports and environmental influences on human resource management (Bamberger and Phillips, 1991), and an investigation of corporate financial disclosure (Gibbins *et al.*, 1990). Interest in grounded theory in accounting research is showing signs of further development and Parker and Roffey (1996) provides a discussion on its epistemological and ontological assumptions as well as a general guide to its use.

In this present chapter the methodology as set out by Strauss and Corbin (1990) is adopted for the conduct of the study. The main source of information was the extensive archives of the ASC and the minutes of all meetings referring to related party transactions of both the main committee and the working party were analysed. In addition, the exposure drafts, the numerous responses to them and the subsequent standard were analysed. To support this activity, nine in-depth, unstructured interviews were conducted with members of the accounting profession who had, in some way, been closely connected with the development of the standard, including two members of the original ASC and the person heading the ASB's development of a related party standard. Finally, participant observation was conducted of the Institute of Chartered Accountants in England and Wales (ICAEW) working party which had been formed to submit responses to FRED 8 issued by the ASB.

Initially the data were coded using both open and axial procedures (Strauss and Corbin, 1990). The data contained in the archival files and gained from the interviews were labelled according to content, with similar items included under the same labels. All references under the same label were then aggregated and stored on computer files. These files became known as 'theme files' and allowed different instances of the same phenomenon to be grouped and analysed together. An example of this coding of the data can be seen in Table 5.1.

Table 6.1 Example of data coding

Accounting Bodies Development of standard Stimuli Accounting Bodies Development of standard Stimuli National Laws and Norms National Laws and Norms Stimuli Level of priority Development of standard	In March 1982, **the ASC** set up a working party to **develop an accounting standard** on related party transactions. The working party developed an initial draft of an exposure draft. Following the **reorganisation** of the **membership of the ASC** and a review of the work program, it was decided in September 1982 **to suspend work on the project.** There were two principle reasons for this decision firstly, the **ASC was unwilling** to develop a standard requiring disclosures beyond that **required by law** at a time when because were having to cope with compliance with the extensive additional disclosures introduced by the **Companies Act 1981**. Secondly, scarce **secretarial resources** necessitated a reconsideration of the projects being undertaken. As the project was at an early stage and considered **not to be of high priority**, it was one of a number of projects which were **suspended**.

Source. Extract from ED 40. ASC (1986) Exposure Draft 40. Disclosures of Related Party Transactions, ASC, p1 (Unpublished. Found in the ASC Archive).

These codes were used to adapt and devise the conditional matrix so that the process of developing the standard over the 15 year period could be followed. In grounded theory, process is considered to be important as it links the static actions and interactions into a dynamic movement of interrelationships and consequential occurrences and responses. To "*capture process analytically, one must show the evolving nature of events by noting why and how action / interaction - in the form of events, doings, or happenings - will change, stay the same or regress*" (Strauss and Corbin, 1994a, p.144). The conditional matrix is an ideal tool for developing and analysing this 'process'. It employs a transactional system to investigate and analyse different levels of conditions which give rise to actions and interactions, of which the consequences in turn constitute a change in conditions to which other corresponding actions and interactions are applied. By tracing conditional paths, an action or event can be directly related to a phenomenon by following the course of events from the action, through the interactions and ensuing consequences.

Figure 6.2 represents the conditional matrix constructed to analyse the process of the development of the related party accounting standard. This model was used to trace conditional paths between different groups and levels of society to examine the impact that each had on the development of ED 46, FRED 8 and FRS 8. The basic framework may be used to analyse the development of any accounting standard.

ANALYSIS AND DISCUSSION

Analysis of the data revealed that ASC originally commenced their work due to developments at the 'International Legislation' level. It was IASC interest in the topic which acted as the initial causal condition and focused ASC's attention; an experience similar to Australia (Walker and Robinson, 1994). As a committee of Consultative Committee of Accounting Bodies (CCAB), which in turn was a member of IASC, the ASC had a responsibility to ensure congruence with international accounting standards. In an internal memorandum on Forward Plans, it stated *"The UK and Irish accounting profession, through its membership on IASC, has undertaken to use its best endeavours to secure compliance with International Accounting Standards through the promulgation of equivalent standards locally, where existing standards so not already cover IASC requirements"* (ASC Archive, 1981).

With such an intent, and based on information that IASC were investigating the issue of related parties, the ASC was conscious that the IASC would possibly be bringing out a standard for which there was no corresponding accounting regulation in the UK. As such, the issue of related party transactions was a *"project undertaken as a result of IASC work on subject"* (ASC Archive, 1982).

This international impetus was verified in an interview by the researchers with a member of the ASC at the time of these initiatives. In response to a question concerning how topics came to the attention of the ASC, the participant responded *"Different ways. ... it could even be a recognition that there are topics that have been dealt with by international standards that we haven't dealt with, and this was the case for the related party exposure draft."* Hence it was the impending changes at the 'International Legislation' level of the conditional matrix which prompted UK action. That action was the formation of a working party to further investigate the issue of related parties. A member of that working party has stated *"We were enthusiasts for disclosing related party transactions, but were aware that our colleagues in the accounting profession did not see the topic as being crucial."*

The impact of developments at the international level on the accounting profession in the UK in general should not be overstated. At that time, the UK was closely enmeshed with company law harmonisation within Europe and the majority of the accounting profession displayed little enthusiasm for developments outside that arena. In the words of one interviewee *"It was one thing for us (the ASC) to recognise that related parties were going to be important, but the rest of the accounting profession was not going to be interested if we issued anything - we had to wait."* It is this comment which suggests that one constraint operating on members of the ASC was the perceived disinterest of its constituents. The progress of the standard, therefore, relied to a large degree on the ASC's belief in changes occurring in the attitude of its constituents.

The data analysis revealed that there were several factors and intervening conditions which affected the development of the standard. These were coded as 'Stimuli' and were usually present at the 'Accounting Bodies' level and outwards

Figure 5.1 *Related party conditional matrix*

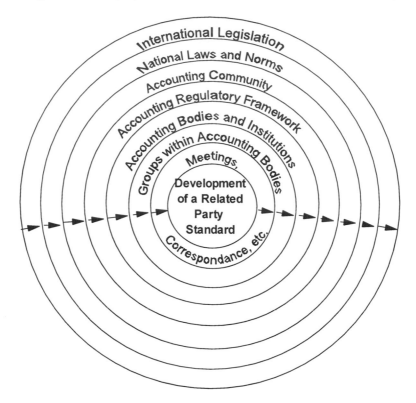

in the conditional matrix: changes in circumstances which impinged on the more innermost circles of the development of an accounting standard - affecting the groups within the accounting bodies and their actions towards evolving a standard.

First of these factors was the low level of priority which was assigned to the related party project by the ASC. Due to the topic being identified by the IASC, rather than being inspired by any actual problems experienced in the UK, it was considered to be of less importance to the ASC's constituents than other issues with which it was simultaneously involved.

The topic of related parties remained a low priority throughout the majority of its time as an ASC project: it was very much a constant intervening condition. Often the topic of related parties was delayed and postponed so that other issues could be considered, for example during a meeting in June 1987 the issue of related parties was deferred due to insufficient time to complete all business. This low priority status for the issue of related parties was remembered by a committee member, interviewed by the researchers, who claimed that "*there wasn't massive pressure*" on the related party working party and commented, that "*they kept*" *putting it off quite a bit until we judged the time was ready*" thus verifying the archives documentation of delays

This judgement as to the appropriate time was not exercised through formal procedures, but through the knowledge, experience and informal soundings of the part-time, voluntary committee members of the ASC. As senior people in their own employing institution, they had ample opportunity to discuss with people outside the committee attitudes to related party disclosures and to assess likely responses to any initiative. In the words of a similar research study it is possible *that "the most critical events in the development of rules on RPTs arose from interactions between key players*" (Walker and Robinson, 1994, p. 35). For the ASC, it was not a matter of refusing to give the project high priority but ensuring that it remained on the agenda until there was some convergence of opinions and, perhaps more importantly, a change in public perception towards the need to disclose related party transactions.

This shift in public opinion occurred too late for the ASC which was disbanded in 1990 and replaced by the ASB. Again the topic of related party transactions was given low priority status. Indeed, initially the ASB had no intention of continuing with work on the standard. Instead, it considered the issue to be within the remit of the DTI and, consequently, preferred to leave the issue to this other body. The revelation of the Maxwell fraud, however, brought the issue of related party transactions very much into public knowledge, changing public ignorance into public outrage. It was this shift that the ASC and ASB had been waiting for and the ASB moved quickly to forward the work of the ASC and issue an exposure draft. This finding corresponds with the views of Walker and Robinson who argue that "*outside events, such as much-publicised corporate failures may also add instability to laboriously negotiated territorial arrangements between government and the profession*" (Walker and Robinson, 1994, p. 40).

In addition to the fraud there were other influences which affected the lengthy development of a standard, one being a lack of resources. A scarcity of appropriate funds represented a change in the intervening conditions at the 'Accounting Bodies' level and had consequences on all three of the more innermost circles of the conditional matrix. Soon after the initial working party was formed it was accordingly disbanded due to a paucity of secretarial support. The ASC Work Programme for 29 September 1982 (ASC Archive, 1982) advised that projects were to be suspended temporarily on the grounds that they were not matters *of "excessive public interest and would divert scarce secretarial resources*" away from those projects considered to be of a higher priority. Among those projects to be postponed was that of related party transactions. Thus the consequence was a suspension of the working party and its actions and, ultimately, an interruption to the process of developing a related party standard.

The suspension of work, however, had consequences of its own. A sister body, the Auditing Practices Board (APB), believed that the issue of related party transactions was of sufficient importance and intervened, in favour of continuing work on the topic. The APB offered its own secretarial resources to ASC to continue with the working party. This provided some evidence to the ASC that the auditing profession were becoming aware of the problem and, combining forces with the APB, the ASC started work on the development of a related party exposure draft again.

A third hindrance on the publication of an exposure draft came from the 'National Laws and Norms' level of the conditional matrix in the form of expected amendments to Companies Act 1980. It was suspected by the ASC that there would be changes to legislation which would be applicable and relevant to an accounting standard on related party transactions regarding directors' material interests in transactions. Therefore, as a result of expected amendments to company law, the work of the joint ASC and APB project was postponed until the alterations were published. The amendments were issued by means of a Statutory Instrument in November 1984 but "*Many believed, however, that the wording of the Statutory Instrument was ambiguous and did not achieve what was intended as set out in the accompanying Explanatory Note. There was some expectation that further clarification might be forthcoming*" (ASC, 1986, p.2). The changes in the Companies Act represented a change in the 'National Laws and Norms' tier in the conditional matrix. However, with the lack of clarity acting as an intervening factor, the ASC felt unable to act on these changes and due to the perceived ambiguity of the Statutory Instrument, the postponement of the working party was continued to await definition. When no clarification was forthcoming, the working party restarted its work in September the following year, 1985: a suspension of work of over a year (ASC, 1986). There is no evidence to indicate that the ASC was provoked into this recommencement and it must be assumed that the reason was the belief of the committee members that the issue had to be addressed.

Another major factor which has hindered the production of an accounting standard is the highly controversial nature of the subject of related parties and their transactions. This was revealed in two ways: firstly, the technical difficulties which the working party had to overcome before it managed to produce an exposure draft which was acceptable to the regulatory bodies, and secondly, for the ASC and ASB to agree an exposure which was acceptable to the accounting community. This latter point can be seen in the myriad of varying responses, which contained several conflicting and contradictory suggestions, from commentators responding to both ED 46 and FRED 8 (ASC, 1990). This was also supported by evidence from the participant observation conducted by the researchers at an ICAEW working party set up in 1994 to comment on the second exposure draft. The former difficulty, however, was apparent from the ASC archives where there is also evidence of much debate about the provisions, many reflecting and mirroring those contained in the reviewers' comments.

Indeed, this research uncovered sixteen separate drafts of a related party standard and the minutes show that an exposure draft was presented by the working party to the full committee three times without approval. Indeed one exposure draft (ED 40) was ready for release as early as 1986 (ASC, 1986), but it was considered by the full committee that it was too contentious at that time. Despite constant reiterations of the drafts by the working party and the presentation of potential exposure drafts to the full committee on three occasions, the actual changes constituted refinements to text rather than major changes in content. The final exposure Draft (ED 46) was very similar to the unpublished exposure draft which in turn was closely based on a research paper presented to the ASC in 1980. Many of the ideas, explanations and terminology had not changed, but the ASC considered the environment into which the ED was being released had shifted to some degree.

The fifth element affecting the development of a related party standard was the replacement of the ASC by the ASB in 1990: a body independent of the accounting profession and with greater regulatory powers. There was major upheaval at the 'Accounting Bodies' level with the end of the ASC era and the start of a new generation with the ASB. This changeover at the 'Accounting Bodies' level had consequences on the options open to the ASC. Consistently favourable responses towards ED 46 might have encouraged the ASC to issue a standard before the ASB began life. As this was not the case, however, the ASC were unable to proceed with publishing the exposure draft as a standard, even in an amended form. Major alterations were needed to make the standard acceptable to those within the accounting community and the working party recommended that the project be deferred and the documentation pass to the new ASB so that it could act as it saw fit. Thus the extinction of the ASC, in conjunction with the discouraging comments from reviewers, led to a suspension of work on the development of a related party accounting standard.

It was action at the 'Accounting Community' level of the conditional matrix that really had a positive impact on the development of a standard. The discovery and subsequent public scandal of the Maxwell fraud decided the ASB to resolve matters. Prior to this, the ASB felt that the topic was out of its remit and had determined to leave the issue in the hands of the DTI. This response is not dissimilar to earlier events in the USA where enthusiasm for accounting standards was *"triggered by the force of external events: the stock market crash of 1929, followed by the suicide of the 'Match King', Ivan Krueger, which revealed the collapse of the international giant Krueger and Toll company"* (Davidson and Anderson, 1987, p. 114).

This discovery of the impact of the Maxwell fraud provided a contrast with the ASC's interest in related parties. The ASC was unconcerned with the issue of fraud, but had taken action because it considered the pressure of an international standard would lead to a responsive environment. In contrast, the ASB gave little weighting to the international perspective but was influenced by the Maxwell fraud at the 'community' / 'national' level. It should not be concluded from this that the ASB believed that the standard would prevent such frauds. An extensive analysis by the researchers of other related party fraud cases in a number of countries suggested that an accounting standard is of little benefit in combating the problem of fraudulently misleading accounts and discussions between the researchers and members of the ASB indicate that they hold the same opinion. The public concern expressed at the Maxwell scandal, however, resulted in an acceptance by various constituents of the ASB of the need for an accounting standard.

Although there is question as to the ASB's motives, its determination cannot be doubted. When the new regulatory body decided that a standard would be produced, it worked very quickly. An exposure draft was released two years later, and the final standard in the following year. Compared to the ASC's nine years to develop an exposure draft and considering the other substantial issues confronting the ASB in its early years, this is a remarkable achievement.

CONCLUSIONS

The regulation of financial accounting and reporting can be better understood by an examination of the reality of the process by which accounting standards are developed. The experiences in the UK of developing a standard for regulating related party transaction may not be typical, but this chapter provides illumination of the processes and offers insights into the decisions and events which take place.

In the terminology of Strauss and Corbin (1990), the original 'causal event' for the development of the standard in the UK was an initiative by the IASC. Over the 15 years there were a number of intervening factors which led to various stages of regression and progression. The technical complexities of the subject, the unwillingness of regulators to commit resources to the project and the perceived attitudes of constituents delayed its development. However, intervention by the APB alleviated the resources problem and a major financial scandal motivated the ASB to overcome the technical problems and to issue a standard which addressed public concern even if it may not combat fraudulent accounts.

A superficial analysis may suggest that the standard setters were merely being reactive: but this opinion does them a disservice. The question is not why they did not take action sooner, but how did they manage to keep the project on the agenda for fifteen years until it reached fruition? The ASC had judged that actions at the international level were insufficient to raise awareness amongst its constituents to make the issue of a standard feasible. Many potential exposure drafts had been written and one, ED 40, had been completed but never issued. The ASC determined, through its informal soundings, that resistance would be too great and it was not until it was about to be disbanded that it decided to issue an Exposure Draft. The ASB also considered that there was insufficient public support to take action, but the Maxwell scandal introduced a dramatic change. Public concern allowed the ASB to issue a standard on related party transactions, although it accepted that, if issued earlier, it would have done little to prevent the Maxwell scandal.

It would be imprudent to generalise from this particular experience in the UK to all forms of financial accounting and reporting regulation in the international arena. The findings do provide support, however, for the work done in Australia (Walker and Robinson, 1994) and New Zealand (Rahman, Ng and Tower, 1994) and further research in respect of other standards and the experiences in other countries is now required. In particular, an inter-country comparative study where standards are being developed on the same topic would prove most valuable.

REFERENCES

Accounting Standards Board (1994). *Financial Reporting Exposure Draft 8: Related Party Disclosures.* London: ASB.

Accounting Standards Board (1995). *Financial Reporting Standard 8: Related Party Disclosures.* London: ASB.

Accounting Standards Committee (1986). *Exposure Draft 40 (ED 40): Disclosure of Related Party Transactions* (unpublished).

Accounting Standards Committee (1989). *Exposure Draft 46 : Related Party Transactions.* London: ASC.

Accounting Standards Committee (1990). *Reviewers' Comments on ED 46.* London: ASC.

Accounting Standards Committee Archive, John Rylands Library, Manchester. Page numbers are unavailable for quotes made from the ASC archive as the archive maintains several loose leaf, unnumbered documents, papers and pages which are in no set order.

American Institute of Certified Public Accountants (1975). Statement on Auditing Standard No 6, *Journal of Accountancy*, Vol.140, September, pp.

Bamberger, P., and Phillips, B. (1991). Organisational environment and business strategy: parallel versus conflicting influences on human resource strategy in the pharmaceutical industry, *Human Resource Management*, Vol. 30, No. 2, Summer, pp.153-82.

Booth, P., and Cocks, N. (1990). Critical research issues in accounting standard setting, *Journal of Business Finance and Accounting*, Vol.17, No.4, pp.511-28.

Brown, P.R. (1981). A descriptive analysis of select input bases of the FASB, *Journal of Accounting Research*, Vol.19, No.1, pp.232-46.

Brown, L., and Feroz, E. (1992). Does the FASB listen to corporations, *Journal of Business Finance and Accounting*, Vol. 18, September, pp.715-29.

Compton, C.D., White, K., and DeWine, S. (1991). Techno-sense: making sense of computer-mediated communication systems, *The Journal of Business Communication*, Vol.28, No.1, Winter, pp.23-43.

Conrad, C. F. (1978), A grounded theory of academic change, *Sociology of Education*, Vol.51, pp.101-12.

Davidson, S., and Anderson, G. (1987). The development of accounting and auditing standards, *Journal of Accountancy*, Vol.163, No.5, pp.110-35.

Davies, M., Paterson, R., and Wilson, A. (1991). *Generally Accepted Accounting Practices.* London: Ernst and Young.

Financial Accounting Standards Board (1982). *Statement of Financial Accounting Standards 57: Related Party Disclosures.* March, New York: FASB.

Fogarty, T.J. (1992). Financial accounting standard setting as an institutionalized action field: constraints, opportunities and dilemmas, *Journal of Accounting and Public Policy*, Vol.11, No.4, pp.331-55.

Foster, W.C. (1975). Disclosure: who needs what?, *Accounting Forum*, Vol.45, May, pp.43-50.

Gibbins, M., Richardson, A., and Waterhouse, J. (1990). The management of corporate financial disclosure: opportunism, ritualism, policies and processes, *Journal of Accounting Research*, Vol.28, No.1, Spring, pp.121-43.

Glaser, B., and Strauss, A. (1967) *The Discovery of Grounded Theory.* Chicago: Aldine.

Gordon, I., and Morris, R. (1996). The equity accounting saga in Australia: cyclical standard setting, *Abacus*, Vol.32, No.2, pp.153-77.

Gummesson, E. (1991). *Qualitative Methods in Management Research.* California: Sage Publications.

Hope, T., and Gray, R. (1982). Power and policy making: the development of a research and development standard, *Journal of Business Finance and Accounting,* Vol.9, No.4, pp. 531-58.

Hussein, M., and Ketz, J.E. (1991). Accounting standards setting in the US: an analysis of power and social exchange, *Journal of Accounting and Public Policy,* Vol.10, No.1, pp.59-81.

Kapnick, H. (1975). Management fraud and the independent auditor, *Journal of Commercial Bank Lending,* Vol.58, December, pp.20-30.

Klumpes, P. (1994). The politics of rule development: a case study of Australian pension fund rule-making, *Abacus,* Vol.30, September, pp.140-59.

Lindahl, F. (1987). Accounting standards and Olson's theory of collective action, *Journal of Accounting and Public Policy,* Vol.6, No.1, pp.59-72.

Mason, A. K. (1979). *Related Party Transactions. A Research Study.* Canadian Institute of Chartered Accountants.

Moody, S.M., and Flesher, D.L. (1986). Analysis of FASB voting patterns: Statement Nos. 1-86, *Journal of Accounting, Auditing and Finance,* Vol.1, No.4, pp.319-30.

Nobes, C. (1991). Cycles in UK standard setting, *Accounting and Business Research,* Vol.21, No.83, pp.265-74.

Nobes, C. (1992). The existence and significance of cycles: a reply, *Accounting and Business Research,* Vol.22, No.88, pp.381-2.

Parker, L.D., and Roffey, B.H. (1996). Back to the drawing board: revisiting grounded theory and the everyday accountant's and manager's reality, *Accounting, Auditing and Accountability Journal,* Vol.

Rahman, A.R. (1992). *The Australian Accounting Standards Review Board: the Establishment of its Participative Review Process.* Garland Publishing.

Rahman, A.R., Ng, L.W., and Tower, G.D. (1994). Public choice and accounting standard setting in New Zealand: an exploratory study, *Abacus,* Vol. 30, No.1, March, pp. 98-117.

Segev, E. (1988). A framework for the grounded theory of corporate policy, *Interfaces,* Vol.18, No.5, pp.42-54.

Strauss, A., and Corbin, J. (1990). *Basics of Qualitative Research: Grounded Theory Procedures and Techniques,* California: Sage Publications.

Strauss, A., and Corbin, J. (1994). Grounded theory methodology: an overview, in Denzin, K., and Lincoln, Y . eds. *Handbook of Qualitative Research.* Thousand Oaks: Sage Publications, pp.273-85.

Tandy, P., and Wilburn, N. (1992). Constituent participation in standard setting: the FASBs first 100 statements, *Accounting Horizons,* Vol.6, No.2, pp.47-58.

Turner, B.A. (1981). *Quality and Quantity.* Amsterdam: Elsever Scientific Publishing.

Turner, B.A. (1983). The use of grounded theory for the qualitative analysis of organisational behaviour, *Journal of Management Studies,* Vol.20, No.3, pp.333-48.

Walker, R.G., and Robinson, S.P. (1994). Related party transactions: a case study of interorganisational conflict over the development of disclosure rules, *Abacus,* Vol.30, No.1, pp.18-43.

7

THE REGULATION OF PUBLIC DISCLOSURE: AN INTRODUCTORY ANALYSIS WITH APPLICATION TO INTERNATIONAL ACCOUNTING STANDARDS

Marco Trombetta*

INTRODUCTION

For the six-month period ending 30 June 1993, Daimler-Benz AG registered as net income a profit of DM168m under German GAAP (Generally Accepted Accounting Principles) and a loss of DM949m under US GAAP.[1] The usual

* The author wishes to thank Meg Meyer for her comments on previous versions. The observations made by Joshua Ronen and Massimo Warglien at the Workshop on Accounting Regulation in Siena were particularly helpful in the final revision.

conclusion, following cases like this, is that there is a need to increase the degree of international harmonisation of accounting regulation in order to prevent such situations from occurring again. In this chapter, with the help of an analytical model, I openly question this conclusion and show that, even if some form of international regulation is certainly needed, the optimal regime does not necessarily exclude the possibility of reporting different results in different countries.

I adopt the decision-usefulness approach to accounting regulation and I compare three possible regimes. In a Strong Harmonisation regime, the same set of GAAP is imposed in each country. In a Weak Harmonisation regime, the choice of which GAAP to follow is left open, but whatever the choice the same set of accounts has to be produced in each country. In a Mutual Recognition regime, the choice of which GAAP to follow is left open and different GAAP's can be followed in different countries. In particular, I judge each regime in terms of the amount of information about the firm that is successfully transmitted in equilibrium. I find that Strong Harmonisation is never the optimal regime in terms of information transmission. The choice between Weak Harmonisation and Mutual Recognition depends on what is assumed about the underlying economic parameters and can be controversial.

THE VALUE OF THE FIRM AND THE ROLE OF FINANCIAL REPORTING

In various economic contests we find an informed agent, who tries to obtain a favourable reaction from a less informed agent by sending a message about his/her private information. A classic example is a seller who describes the goods to be sold to a buyer, who is in the process of deciding whether to buy or not. Another example, which is the object of this chapter, is the case of a firm releasing its annual financial report and a group of potential investors who use the report in order to value the firm.

These situations can be modelled as 'persuasion games' (Milgrom, 1981; Milgrom and Roberts, 1986). In these games, the informed agent (the sender) makes an announcement about his/her private information. This announcement is used by one (or more) agent(s), the receiver(s), in order to take a decision. The outcome of this decision enters in the sender's payoff function. Hence the sender can use the announcement strategically in order to shape the receiver's beliefs. Consequently, we have a potential information transmission problem because the sender can misrepresent his/her original information and the receiver can be misguided while taking his/her decision.

This is the reason why usually the release of information by the sender is not completely free, but has to comply with specific rules imposed by some regulatory body. For example, the seller is usually responsible for the conformity of the goods sold with what was stated at the time of the purchase. In the application considered here, the financial reporting activity is regulated by what are called 'Generally Accepted Accounting Principles', which are usually defined by a public or private regulatory body and have some form of legal value.

In what follows, I analyse the information transmission problem between the managers of a firm and potential investors with the help of a simple persuasion game, and I evaluate the performance of possible disclosure rules in terms of their ability to minimise the information loss in equilibrium.

The state of nature that is the object of the financial disclosure might be interpreted in many different ways. In what follows, I will assume that the state of nature is the 'true' value of the firm. Items like 'intangible assets', 'deferred taxation', 'risky credits', 'long-term loans' and 'exchange rate risk' are controversial and different treatments of these items can lead to different reported figures for 'income' and 'net assets' in the financial statements of the firm.[2] This is also the reason why we observe different GAAP in different countries, given that different regulatory bodies can make different choices and decide to recommend different accounting treatments for controversial items.[3] If we accept that these items are genuinely controversial, *i.e.*, there is no objectively correct valuation and accounting treatment of them, then there is no reason why the managers of the disclosing firm should be fully aware of the true value of the firm. They certainly possess information about it and they have an information advantage with respect to financial statement users because they have access to the original raw data concerning the firm. But they may themselves be not completely certain about the true value of the firm.

If the information possessed by the firm was perfect, and the objective function was monotone, the well known 'unravelling result' would hold. This result says that, whenever disclosure is 'verifiable' (*i.e.*, compatible with the information possessed by the firm), then in equilibrium we have perfect transmission of information (*i.e.*, the receiver infers correctly all the relevant information).[4] Hence we would already know the way of solving the information transmission problem: to implement a set of rules and procedures which guarantees verifiability. In the accounting standards case, the design of such a system of rules is likely to be possible, especially if we consider the auditing process as a part of this system.

Many disclosure models in the analytical accounting literature have already explored the consequences of adding the possibility that managers may not be informed.[5] The unravelling result does not hold anymore and we do not have perfect transmission of information in equilibrium. The consequences of such an approach for international accounting regulation, however, have never been explored.

A considerable literature has been produced on international harmonisation of accounting, especially within the European Union, but not many papers exist where the problem is addressed within an economic theory approach.[6] An exception is Gigler et al. (1994) where the effects of the introduction of an international standard imposing line of business reporting on product market competition are explored.

More effort has been spent in analysing the optimal choice of GAAP at a national level in order to decide whether rigid or flexible GAAP should be imposed.[7] However there is a fundamental difference between regulation at the national level and regulation at the international level. At the national level, only one set of GAAP is adopted. The GAAP can be flexible, but only one set of accounts is produced. At the international level, Strong Harmonisation is not the only choice. It is possible to recognise and accept different GAAP for different countries and the firm can be allowed to produce two different sets of accounts in two different countries. This has generally been recognised as a problem because it adds confusion to the analysis of the performance of the firm. However, in the following sections I will show that, if the international regulation regime is correct, two sets of accounts for the same firm in two different countries can provide valuable information, which would be lost if Strong Harmonisation was imposed.

THE PERSUASION GAME

We have two players: one sender (F) and one receiver (M). The state space is made only of two elements, *i.e.*,

$$X = \{x_L, x_H\} \quad with \ x_L < x_H$$

and $p(x_i) = p_i$ where $i = L, H$ is the probability that state x_i is the true state. If we let $p_L = p$ then we have $p_H = 1\text{-}p$. As mentioned in the introduction, this state of nature can be interpreted as the true value of the firm.

Before releasing his/her statement (message), F can observe one signal σ such that:

$$\sigma = \begin{cases} 0 & if \ x^* = x_L \\ 1 & if \ x^* = x_H \end{cases} \tag{1}$$

where x^* is the true state and the probability of receiving this signal is θ. Hence F's information set, I, can assume only one of the following three values:

$$I = [x_L] \qquad \text{with probability } p\theta$$
$$I = [x_H] \qquad \text{with probability } (1-p)\theta$$
$$I = [x_L, x_H] \quad \text{with probability } 1-\theta.[8]$$

The information set possessed by F can be interpreted as the type of sender, whose strategy consists of a disclosure D as a function of his/her type, *i.e.*, $D(I)$.

After the disclosure, M values the business of F. Then F sells part of the business to M in accordance with this value. Afterwards, M can re-trade shares of F at the same value at which the shares were traded between F and M. After this second round of transactions, the true state is revealed. The payoff functions of the two players are as follows:

$$\pi^F = V - x^*$$ (2)

$$\pi^M = -(x^* - V)^2$$ (3)

where V is the valuation of F's business given by M. M's optimal strategy consists of setting V equal to the expected value of x given the announcement D. If V is greater than this expected value, then M will be willing to sell shares, but nobody will be willing to buy. If V is less than this expected value, then M will be willing to buy shares but nobody will be willing to sell. This is the rationale of expression (3). F's strategy consists in choosing D in order to influence M's beliefs and obtain a valuation as high as possible. F's payoff is obviously positive monotone in V.

The 'verifiability' rule

At first we assume that the only constraint on the disclosure is given by the verifiability assumption:

Assumption 1: $I \subseteq D(I)$. In other words, the disclosed set must contain the information set, but F is free to add some 'noise' (*i.e.*, 'enlarge' the information set) that may mislead M.

Hence if $I = [x_L]$ or $I = [x_H]$, then a disclosure $D(I) = [x_L, x_H]$ is accepted according to the verifiability rule.

This is simply the two-state case of Shin's (1994) model. Hence an equilibrium of the model is as follows:

• F adopts the 'sanitization' strategy, *i.e.*, $\sigma \in D \Leftrightarrow \sigma = 1$. In other words F hides 'bad news' ($\sigma = 0$) and discloses only 'good news' ($\sigma = 1$).
• M values the business according to the rule $V = E_\beta(x \mid D)$
• The distribution $\beta(x)$ is given by:

$$\beta(x) = \begin{cases} \dfrac{p}{p + (1 - \theta)(1 - p)} = \beta_L \text{ if } x = x_L \\ \dfrac{(1 - \theta)(1 - p)}{p + (1 - \theta)(1 - p)} = \beta_H \text{ if } x = x_H \end{cases}$$ (4)

The proof of this statement can be found in Shin (1994). Given that this notation will be used again, it is useful to express the optimal strategy in the following way:

$$D(I) = \begin{cases} [x_L, x_H] & \text{if } I = [x_L, x_H] \text{ or } [x_L] \\ [x_H] & \text{if } I = [x_H] \end{cases} \tag{5}$$

which makes clear the hybrid nature of the equilibrium because type $[x_H]$ separates from the others, but types $[x_L]$ and $[x_L, x_H]$ pool together and send the same message. The corresponding equilibrium belief profile for M is:

$$\mu(x|D) = \beta(x) \quad \text{if } D = [x_L, x_H] \tag{6}$$

$$\mu(x|D) = \begin{cases} 0 & \text{if } x = x_L \\ 1 & \text{if } x = x_H \end{cases} \quad \text{if } D = [x_H] \tag{7}$$

Consequently the equilibrium value of V is given by:

$$V = E_\beta(x|D) = \begin{cases} \beta_L x_L + \beta_H x_H & \text{if } D = [x_L, x_H] \\ x_H & \text{if } D = [x_H] \end{cases} \tag{8}$$

This completes the description of this equilibrium when only verifiability of the disclosure is required.

The 'one state' rule

Let us now analyse a different rule. From the previous case we can notice that the 'pooling' nature of the equilibrium is due to the fact that, when the true type is $[x_L]$ (*i.e.*, the true state is x_L and F knows it), F has an incentive to misreport it and announce $[x_L, x_H]$ without breaking any rule. If we imposed an upper limit to the number of states that can be part of the disclosure (in this case, this limit is forced to be one), then type $[x_L]$ would be forced to tell the truth.

However, when the true type is $[x_L, x_H]$, such a rule forces F to be more precise than he/she could be by telling the whole truth. The situation can be seen as one where the manager of a firm has to decide under which category to report a certain accounting figure. His/her decision is constrained by some existing accounting standard which forces him/her to make a choice even if it might not be clear which is the most appropriate category. In other words, the manager is forced to make a choice even if he/she is unsure which choice is right. An example is the case of a risky debt, which has 50% probability of being cashed and 50% of remaining unpaid. Should it be registered as a bad debt or as a realisable asset? There is no clear answer to this question, but it might be possible that existing rules force the manager to make a choice anyway. This example is rather extreme, but it gives the flavour of the kind of rules that can be modelled in this way.

Obviously the verifiability assumption must be modified because, when the true type is $[x_L,x_H]$, it is not possible for F to include the complete information set in the disclosure. We will assume the following:

Assumption 2: only one state can be disclosed, but it has to be contained in the information set, *i.e.*, $[x_L]$ cannot send the message $D = [x_H]$.

Lemma 1
In the persuasion game with the 'one state' rule (assumption 2), an equilibrium is described as follows:

F's strategy is given by:

$$D(I) = \begin{cases} [x_L] & \text{if } I = [x_L] \\ [x_H] & \text{if } I = [x_L, x_H] \text{ or } [x_H] \end{cases} \tag{9}$$

M's belief profile is given by:

$$\mu_S(x|D) = \delta(x) = \begin{cases} \delta_L = \dfrac{(1-\theta)p}{(1-\theta)p+(1-p)} & \text{if } x = x_L \\ \delta_H = \dfrac{(1-p)}{(1-\theta)p+(1-p)} & \text{if } x = x_H \end{cases} \quad \text{if } D = [x_L, x_H] \tag{10}$$

$$\mu_S(x|D) = \begin{cases} 1 & \text{if } x = x_L \\ 0 & \text{if } x = x_H \end{cases} \quad \text{if } D = [x_L] \tag{11}$$

Consequently, the equilibrium value of V is:

$$V = E_{\mu_S}(x|D) = \begin{cases} x_L & \text{if } D = [x_L] \\ \delta_L x_L + \delta_H x_H & \text{if } D = [x_H] \end{cases} \tag{12}$$

Proof:
If we call $\mu([x_i]|x^*)$ the probability of disclosing $[x_i]$ when the true state is x^*, then the prospective equilibrium strategy can be expressed as follows:

$$\mu\big([x_L]\big|x^*\big)=\begin{cases}\theta & \text{if } x^* = x_L \\ 0 & \text{if } x^* = x_H\end{cases} \tag{13}$$

$$\mu\big([x_H]\big|x^*\big)=\begin{cases}(1-\theta) & \text{if } x^* = x_L \\ 1 & \text{if } x^* = x_H\end{cases} \tag{14}$$

It is now clear that the belief profile (10) is consistent with Bayesian updating of the prior given this strategy. On the other hand, given the belief profile, the strategy described by (9) is optimal. In order to prove this claim, it is enough to show that when the true type is $[x_L,x_H]$ the message $[x_L]$ is dominated by $[x_H]$. It is straightforward to check that, given that $x_L < x_H$, then

$$E(V|[x_L]) = x_L \le E(V|[x_H]) = \delta_L x_L + \delta_H x_H \tag{15}$$

It remains to be shown that the equilibrium belief profile is consistent.[9] This is demonstrated in the appendix. QED

Comparisons between the two rules

Looking at the equilibrium of the second game, we can notice that the introduction of the rule has 'reversed' the outcome in comparison to the old equilibrium. When the true type is $[x_L]$, F is forced to reveal his/her information, but when the true type is $[x_L,x_H]$ he/she is 'free' to claim that the true type is $[x_H]$. On the other hand, type $[x_H]$ reveals his/her information as before. Hence, once again, we have a hybrid equilibrium where $[x_L,x_H]$ and $[x_H]$ pool at $[x_H]$, whereas $[x_L]$ is 'forced' to separate at $[x_L]$.

It is also easy to check that: $\delta_L < p_L < \beta_L$ and $\delta_H > p_H > \beta_H$. In other words, when we assume verifiability only, we have a 'sceptical' belief profile, because, when the pooling message is received, post-disclosure beliefs shift probability from the highest state to the lowest state. On the other hand, when we impose the 'one state' rule, we end up with an 'optimistic' belief profile because the receipt of the pooling message shifts probability from the lowest state to the highest state. An illustration of the difference between the two games is provided in Table 7.1

Assume that $p < 1/2$, i.e. $p_L < p_H$. Suppose that our aim is to minimise the difference between the true type and the equilibrium valuation. Ex-ante this expected loss is given by the following product:[10]

$E_p(\text{information loss}) = E_p(\text{loss}|\text{pooling message})\text{pr}(\text{pooling message})$
$\qquad\qquad + E_p(\text{loss}|\text{separating}) \text{ pr (separating message)}$
$\qquad\qquad = E_p(\text{loss}|\text{pooling message})\text{pr}(\text{pooling message})$

Table 7.1 Loss functions for the 'verifiability' and 'one state' rules

'Verifiability' rule

Type X_L	X_H	Disclosure X_L	X_H		Pr(Type)	E(x|I)[a]	V(x|D)[b]
X					θ p	x_L	$\beta_L x_L + \beta_H x_H$
X	X ⇒	X	X	(a)	(1-θ)	$p_L x_L + p_H x_H$	$\beta_L x_L + \beta_H x_H$
	X ⇒		X	(b)	θ (1-p)	x_H	x_H

'One state' rule

Type X_L	X_H	Disclosure X_L	X_H		Pr(Type)	E(x|I)[a]	V(x|D)[b]
X		X		(a')	θ p	x_L	x_L
	X ⇒				θ(1-p)	x_H	$\delta_L x_L + \delta_H x_H$
X	X ⇒		X	(b')	(1-θ)	$p_L x_L + p_H x_H$	$\delta_L x_L + \delta_H x_H$

[a] Expected value given the information set of the sender
[b] Expected value given the message observed

If we switch from the first game to the second, the first component decreases because the belief profile is more similar to the prior ($\delta_L < \delta_H$ whereas $\beta_L > \beta_H$), but the second increases because the 'pooling' state [x_H] becomes more likely than the 'separating' one [x_L]. Hence it is not immediately obvious which one of the two games is better than the other.[11]

To decide which is the best rule, we have to compute the exact value of the loss function. Let us suppose that there exist social losses caused by an incorrect valuation of the firm.[12] If this is the case, then the regulator wants to reduce as much as possible the difference between the market value of the firm, V, and the actual true state x^*. In other words, he/she tries to minimise the informational loss due to possible misreporting by F.

Formally, we can assume that the regulator's objective function is exactly the same as the market, but that the regulator chooses which game is preferable to play from the point of view of the amount of information transmitted in equilibrium. Hence the regulator and the market share the same objective but have different strategy spaces. Thus, formally, we assume that the objective of the regulator is to minimise the following ex-ante loss function:

$$L = E_p[(x^* - V)^2] \qquad (16)$$

We will use the following notation:

L_v = expected loss when we assume only verifiability
L_1 = expected loss when only one state can be disclosed

The expression for these three quantities can be calculated in each of the models presented before.

Case 1: Verifiability

$$L_v = [(x_L - (\beta_L x_L + \beta_H x_H))^2]p + [\theta(x_H - x_L)^2 + (1-\theta)(x_H - \beta_L x_L - \beta_H x_H)^2](1-p)$$

After some algebraic manipulation and exploiting the fact that $\beta_L = 1 - \beta_H$, we can re-express the above as follows:

$$L_v = (x_H - x_L)^2[\beta_H^2 p + (1-\theta)(1-\beta_H)^2(1-p)] \tag{17}$$

Case 2: One state

$$L_1 = [\theta(x_H - x_L)^2 + (1-\theta)(x_L - \delta_L x_L - \delta_H x_H)^2]p + [(x_H - (\delta_L x_L + \delta_H x_H))^2](1-p)$$

Again this expression can be simplified into:

$$L_1 = (x_H - x_L)^2[(1-\theta)\delta_H^2 p + (1-\delta_H)^2(1-p)] \tag{18}$$

Using expressions (4) and (10), we can notice that, as expected, when $\theta = 1$ (perfect information), we have $\beta_H = \delta_L = 0$ and the expected loss is always zero. Once again, this is another way of proving the 'unravelling result'. In this case, verifiability is enough to obtain perfect transmission of information. However when $\theta \neq 1$, this is not true anymore. Consequently the question of which rule performs better is not trivial anymore.

For a given θ, all the variables can be expressed as functions of p only and it is fairly easy to check that for any p we have

$$L_v(p) = L_1(1-p) \tag{19}$$

In other words the loss function for the first game (verifiability only) and the loss function for the second game (fixed number of states to disclose) are symmetric with respect to the value $p = 1/2$. This symmetry property is enough to prove the following proposition.

Proposition 1
The 'one state' rule is better (worse) than the 'verifiability' rule if and only if $p<1/2$ ($p>1/2$) or, equivalently, if and only if $p_L < p_H$ ($p_L > p_H$).

Proof:

From expression (4), we have that $\qquad \beta_H = \dfrac{(1-\theta)(1-p)}{p+(1-\theta)(1-p)}$

If we substitute this expression into (17) we get

$$L_v(p) = (x_H - x_L)^2 (1-\theta)(1-p)\frac{p}{1-\theta(1-p)} \qquad (20)$$

from which we have that

$$L_v(1-p) < L_v(p) \Leftrightarrow p < \frac{1}{2} \qquad (21)$$

This means that the loss function in the first game is skewed to the left with respect to $p = 1/2$. But given that the loss functions for the two games are symmetric with respect to this value we have that:

$$L_v(p_0) > L_v(1-p_0) = L_1(p_0) \Leftrightarrow p_0 < \frac{1}{2} \quad . \text{QED}$$

Proposition 1 confirms the intuition that, given the shape of belief profiles, from the point of view of the regulator, the second rule ('one state') is preferred to the first ('verifiability') when the lower state is less likely than the higher state. With respect to the two effects outlined before, the result states that the reduction in the expected loss in case of pooling more than compensates for the increase in the probability of observing the pooling message. But the importance of the proposition is more general. It tells us that the optimal rule depends on the prior distribution. Hence we were able to show that there is not a rule that is optimal for every environment, but that the optimal rule depends on the prior distribution.

IMPLICATIONS FOR INTERNATIONAL ACCOUNTING REGULATION

Let us now examine the implications of the previous analysis for international accounting regulation. Consider again the example of Daimler-Benz provided in the introduction.

Suppose that the true value of Daimler-Benz can be either x_H or x_L. With no international regulation, Daimler-Benz is forced to adopt US GAAP in the US and German GAAP in Germany.

Assume now that an international regulatory board is set up and the following three regimes are considered.

- Strong Harmonisation. In this case, the same GAAP are imposed for both countries. Whatever these principles are, Daimler-Benz produces only one set of accounts and there is no choice.

- Weak Harmonisation. The choice of which GAAP to follow is left open, but whatever the choice, Daimler-Benz has to produce the same set of accounts in both countries.
- Mutual Recognition. Both German GAAP and US GAAP are declared acceptable and Daimler-Benz is free to choose which GAAP to follow in each country as long as it declares its policy. In other words Daimler-Benz can present the same set of accounts in both countries, or two different sets of accounts, *i.e.*, one for each country.

Message interpretation

It is important to clarify how the analytical setting presented before can be used to analyse the choice between these three regimes.

The importance of the bottom line figure of the Profit and Loss account (Income statement) for users of financial statements is well known. The proof is given by the constant discussion, between regulators and preparers and users of these statements, about where to draw the line and what goes above and below the line.[13]

The choice between adopting US GAAP and adopting German GAAP is the choice between reporting a bottom line figure of 'Loss of DM 949m' and reporting a bottom line figure of 'Profit of DM 168m'. Given the importance of this bottom line figure, I claim that this choice can be seen as a choice between sending respectively either the message '$x=x_L$' or the message '$x=x_H$' about the true value of the firm.

Strong Harmonisation forces the company to choose one of these messages. Weak Harmonisation asks the company to choose only one of these messages without specifying which one. Mutual Recognition leaves the company free to choose a different message in each of the two different countries.[14]

Consider now the possible information sets in the Daimler-Benz case.

Perfect information

We can assume that a firm such as Daimler-Benz knows for sure its true value. Then we have only two possible alternatives.

One possibility is that there is only one correct way of presenting the accounts and that such a firm is openly misrepresenting the situation in one or in both countries. Then it is not at all clear why any form of international harmonisation should prevent this from happening again. The only way to justify such a statement would be to assume that an international board can police firm behaviour better than a national board and, given the historical experience of many international organisations, this is a strong assumption.

The other alternative is that the same true value can be represented in two acceptable ways and there is no obvious way to decide which one is correct. In that case, with no international regulation or with the strong version of harmonisation, the firm has no choice. The fact that we observe two different sets of accounts with no international regulation is not informative. The only advantage of international regulation would be that it would save the cost of producing two sets of accounts.

The weaker version of harmonisation instead would be equivalent to the 'one state' rule of the model, because the firm would be free to choose which GAAP to follow, but could not send more than one message. Mutual Recognition would be equivalent to the verifiability case of the model, because the firm can choose whether to send only one message, and if so which one, or to send a two-valued message.

Both with Weak Harmonisation and Mutual Recognition, the message 'Profit of DM168m' in both countries could be interpreted as $D=[x_H]$. The message 'Loss of DM949m' in both countries could be interpreted as $D=[x_L]$. Finally if Mutual Recognition is the regime, then the message 'Profit of DM168m' in one country and 'Loss of DM949m' in the other could be interpreted as $D=[x_L,x_H]$.

Hence, if we dismiss the case of open misrepresentation and we assume that the firm knows for sure its true value, then Weak Harmonisation or Mutual Recognition are equivalent in the sense that both guarantee perfect transmission of information in equilibrium.

Non perfect information

Assume now that it is possible that the firm does not know for sure its true value. In the case of Strong Harmonisation or no regulation, there is still no choice and no information can be deduced from the observation that two different sets of accounts have been produced. For Weak Harmonisation and Mutual Recognition, the interpretation of the accounts would be the same as before and the choice of the optimal regime depends on the prior distribution of the possible values of the company. If the firm is more likely to be a low-value company, then Mutual Recognition is the optimal regime. If the firm is more likely to be a high-value company, then Weak Harmonisation is the optimal regime.

SUMMARY AND CONCLUSIONS

I have provided an attempt to evaluate the performance of different possible rules when the imperfect nature of the information possessed by the reporting firm prevents the possibility of having perfect information transmission in equilibrium. The rules have been judged with regard to a quadratic loss function that measures the amount of information lost in equilibrium. This loss is due to the possibility that the firm may manipulate its accounting data.

The rule that requires the firm to disclose only a fixed number of possible states has been compared with the verifiability rule that simply excludes open misrepresentation. The two rules perform in exactly the same way if the prior is uniform. Otherwise the ranking depends on the shape of the prior.

These results have been used to draw some conclusions about the international harmonisation of GAAP. Strong Harmonisation is not the best regime, in terms of the amount of information that it is successfully communicated in equilibrium. A regime of Weak Harmonisation or Mutual Recognition of GAAP is always preferable.

In general, the analysis shows that what matters is not the face value of the financial reporting information. If this were the case, then the strictest regime should be the best because it minimises the uncertainty surrounding the face value. But this is not the case because published financial statements are 'interpreted' by expert users and therefore the more precise statements can be as informative as those that are less precise. If the decision usefulness approach to accounting regulation is adopted, then the way in which information is to be processed by potential users of the accounts needs to be taken into consideration. This chapter has shown that, if this approach is adopted, some common sense statements on international harmonisation of GAAP can be questioned on the grounds of information economics.

Moreover, the simple model presented here also shows how a decision concerning which regulatory regime is optimal depends crucially on prior beliefs about the state of the world. Given that these beliefs may vary among different agents, it is not surprising that the debate on international accounting standards can prompt comments like the following: *"Bean-counters may have a reputation for dullness, but they can be as stubborn and quarrelsome as any stock-exchange boss"* (The Economist, January 30th 1999, p.83, UK edition).

APPENDIX

Consistency of beliefs in Lemma 1

Suppose that, when $I=[x_L,x_H]$, F can make a 'mistake' and play strategy $[x_L]$ with positive probability η. Formally:

$$\hat{\mu}\big([x_L]\big|x^*\big) = \begin{cases} \theta + (1-\theta)\eta & \text{if } x^* = x_L \\ (1-\theta)\eta & \text{if } x^* = x_H \end{cases} \tag{A.1}$$

$$\hat{\mu}\big([x_H]\big|x^*\big) = \begin{cases} (1-\theta)(1-\eta) & \text{if } x^* = x_L \\ 1 - (1-\theta)\eta & \text{if } x^* = x_H \end{cases} \tag{A.2}$$

Bayesian updating would give us the following belief profile:

$$\hat{\mu}_S\left(x\middle|[\,x_L\,]\right)=\begin{cases}\dfrac{[\theta+(1-\theta)\eta]p}{[\theta+(1-\theta)\eta]p+(1-\theta)\eta(1-p)} & \text{if } x=x_L\\[2mm]\dfrac{(1-\theta)\eta(1-p)}{[\theta+(1-\theta)\eta]p+(1-\theta)\eta(1-p)} & \text{if } x=x_H\end{cases}\tag{A.3}$$

$$\hat{\mu}_S\left(x\middle|[\,x_H\,]\right)=\begin{cases}\dfrac{(1-\theta)(1-\eta)p}{(1-\theta)(1-\eta)p+[1-(1-\theta)\eta](1-p)} & \text{if } x=x_L\\[2mm]\dfrac{[1-(1-\theta)\eta](1-p)}{(1-\theta)(1-\eta)p+[1-(1-\theta)\eta](1-p)} & \text{if } x=x_H\end{cases}\tag{A.4}$$

It easy to check that

$$\eta\to 0\Rightarrow \hat{\mu}_S(\,x\middle|[\,x_i\,])\to\mu_S(\,x\middle|[\,x_i\,])i=L,H\,.\quad\text{QED}$$

NOTES

[1] The example is taken from Broby (1995).

[2] 'Income' and 'Net Assets' are used here in a broad sense and simply mean a measure of the performance of the firm during the reporting period (income) and an evaluation of the position of the firm in terms of net wealth at the end of the reporting period.

[3] Amir *et al.* (1993) study the effect of these different treatments on firms' market value.

[4] The 'unravelling result' is presented in Milgrom (1981). Another presentation of the result, along with many interesting applications, can be found in Okuno-Fujiwara *et al* (1990)

[5] *e.g.* Dye (1985a), Jung and Kwon (1988).

[6] See, for example, the collection of papers edited by Nobes (1996) and Blake and Hossain (1996).

[7] Two examples are Dye (1985b) and Dye and Verrechia (1995).

[8] We assume that the realisation of the state and the realisation of the signal are independent events.

[9] In fact, it is not necessary to prove consistency in this case. Given that there are only two stages in the model, Theorem 8.2 of Fudenberg and Tirole (1991) states that Perfect Bayesian Equilibrium (PBE) and Sequential Equilibrium (SE) are equivalent. The proof of the optimality of the equilibrium strategy and belief profile already assures that the equilibrium is a PBE. It is useful, however, to understand the idea behind the consistency requirement and in this case the proof is easy. This is the reason why it is provided in the appendix.

[10] The notation $E_p(\bullet)$ indicates an expected value taken according to the original prior distribution p and *(1-p)*.

[11] This interpretation of the result was suggested by Meg Meyer.

[12] For example, potential investors may become sceptical about the market process and find alternative uses for their savings.

[13] In January 1999, Andrew Lennard (deputy technical director of the ASB, the UK regulatory body), gave a talk on 'Accounting regulation in the third millenium' to the Financial Reporting Discussion Group, in London. One of the issues which he indicated as crucial to the future activity of the ASB is how to report financial performance. This was certainly the most debated issue during question time.

[14] The possibility of deriving one message from the other is not relevant. What is important is the choice made by the company between the option of choosing the same message in both countries or choosing a different message for each country.

REFERENCES

Amir, E., Harris, T.S., and Venuti, E. (1993). A comparison of the value-relevance of US versus non-US GAAP accounting measures using form 20-F reconciliations, *Journal of Accounting Research*, Vol.31, Supplement, pp.230-64.

Blake, J., and Hossain, M. (1996). *Readings in International Accounting*. London: International Thomson Business Press.

Broby, D.P. (1995). A fund manager's view of financial reporting, in *Financial Reporting 1995-96: A Survey of UK Reporting Practice*. Milton Keynes: Accountancy Books.

Dye, R.A. (1985a). Disclosure of nonproprietary information, *Journal of Accounting Research* Vol. 23, No.1, pp.123-45.

Dye, R.A. (1985b). Strategic accounting choice and the effects of alternative financial reporting requirements, *Journal of Accounting Research*, Vol. 23, No.2, pp.544-74.

Dye, R.A., and Verrecchia, R.E. (1995). Discretion vs uniformity: choices among GAAP, *The Accounting Review*, Vol. 70, No.3, pp.389-415.

Fudenberg, D., and Tirole, J. (1991). *Game Theory*. Cambridge Massachusetts: MIT Press

Gigler, F., Hughes, J.S., and Rayburn, J. (1994). International accounting standards for line-of-business reporting and oligopoly competition, *Contemporary Accounting Research*, Vol. 11, No. 1-2, pp.619-32.

Jung, W.O., and Kwon, Y.K. (1988). Disclosure when the market is unsure of information endowment of managers, *Journal of Accounting Research*, Vol.26, No.1, pp.146-53.

Milgrom, P. (1981). Good news and bad news representation theorems and applications, *Bell Journal of Economics*, Vol.12, No. 2, pp.380-91.

Milgrom, P., and Roberts, J. (1986). Relying on the information of interested parties, *Rand Journal of Economics*, Vol.17, No.1, pp.18-32.

Nobes C.W. (1996). *International Harmonization of Accounting*, Cheltenham: Edward Elgar Publishing.

Okuno-Fujiwara, M., Postlewaite, A., and Suzumura, K. (1990). Strategic information revelation, *Review of Economic Studies*, Vol.57, No.1, pp.25-47.

Shin, H.S. (1994). News management and the value of firms, *Rand Journal of Economics*, Vol.25, No.1, pp.58-71.

8

IS THE USEFULNESS APPROACH USEFUL? SOME REFLECTIONS ON THE UTILITY OF PUBLIC INFORMATION

Klaus Schredelseker

THE PROBLEM

Whether or not the disclosure of a firm's accounting data should be mandatory is one of the most controversial topics debated in law and economics. The positions taken are quite diverse (Easterbrook and Fischel, 1991, pp.276-314):

- *The market view*: If investors prefer firms which deliver reliable and detailed information about their current position and future prospects, then the better the public accounting information provided by a firm, the lower the firm's capital cost will be. Each firm will thus have a natural incentive to disclose information: there will be no need for regulation that makes disclosure mandatory.

- *The regulator's view*: The advocates of regulation argue that legislation requiring the disclosure of a certain amount of accounting data in a well defined format is necessary. Otherwise, the self-interest of managers would lead them not to disclose true and fair information, but rather to adopt a marketing approach where managers let the public know what they want them to know and keep secret what they don't want the public to be aware of.

Both sides, however, take for granted the usefulness of public information to market participants, an assumption that is also made by the Financial Accounting Standards Board in FASB Statement No.1: "*Financial reporting should provide information that is useful to present and potential investors and creditors and other users in assessing the amounts, timing, and uncertainty of prospective cash receipts.*"

This chapter will show that this is far from unquestionable. Indeed, it will be shown that what the accounting literature usually assumes is not necessarily true: that is, it is not always the case that the better a market is endowed with public information, the higher the welfare of investors and other users will be. It will further be shown that the lower the average information level of the market participant, the higher the allocational efficiency of the market may be. Finally, it will be shown that it is easily possible that the worse off an investor is, the better that investor's skills in financial analysis will be.

For the past three decades, market efficiency has provided the basic paradigm of modern financial economics: if markets were to be informationally efficient, and thus all information would be fully reflected in prices, there would be no basis for expecting excess returns.[1] To begin with, researchers came up with overwhelming empirical evidence that real markets show a high level of informational efficiency, at least with respect to publicly available information. This was a hard time for accountants.

Within the last two decades, however, the efficient markets hypothesis has come under serious pressure. Firstly, empirical research has increasingly pointed at phenomena contradicting the hypothesis: various factors such as calendar effects, a size effect, autocorrelation effects and a book-to-value-effect have been referred to as anomalies, *i.e.*, something that should not happen, given the efficient markets paradigm. Secondly, there is a growing body of theoretical literature, mainly based upon information economics, which deals with markets under conditions of costly information, asymmetric distribution of knowledge and negative information values. These theoretical approaches seek to resolve the well-known information paradox originally formulated by Grossman (1976); that is, if stock prices fully reflect all available information in accordance with Fama (1970), there will be no incentive to acquire costly information. This is because, in the case of a fully revealing market, prices will become redundant with respect to investors' private information and no investor would pay even a cent for it. Conversely, if nobody processes information, there is no reason why prices should convey any of it. Up to now, research has taken a number of directions in seeking to resolve this paradox

(Grossman and Stiglitz, 1980; Diamond and Verrecchia, 1981; Hellwig, 1982; Kyle, 1989; Jackson, 1991; Yu, 1993).

The more the efficient markets hypothesis has weakened, the more accountants have got the upper hand. Indeed, there is a widespread belief that, if prices do not reflect all available information, it should be useful to traders to be informed. We believe, however, that the real challenge for accounting comes not from the efficient markets hypothesis, but from its counterpart, the assumption that markets could be somewhat less than efficient. The simple equation 'more information = better investment performance' overlooks the fact that investment decisions have to be considered within a complex (let us say 'game theoretical') market environment and not as a decision against nature. There is no doubt that, in decisions against nature, information always has a positive value: the better one is informed, the better the decisions will be. In markets, however, this is no longer the case; if, *ceteris paribus*, one person's decision quality improves, there has to be at least one other person whose decision quality decreases, as markets are zero-sum games with complex information structures.

METHODOLOGY

In this chapter, I develop some basic relationships between public information and the quality of investment decisions by using an extremely simple, but quite powerful, simulation approach.[2] The model simulates a one-period pure exchange economy in which only one security is traded, a security whose net supply is zero as in a futures or options market. In each run of the simulation, the security's value (its intrinsic value, V) is the sum of the values of eleven Laplace coins showing either zero or one. V is thus a random variable, drawn from a binomial distribution with realizations from zero to eleven. Trading takes place in a call market with ten traders; the traders place their orders and the price is fixed in such a way that the number of sellers equals the number of buyers (five on each side).

The traders are risk-neutral, expected-wealth maximizers who are bound to trade exactly one security each run. Information is exogenously given, but not distributed equally. Before trading, each trader T_t receives information about a certain number of coins (the trader's information level, IL_t) and a trader-specific noise term. We suppose information asymmetry to be cumulative: $IL_{t-y} \in IL_t$ for every $t>y>0$. If we disregard noise, the following premise holds: what is known to any trader is known to each of the well informed traders as well.

A trader who decides whether to go long or to go short upon the signal received is referred to as 'active' (a passive trading strategy will be introduced later). If an active trader with IL_n sees n coins of which x show up one (and $n-x$ show up zero), he expects the security's value to be

$\quad E_t(V) = x + 5.5 - n/2 + d_t\varepsilon,$

where x is the sum of what he sees, the expected value of the coins he does not see is equal to $5.5 - n/2$, and $d_t\varepsilon$ is the trader-specific noise term. In our simulations,

$d_t\varepsilon$ is composed of ε, an equally distributed 15-digit-random variable between -0.5 and 0.5, and d_t, a non-zero dispersion parameter which measures trader t's capability to extract the information content from the signals received; in more practical terms, $d_t\varepsilon$ represents the investor's skill in financial analysis: the higher d_t is, the more mistakes an investor makes in assessing the information received. To begin with, d is equal for all ten traders and therefore very low. The noise term $d_t\varepsilon$ also exists for a purely technical reason: as d_t will never be zero, the case that two or more traders will arrive at the same estimate of V is practically ruled out.

The market price P is calculated as the median of the traders' orders. When all traders adopt an active investment strategy, their orders correspond to their estimations $E_1(V)...E_{10}(V)$: as the traders are assumed to be strictly risk-neutral, each trader buys the security at any price P if $P < E_t(V)$ and sells it if $E_t(V) < P$. In the first case, the trader expects the security to be underpriced; in the second case, he expects it to be overpriced. With $d_t \neq 0$, there are always five traders buying and five traders selling (the probability that in one run there will be two equal random numbers is close to zero). With $d_t \neq 0$, we will never have full informational efficiency: the difference between price and value will not be zero. Thus, in each run, we can calculate the gains and losses G_t for the traders as follows:

- in the case of $P<V$ (underpricing), the buyers gain $G_{buy} = V-P$ and the sellers lose $G_{sell} = P-V$
- in the case of $P>V$ (overpricing), the buyers lose $G_{buy} = V-P$ and the sellers gain $G_{sell} = P-V$.

Our market will be informationally inefficient not only because of these minor technical reasons, but to a much greater extent because of it's thinness: with only ten market participants, the traders are not price-takers, and they have some noticeable impact on market prices. As we wish to study markets which are somewhat less than efficient, this is not a shortcoming but a welcome feature that will drive some of the main results.

A short example will further clarify how the simulation works. Let the distribution of the coins be 11000101101 ($V=6$) and let us assume that each trader t sees the first t coins; d is 0.1 and from the noise term $d_t\varepsilon$ we see only three digits, as in Table 8.1.

Given the distribution of orders $E_1(V)...E_{10}(V)$, the market clearing price (the

Table 8.1 Example of market simulation

T	Trader t	1	2	3	4	5	6	7	8	9	10
N	Number of coins seen	1	2	3	4	5	6	7	8	9	10
X	Coins showing 1	1.000	2.000	2.000	2.000	2.000	3.000	3.000	4.000	5.000	5.000
$5.5-n/2$	E(remainder)	5.000	4.500	4.000	3.500	3.000	2.500	2.000	1.500	1.000	0.500
$d_t\varepsilon$	$(-\frac{1}{2}...\varepsilon..\frac{1}{2}; d_t=0.1)$	0.029	-0.008	-0.026	-0.013	0.021	0.043	0.017	-0.006	0.002	-0.035
Orders	$E_t(V) = x+5.5-n/2+ d_t\varepsilon$	6.029	6.492	5.974	5.487	5.021	5.543	5.017	5.494	5.998	5.465
$P=5.519$	Buyer / Seller	B	B	B	S	S	B	S	S	B	S

median price) is 5.519, which means that the security, which has an intrinsic value of 6.0, is undervalued by 0.481: buyers (B) gain 0.481; sellers (S) lose the same amount.

Each of the following tables exhibits the results of 2^{11} (=2048) runs: all 2048 possible states of the binomial distribution were calculated, so that the results would be free from estimation errors with respect to the distribution itself. The only remaining stochastics are due to $d\varepsilon$, but as d is quite small (from now on $d = 0.01$) the noise term does not have much significance but only serves to guarantee a unique market clearing price. Nevertheless, in order to rule out casual results, the simulation procedure is repeated five times and the results reported here are the averages of the five simulations.

THE PRIVATE VALUE OF PUBLIC INFORMATION

We call information 'public' if everybody has access to it. If we assume that every trader t sees exactly t of the eleven coins, the public information level is very low with $PIL = 1$: only the first coin is observed by everybody. If all the traders adopt an active strategy and if they all have high skills in assessing the information received (d=0.01 for all traders), the gains and losses will be allocated as in Table 8.2:

Table 8.2 Gains and losses when the level of information is very low

Public information level PIL = 1; d=0.01; all traders adopt an active strategy										
Trader t	1	2	3	4	5	6	7	8	9	10
Trader t's information level IL_t	1	2	3	4	5	6	7	8	9	10
Trader t's gains per round G_t	-0.35	-0.39	-0.41	-0.38	-0.33	0.02	0.22	0.40	0.54	0.68

Looking at the expected gains (*i.e.*, calculated gains per run), we observe the following result: there are winners and losers and the gains and losses sum to zero. Furthermore, we see that the winners are those with a high standard of information whereas the losers are the less informed traders. However, a somewhat puzzling result is that, at least at a first glance, T_2 does worse than T_1, and T_3 does worse than T_2, despite the fact that they are better informed. For T_2 and T_3, the marginal utility of information is negative, whereas for all traders with an $IL_t \geq IL_4$ we have the expected situation of positive marginal utilities of information. How can this be the case?

We have assumed information asymmetry to be cumulative: therefore, the traders partly rely upon the same subsets of information. If these information subsets are somewhat biased with respect to the entire information, traders making decisions on the basis of such subsets will make the same mistakes and will cause prices to deviate from their intrinsic values to a noticeable extent. Traders who have high levels of information will recognize these mispricings and will profit from them. Traders who have very low levels of information will avoid losses as they will not know enough to fall into the trap.

Let us clarify this by looking at four examples, each of which shows a different distribution of the coins, but always with the same intrinsic value $V = 6$:

- in the first two examples (Panels A and B), we have unbiased distributions: a trader who knows only a subset of the whole information knows roughly as much as if he knew the whole set;
- in the last two examples (Panels C and D), we have extremely biased distributions: a trader who knows only a subset of the whole information may be very misled compared to those who know the whole information.

In order to obtain pure results, we let the dispersion parameter d be very small. The preliminary results are that:

- if the information is unbiased, there is no significant relationship between a trader's information level and performance: in Panels A and B, well informed traders are as likely as less informed traders to be among the winners or losers;
- if, however, the information is biased, we will have three groups of traders: (i) those who are very well informed will win; (ii) those who have an average

Table 8.3 Biased and unbiased information sets

Public information level $PIL = 1$; $d=0.0001$; all traders adopt an active strategy										
Trader t with IL_t	1	2	3	4	5	6	7	8	9	10
Panel A $V = 6.00$ Distribution: 10101010101 $P = 5.75$ (undervaluation)										
$E_t(V)$ Trader t's estimation of V	6.00	5.50	6.00	5.50	6.00	5.50	6.00	5.50	6.00	5.50
G_t Trader t's gain/loss:	0.25	-0.25	0.25	-0.25	0.25	-0.25	0.25	-0.25	0.25	-0.25
Panel B $V = 6.00$ Distribution: 01010101011 $P = 5.25$ (undervaluation)										
$E_t(V)$ Trader t's estimation of V	5.00	5.50	5.00	5.50	5.00	5.50	5.00	5.50	5.00	5.50
G_t Trader t's gain/loss:	-0.75	0.75	-0.75	0.75	-0.75	0.75	-0.75	0.75	-0.75	0.75
Panel C $V = 6.00$ Distribution: 11111100000 $P = 7.25$ (overvaluation)										
$E_t(V)$ Trader t's estimation of V	6.00	6.50	7.00	7.50	8.00	8.50	8.00	7.50	7.00	6.50
G_t Trader t's gain/loss:	1.25	1.25	1.25	-1.25	-1.25	-1.25	-1.25	-1.25	1.25	1.25
Panel D $V = 6.00$ Distribution: 00000111111 $P = 4.25$ (undervaluation)										
$E_t(V)$ Trader t's estimation of V	5.00	4.50	4.00	3.50	3.00	3.50	4.00	4.50	5.00	5.50
G_t Trader t's gain/loss:	1.75	1.75	-1.75	-1.75	-1.75	-1.75	-1.75	1.75	1.75	1.75

level of information will lose because they will make the same errors as many others do; and (iii) those who win because they know too little will become victims of the biased information.

These results are plotted in Figure 8.1. We see that, in the case of a very low level of public information, it generally pays to be well informed. For some less informed traders, however, more information may be of no or even of negative value.

Figure 8.1 *Gains and losses when the level of public information is very low*

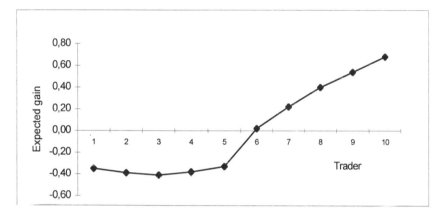

Let us now look at what happens if the public information level (*PIL*) rises. The law and economics literature usually argues that an improvement in public information (stricter disclosure requirements) reduces the information span, *i.e.*, the gap between the most informed and the least informed actors in a given market. The horizontal axis of Figure 8.2 shows all the traders in a market, arranged according to their own information level *IL*. The vertical axis gives the absolute value of *IL*, from the least informed to the most informed. If we assume a market with no public information at all, with each trader having a different *IL*, we will get by definition a relationship as in Figure 8.2, although not necessarily linear. The least informed traders have a very low *IL*, the most informed have a very high *IL*, and the information gap is thus very large.

Figure 8.2 Information gap before and after the introduction of public information

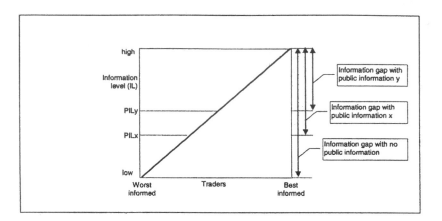

Now let the law introduce a minimum information disclosure requirement, where everybody receives the minimum information free of charge:

*   if we introduce PIL_x, the IL function firstly follows the horizontal dotted line at PIL_x and then follows the previous slope: the IL of all traders t with $IL_t < PIL_x$ improves whereas the IL of traders with $IL_t > PIL_x$ remains unchanged;
*   if we introduce PIL_y ($y>x$), the IL function firstly follows the horizontal dotted line at PIL_y and then follows the previous slope: the IL of all traders t with $IL_t < PIL_y$ improves.

As can easily be seen, as the level of public information rises, there are two consequences: the higher PIL is, (i) the smaller the information gap will be, and (ii) the more traders will make their decisions by using PIL. Traditionally, the law and economics literature only pays attention to the first effect, but it may be the second that is more important. This is shown in Table 8.4, where we successively improve PIL from PIL_1, as in the basic model, to PIL_{10} where all traders have the same information. The results obtained by using PIL are printed in bold; the others are calculated with $IL_t > PIL$.

From PIL_1 to PIL_5, any improvement in public information is accompanied by a lower expected gain for those traders who base their decisions upon PIL. If we directly compare the situations when moving from PIL_1 (diamond plot symbols in Figure 8.3) to PIL_5 (circle plot symbols in Figure 8.3), we observe a fall in performance of those traders whose IL has improved ($T_1...T_4$), whereas the performance of those traders whose IL has remained unchanged ($T_6...T_{10}$) improves.

Table 8.4 *The level of public information*

Public information level PIL = $PIL_1...PIL_{10}$; $d=0.01$; all traders adopt an active strategy									
Trader t	1	2	3	4	5	6	7	8	9	10
Public Information PIL_1	-0.35	-0.39	-0.41	-0.38	-0.33	0.02	0.22	0.40	0.54	0.68
Public Information PIL_2	-0.40	-0.40	-0.41	-0.40	-0.30	0.01	0.26	0.40	0.56	0.68
Public Information PIL_3	-0.47	-0.47	-0.47	-0.36	-0.33	0.13	0.24	0.46	0.56	0.72
Public Information PIL_4	-0.52	-0.52	-0.52	-0.52	-0.25	0.06	0.43	0.46	0.66	0.71
Public Information PIL_5	-0.56	-0.56	-0.56	-0.56	-0.56	0.41	0.26	0.65	0.64	0.84
Public Information PIL_6	-0.41	-0.41	-0.41	-0.41	-0.41	-0.41	0.50	0.43	0.75	0.75
Public Information PIL_7	-0.25	-0.25	-0.25	-0.25	-0.25	-0.25	-0.25	0.50	0.46	0.75
Public Information PIL_8	-0.12	-0.12	-0.12	-0.12	-0.12	-0.12	-0.12	-0.12	0.50	0.50
Public Information PIL_9	-0.05	-0.05	-0.05	-0.05	-0.05	-0.05	-0.05	-0.05	-0.05	0.50
Public Information PIL_{10}	0.00	0.00	0.00	0.00	0.00	0.00	0.00	0.00	0.00	0.00

The intention of the law that induced the improvement in *PIL* was surely to flatten the information span in order to flatten the expropriation span: the position of the less informed market participants should therefore be strengthened and the advantage of the well informed traders should be weakened. The effect of the law, however, is the contrary. The reason for this somewhat puzzling fact is similar to the cause of the negative marginal utility of information for traders $T_1..T_3$ in Table 8.2: that is, if *PIL* rises, traders who rely upon *PIL* may make smaller errors in estimating the intrinsic value of the security, but those errors will be similar to the errors made by many other traders who likewise base their decisions upon *PIL*.

Figure 8.3 *The effect of increasing the information level from PIL = 1 (♦) to PIL = 5 (●)*

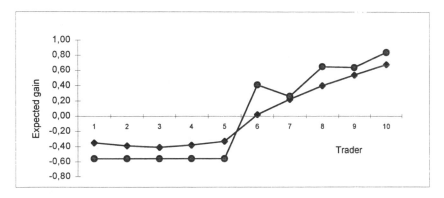

To a certain extent, the second factor dominates the first, which is not surprising. The techniques of financial analysis, especially the analysis of balance sheets, income statements, cash flow statements, etc., are basically the same wherever practised. Thus, the decisions of traders analyzing the same financial statements using the same techniques will be highly correlated.

Published financial statements can be seen as just a sample drawn from the total information about a firm's future prospects. A sample, however, can be biased or unbiased. If the sample is unbiased, it holds that those who know about the sample know as much as if they possessed all the information concerning the company, and agents who trade on this information will make no mistakes. But it is at least as likely that the company's financial statements will be somewhat biased. In this case, all agents who decide upon this biased information will come to the same incorrect conclusion. From portfolio theory, we have learned that it is not variance but covariance that drives basic financial returns and it seems that we have a similar effect here: if the errors made by traders in assessing the information which they possess are uncorrelated, these at least partially diversify away; if, instead, the errors are correlated, they result in much higher mispricings than if decisions had been taken without public information.

In order to clarify this, let us look at the example in Table 8.5. We take the same setting as in Panels C and D of Table 8.3, but instead of PIL_1 we consider PIL_5.

As we now have at least five traders whose estimations are different only with respect to the noise term $d\varepsilon$, we meet a technical problem: it may be random whether a trader is on the winning or the losing side. In Panel A, traders $T_1...T_5$ and T_7 all receive the same signal. The market clearing price (the median) depends upon $d\varepsilon$ and will be either slightly under or slightly over 8.00; thus, with a small d, T_6 will in any case be a buyer (and lose) while $T_8...T_{10}$ will be sellers (and win). For traders $T_1...T_5$, and T_7, their $d\varepsilon$ will determine whether they are buyers (winners) or sellers (losers). As the probability that they will be buyers is 2/3, and 1/3 that they will be sellers, we allocate an expected loss of -2*0.67 + 2*0.33 = -0.67, and the zero-sum property of the game is maintained.

Table 8.5 *Biased information sets and a higher level of public information (PIL=5)*

Public information level PIL = 5; $d=0.001$; all traders adopt an active strategy										
Trader *i*	1	2	3	4	5	6	7	8	9	10
Panel A　$V = 6.00$　Distribution: 11111100000　$P \approx 8.00$ (large overvaluation)										
$E_i(V)$　Trader *i* 's estimation of V	8.00	8.00	8.00	8.00	8.00	8.50	8.00	7.50	7.00	6.50.
G_i　Trader *i* 's gain/loss:	-0.67	-0.67	-0.67	-0.67	-0.67	-2.00	-0.67	2.00	2.00	2.00
Panel B $V = 6.00$ Distribution: 00000111111　$P \approx 3.25$ (large undervaluation)										
$E_i(V)$　Trader *i* 's estimation of V	3.00	3.00	3.00	3.00	3.00	3.50	4.00	4.50	5.00	5.50
G_i　Trader *i* 's gain/loss:	-2.75	-2.75	-2.75	-2.75	-2.75	2.75	2.75	2.75	2.75	2.75

If we compare the earlier results from Panels C and D of Table 8.3 with those now shown in Table 8.5, we observe that

- the least informed traders who were among the winners when without public information now show up among the losers (T_1, T_2 and T_3 in Tables 8.3C and 8.5A; T_1 and T_2 in Tables 8.3D and 8.5B);
- the less informed traders who were among the losers when without public information remain as losers despite the fact that their *IL* has improved (T_4 in Tables 8.3C and 8.5A; T_3 and T_4 in Tables 8.3D and 8.5B);
- traders in the middle who were among the losers when without public information remain as losers (T_5, T_6, and T_7 in Tables 8.3C and 8.5A; T_5 in Tables 8.3C and 8.5A);
- the well informed traders who were among the losers when without public information are now winners (T_8 in Tables 8.3C and 8.5A; T_6 and T_7 in Tables 8.3D and 8.5B);
- the most informed traders who were among the winners when without public information remain as winners (T_9 and T_{10} in Tables 8.3C and 8.5A; T_8, T_9, and T_{10} in tables 8.3D and 8.5B)
- the improvement in *PIL* induces higher mispricings: in Tables 8.3C and 8.5A, the overpricing is 2.00 instead of 1.25; in tables 8.3D and 8.5B, the underpricing is 2.75 instead of 1.75.

From a certain level of public information onwards, however, a further improvement of *PIL* leads to the desired results: if the level of public information exceeds *PIL*$_5$, the performance of traders using public information improves. If all traders have reached the same level of information, prices reflect all available information and nobody can improve the situation by trading upon their own information.[3]

DOES IT PAY TO BE A GOOD FINANCIAL ANALYST?

Until now, it has been assumed that all agents have the same capabilities in assessing the information content of a given signal. In order to avoid random deviations from the 'economically pure' results, the dispersion parameter d has been equal for every trader and very small. In real markets, however, investors have different capabilities of digesting and interpreting the signals they receive: some are experts in accounting and extract the maximum information content from the firm's financial statements; others have at their disposal only a few basic techniques and capture only a part of the information.

Let us thus return to the *PIL* = 5 simulation and let us assume that traders $T_6...T_{10}$ have a higher information level than *PIL*$_5$ and are excellent analysts with a dispersion parameter $d = 0.10$ (misinterpretation of the given information is never higher than ± 0.05). Traders $T_1...T_5$, on the other hand, only have *PIL* and differ with respect to their abilities to correctly interpret the information they receive, as follows:

- T_5 is an excellent analyst: d_5=0.10
- T_4 is a good analyst who makes minor mistakes; d_4=0.40
- T_3 is a reasonable analyst but is prone to error; d_3=0.70
- T_2 is a less competent analyst who makes more serious mistakes; d_2=1.00
- T_1 is the weakest analyst who makes major mistakes; d_1=1.30.

Table 8.6 shows what will happen if these ten traders form the market. As can be seen – and this may surprise some readers – out of those traders who rely upon *PIL*, the most successful are those who have very low skills in assessing the information they receive.

Table 8.6 Allowing for differences between traders in their ability to assess information

Public information level PIL = 5; d=different;						all traders adopt an active strategy				
Trader *t*	1	2	3	4	5	6	7	8	9	10
Trader *t*'s dispersion d_t	1.30	1.00	0.70	0.40	0.10	0.10	0.10	0.10	0.10	0.10
Trader *t*'s information level IL_t	5	5	5	5	5	6	7	8	9	10
Trader *t*'s gains per round G_t	-0.35	-0.42	-0.46	-0.49	-0.53	0.25	0.16	0.540	0.56	0.75

The results are even clearer if we allow for greater differences in d_t, as shown in Table 8.7. Indeed, with diminishing professional skills in financial analysis, the performance gap between users of *PIL* and the well informed traders becomes smaller.

Table 8.7 Increasing the difference between traders in their ability to assess information

Public information level PIL = 5; d=very different; all traders adopt an active strategy										
Trader *t*	1	2	3	4	5	6	7	8	9	10
Trader *t*'s dispersion d_t	2.10	1.60	1.10	0.60	0.10	0.10	0.10	0.10	0.10	0.10
Trader *t*'s information level IL_t	5	5	5	5	5	6	7	8	9	10
Trader *t*'s gains per round G_t	-0.24	-0.31	-0.39	-0.45	-0.49	0.05	0.14	0.46	0.53	0.70

Why should this be so? Let us try to give an intuitive answer. Public information such as the annual report published by a firm is only a subset of all the information which is needed to evaluate the firm's equity: some of the necessary information is given in the accounts, but most is not. This information subset can be biased or unbiased with respect to the whole. If it is not biased, then what we know about the sample, we know about the whole population. If, however, the sample is biased, the same conclusion does not apply. Figures 8.4 to 8.6 should help to clarify why this is the case. First, let us compare three groups of traders:

a) traders who base their decisions upon public information (*PI*), and who have low skills in financial analysis: the variance of $E_a(V)$ is very large;

b) traders who base their decisions upon public information, and have reasonable skills in financial analysis: the variance of $E_b(V)$ is large;

c) traders who have superior information and excellent skills in assessing the information: the variance of $E_c(V)$ is small.

The distributions of the estimated security values $E(V)$ in each of the three groups are indicated in the respective graphs. V is the intrinsic value of the security and P a market clearing price.

Case 1 Non-biased public information

If the public information is not biased (Figure 8.4), each group of traders will estimate the security's price with the same expected value; let us assume this to be the intrinsic value V. Thus, the market clearing price P will be close to V: casual

Figure 8.4 Non-biased public information

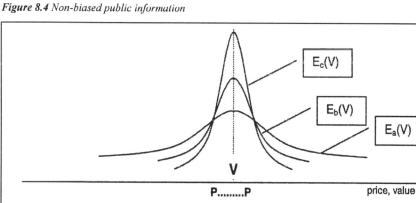

mispricings will be small and, for every trader regardless of the group that trader belongs to, it holds that the probability of being on the right side of the market (buy if $P<V$; sell if $P>V$) is equal to the probability of being on the wrong side of the market (buy if $P>V$; sell if $P<V$). Whether or not you study the financial reports, and whether or not you are a good and experienced financial analyst, the expected returns are always the same.

Case 2 Upward-biased public information

If the public information is upward-biased (Figure 8.5), the estimates of traders who rely upon such information will tend to be relatively high with respect to the intrinsic value: they will overestimate the security's value. The market clearing price will be between *V* and *PI*, say at *P*. As can easily be seen:

- the estimates of most of the traders with superior information (type c) are lower than *P*, which induces them to go short; only a few will estimate a value higher than *P* and end up on the wrong side of the market by going long;
- the estimates of most of the *PIL*-traders (types a and b) are higher than *P*, which induce them to buy on the wrong side of the market: they believe the overpriced security to be underpriced;
- only a few *PIL*-traders estimate a value lower than P and end up by going short on the right side of the market; among these, there are many more traders with low skills in financial analysis (type a) than traders with higher skills (type b).

Figure 8.5 *Upward-biased public information*

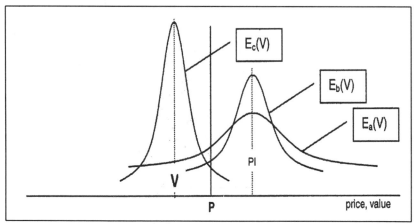

Case 3 Downward-biased public information

If the public information is downward-biased (Figure 8.6), the estimates of traders who rely upon such information will tend to be relatively low with respect to the intrinsic value: they will underestimate the security's value. Again, the market clearing price will be between *V* and *PI*, say at *P*. The results are similar to before:

- the estimates of most of the traders with superior information (type c) are higher than *P*, which induces them to go long; only few estimate a value lower than *P* and end up on the wrong side of the market by going short;
- the estimates of most of the *PIL*-traders are lower than *P*, which induces them to go to the wrong side of the market by selling the security: they believe the underpriced security to be overpriced;
- only a few *PIL*-traders estimate a value higher than *P* and end up on the right side of the market by going long; among these, there are more traders with low skills in financial analysis (type a) than traders with higher skills.

If it is better to be a lousy analyst than a good one, wouldn't the best thing be to ignore the information altogether and relegate decision making to a random machine? If we look back at Table 8.2, where public information is at a very low level, we see that trader T_6 makes an average return close to zero (0.02, to be precise). This is because the level of information received enables that trader to be

Figure 8.6 Downward-biased public information

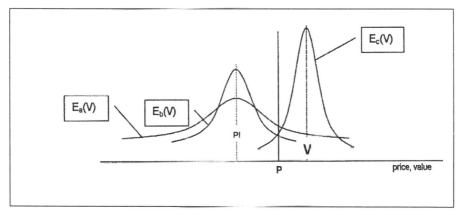

on the right side of the market as often as on the wrong side. However, a trader who decides by flipping a coin whether to go long or short is equally as often on the right side of the market as on the wrong side; so that trader should also make an average return of zero which is much more than the return traders with a considerable amount of information can expect to make.

For practitioners, this kind of passive investment seems to be rational only in the case of efficient markets: here, any kind of information processing is equivalent and passive investment turns out to be advantageous because of its zero cost. But, isn't passive investment much more valuable in markets that are somewhat less than efficient? For at least one half of the investors, it provides both lower cost *and* higher returns.!

The same holds if we have a higher level of public information, say $PIL = 5$. A trader who decides randomly avoids the negative consequences of making the same mistakes as others and adopts the virtual position of the average trader, and thus is more successful than the PIL-trader.

As can be seen in Table 8.8, it is rational for T_1 to switch to a passive strategy: instead of losing 0.56 (see Table 8.4), T_1 now loses only 0.09. The return is not zero because of the very thin market that we have simulated. Naturally, the traders are not price-takers, but they have considerable impact upon the market prices: if a passive trader buys or sells, the price changes and causes a slight mispricing with reference to the price obtained without the passive trader's involvement. Nevertheless, it holds that knowing nothing seems to be much better than knowing what others know.

Summarizing, we see that public information is either of no value to its users (in an efficient market and/or with unbiased public information), or it is of negative

Table 8.8 *The effect of a passive trading strategy*

Public information level $PIL = 5$; $d=0,01$; one trader adopts a passive strategy										
Trader t		1	2	3	4	5	6	7	8	9	10
Trader t's dispersion d_t:		0.01	0.01	0.01	0.01	0.01	0.01	0.01	0.01	0.01	0.01
Trader t's information level IL_t	Passive	5	5	5	5	6	7	8	9	10
Trader t's gains per round G_t:		-0.09	-0.49	-0.49	-0.49	-0.49	0.07	0.17	0.52	0.54	0.74

value (in an inefficient market and with biased public information). A scenario under which public information creates a positive value for those who rely upon it seems to be unattainable.

ON THE SOCIAL VALUE OF PUBLIC INFORMATION

Until now, we have only examined whether and to what extent public information may be useful to its individual users. Often, and usually with respect to the efficient markets debate, it is argued that this is not the appropriate question: even if we admit that the *individual* value of information may be questionable, what really counts is the *social* value of public information; only if we have a certain standard of financial reporting, can we expect the markets to be a fair game which is attractive not only to smart money but to the mass of small investors as well. As Beaver states, "*the rationale for disclosure regulation rests on efficiency or equity considerations*" (Beaver, 1989, p.179).

Can we really expect that, with a high level of public information, the allocational efficiency of the market will be improved? Does an improvement in the disclosure laws really resolve the problem that "*asymmetry of access to information is inherently unfair and violates the meaning of 'fair' disclosure under the Securities Acts*" (Beaver, 1989, p.184)? It has been shown that, with more public information, inequality among the traders can actually be enlarged instead of diminished: it may quite easily be the case that the gain in information is offset by the growing danger of making the same wrong decisions as others do.

Neither is there much hope that the allocational efficiency of the market will be enhanced by procuring more public information. In our model, full market efficiency (intrinsic value efficiency) is given if in any run it holds that $P = V$. Calculating the variance of the market's mispricings over all m runs, $\sigma_M^2 = {}_s\Sigma^m (P_s - V_s)^2/m$, we thus obtain a perfect indicator for market efficiency (in the strongest case, of intrinsic value efficiency): if $\sigma_M^2 = 0$, the market is highly efficient, and the larger σ_M^2 becomes, the more inefficient the pricing system will be. Table 8.9 shows how market efficiency is associated with different levels of public information:

As can be seen, market efficiency is at its maximum if all traders are endowed with the same high level of information. Under PIL_{10}, the market is efficient in the usual sense: market prices fully reflect all available information (10 from 11 coins) and nobody is permitted to improve their situation by deciding upon which information is publicly available; but as there is still information not yet reflected in the prices (*i.e.*, the eleventh coin), the market has not yet reached intrinsic value efficiency and our measure shows 0.5.

However, market efficiency is not at its lowest level at PIL_1, where we have very little public information, but at PIL_5, a situation with a considerably high level of public information. This again can be traced back to the errors that are made

Table 8.9 Public information and market efficiency

Public information level (PIL)	1	2	3	4	5	6	7	8	9	10
Market efficiency	1.01	1.02	1.04	1.07	1.13	1.12	1.00	0.86	0.71	0.50

jointly. Under PIL_1, there are some less informed traders whose decisions are made with nearly no information: in estimating V they make substantial mistakes with respect to the true intrinsic value, but fortunately those mistakes are independent from each other and diversify away. The more their information level rises with increasing PIL, the more they will tend to make the same errors that are made by other investors using PIL: the mistakes become correlated. The consequence is not only that their expected returns will fall but also that occasional mispricings will get much larger. For instance, compare the results in Table 8.3 (Panels C and D) with those in Table 8.5 (Panels A and B): under PIL_5, the overvaluation and undervaluation were much larger than under PIL_1.

Naturally, just as when interpreting the results for the individual investor, we cannot say for sure whether in real markets the current disclosure standards have achieved a situation comparable to that below or above PIL_5. But, as previously, it is fairly convincing that the former is the case.

CONCLUSIONS

Perhaps markets are efficient in the sense of the Efficient Markets Hypothesis. If this is the case, then the reflections in this chapter are as useless as is the 'usefulness-approach' itself. However, we have endeavoured to show that, if the efficiency assumption does not hold, we cannot go back to a pre-EMH world. It is not the case that, by giving up EMH, financial analysis is able to return to the halcyon days where information is always valuable and worthy of being produced, and especially worthy of being acquired. Probably, it is much easier for accountants, financial analysts and investment advisers to live with the Efficient Markets Hypothesis than to live with its counter-model, the Inefficient Markets Hypothesis.

In summary, what we have done here is to simulate a small artificial market with many restrictions of the sort that are usually made by economists modelling in their ivory towers. Does this have anything to do with real markets? We hope so, but we do not know with certainty. We suppose that we have captured the main features of markets: the competitiveness, the asymmetry of information and beliefs, and the asymmetries of skills and personal capabilities. What we have not considered, however, are other important factors such as information cost, risk aversion, lying and cheating, budgetary constraints, and so on. Simulation is a powerful instrument in dealing with highly complex problems, but its weakness is that it only provides insights into what *can be* the case and does not deliver proof of what *has to be* the case. Nevertheless, what gives us confidence in our findings is that we do not know of any other model of a market where information always has a positive value, and where people with higher skills perform more successfully than those with lower skills.

A last word on regulation: if people who agree on the usefulness of accounting data nonetheless deny the necessity of making disclosure mandatory, what should those people do who believe that this kind of information has no positive but rather a negative value to its users?

NOTES

[1] In this context, Hirshleifer (1971) has shown that, if prices react simultaneously to new information, information is of no value to any trader and is thus of no social value either.

[2] Simulation is generally adopted if the problems being studied are too complex to be resolved in a closed-form model, or if the researcher's intellectual abilities are too poor to do this.

[3] We cannot determine precisely whether real markets are before or after the peak, but we strongly assume they are before. If you consider that financial statements are historical data based on the historical cost principle, requiring subjective judgements, and being subject to the political will of the

firm's managers (*viz.* creative accounting), we are convinced that in financial report analysis the vices dominate the virtues

REFERENCES

Beaver, W. H. (1989). *Financial Reporting: An Accounting Revolution.* 2nd ed.. New York: Prentice-Hall.

Diamond, D. W., and Verrecchia, R. E. (1981). Information aggregation in a noisy rational-expectations economy, *Journal of Financial Economics*, Vol.9, No.3, pp.221-35.

Easterbrook, F. H., and Fischel, D. R. (1991). *The Economic Structure of Corporate Law*, Cambridge, Massachusetts: Harvard University Press.

Fama, E. F. (1970). Efficient capital markets: a review of theory and empirical work, *Journal of Finance*, Vol.25, May, pp.383-417.

Grossman, S. J., and Stiglitz, J. E. (1980). On the impossibility of informationally efficient prices, *American Economic Review*, Vol.70, June, pp.393-408.

Grossman, S. J. (1976). On the efficiency of competitive stock markets where traders have diverse information, *Journal of Finance*, Vol.31, May, pp.573-85.

Hellwig, M. (1982). Rational-expectations equilibrium with conditioning on past prices: a mean variance example, *Journal of Economic Theory*, Vol.26, No.2, pp.279-312.

Hirshleifer, J. (1971). The private and social value of information and the reward to inventive activity, *American Economic Review*, Vol.61, September, pp.561-74.

Jackson, M. O. (1991). Equilibrium, price formation, and the value of private information, *Review of Financial Studies*, Vol.4, No.1, pp.1-16.

Kyle, A. S. (1989). Informed speculation with imperfect competition, *Review of Economic Studies*, Vol.56, No.3, pp.317-56.

Yu, G. (1993). Information revelation and aggregation in financial markets, in *Financial Markets, Institutions & Instruments*, New York: NYU Salomon Center / Blackwell, pp.29-54.

9

CORPORATE GOVERNANCE AND CREATIVE ACCOUNTING: A COMPARISON BETWEEN SPAIN AND THE UK

John Blake and Oriol Amat Salas

INTRODUCTION

A particularly sensitive area of corporate governance is the extent and legitimacy of manipulation of accounting rules. This process, which has come to be known as 'creative accounting', involves accountants using their knowledge of accounting rules to manipulate and distort figures reported in the accounts of a business. This process has been seen as arising in the context of the flexibility that is permitted in the USA and the UK in order that financial statements may be 'fairly presented' or may give a 'true and fair view'. By contrast, accounts that are presented in the continental European tradition of legalistic and rigid rules have been seen as less subject to such manipulation. In this article, we compare the experiences of Spain, a country whose accounting approach falls firmly within the continental European tradition, with the United Kingdom. In exploring this issue, we:

(a) consider the definition and nature of 'creative accounting', placing this within the contrasting Anglo-American and continental European accounting traditions;

(b) identify the types of creative accounting technique that can be used, how accounting regulators can control abuse, and compare how controls can be applied within each of the accounting traditions;

(c) review the motivations for companies to engage in creative accounting;

(d) report some evidence on the extent of, and attitudes towards, creative accounting in Spain and the United Kingdom.

CREATIVE ACCOUNTING - DEFINITION AND NATURE

'Creative accounting' is a term used to describe a process whereby accountants use their knowledge of accounting rules to manipulate the figures reported in the accounts of a business. Four authors in the UK, each writing with a different perspective, have identified this issue:

- Griffiths (1986, p.1), writing from the perspective of a business journalist, observes that *"Every company in the country is fiddling its profits. Every set of published accounts is based on books which have been gently cooked or completely roasted. The figures which are fed twice a year to the investing public have all been changed in order to protect the guilty. It is the biggest con trick since the Trojan horse .... In fact this deception is all in perfectly good taste. It is totally legitimate. It is creative accounting."*

- Jameson (1988, pp.7-8), writing from the perspective of the accountant, argues that: *"The accounting process consists of dealing with many matters of judgement and of resolving conflicts between competing approaches to the presentation of the results of financial events and transactions ...... this flexibility provides opportunities for manipulation, deceit and misrepresentation. These activities - practised by the less scrupulous elements of the accounting profession - have come to be known as 'creative accounting'."*

- Smith (1992, p.4) reports on his experience as an investment analyst as follows: *"We felt that much of the apparent growth in profits which had occurred in the 1980's was the result of accounting sleight of hand rather than genuine economic growth, and we set out to expose the main techniques involved, and to give live examples of companies using those techniques."*

- Naser (1993, p.2), presenting an academic view, offers the following definition: *"Creative accounting is the transformation of financial*

> *accounting figures from what they actually are to what preparers desire by taking advantage of the existing rules and/or ignoring some or all of them.*"

It is interesting to observe that Naser perceives the accounting system in Anglo-American* countries as particularly prone to such manipulation because of the freedom of choice it permits, observing that *"The freedom of choice provided by the Anglo-Saxon accounting system could be abused ...."* (*op cit*, p.1).

Various approaches to classifying national accounting systems place the UK and Spain in contrasting groups. Thus, in 1911, Henry Rand Hatfield, in a first attempt to provide such a classification, placed Spain in a group of countries led by France, in contrast to an English speaking tradition (Hatfield, reprinted 1966). A series of systematic cluster studies based on the international surveys of national accounting practice by Price Waterhouse, the leading international accounting firm, in 1973, 1975 and 1979 each placed the UK and Spain in different clusters (Da Costa *et al*, 1978; Nair and Frank, 1980; Nair, 1982) for a total of 7 different analyses. Nobes (1992) offers a characterisation of an 'Anglo-Saxon' grouping, including the UK, focusing on fair presentation, extensive disclosure, and a 'substance over form' approach, and contrasts this with a 'continental' grouping, including Spain, with a legal orientation, a respect for secrecy, and a 'form over substance' approach.

Waller (1990), addressing the problem of 'creative accounting' in the UK, advocates a move to the more legal and prescriptive continental tradition as a solution. However, in recent years, a number of articles have appeared identifying creative accounting as an issue in Spain (Giner 1992; Rojo, 1993; Amat *et al*, 1997). We therefore consider next the extent to which creative accounting is practical, and can be restricted, within each of the Anglo-American and the continental European accounting traditions.

THE PROCESS OF CREATIVE ACCOUNTING

Creative accounting techniques can be considered under four broad headings.

1) Sometimes the accounting rules allow a company to choose between different accounting methods. For example, in many countries (including both Spain and the UK), a company is allowed to choose between a policy of writing off development expenditure as it occurs and amortising it over the life of the related project. A company can therefore choose the accounting policy that gives the desired impression.

2) Certain entries in the accounts involve an unavoidable degree of estimation, judgment, and prediction. In some cases, such as the estimation of an asset's useful life made in order to calculate depreciation, these estimates are normally made inside the business and the creative accountant has the

---

* Editors' Footnote. The authors of this chapter make use of the term 'Anglo-American' with regard to accounting in the English-speaking countries, whilst many others refer to 'Anglo-Saxon' accounting - a common generalisation in the literature. The present usage seems to be more appropriate: the Anglo-Saxons pre-dated bookkeeping, let alone the use of creative accounting in financial reports.

opportunity to err on the side of caution or optimism in making the estimate. In other cases, an outside expert is normally employed to make estimates: for example, an actuary would normally be employed to assess the prospective pension liability. In this case, the creative accountant can manipulate the valuation both by the way in which the valuer is briefed and by choosing a valuer known to take a pessimistic or an optimistic view, as the accountant prefers.

3) Artificial transactions can be entered into both to manipulate balance sheet amounts and to move profits between accounting periods. This is achieved by entering into two or more related transactions with an obliging third party, normally a bank. For example, supposing an arrangement is made to sell an asset to a bank then to lease that asset back for the rest of its useful life. The sale price under such a 'sale and leaseback' arrangement can be pitched above or below the current value of the asset, because the difference can be compensated for by increased or reduced rentals.

4) Genuine transactions can also be timed so as to give the desired impression in the accounts. As an example, suppose a business has an investment of one million pesetas at historic cost that can easily be sold for its current value of three million pesetas. The managers of the business are free to choose in which year they sell the investment and so increase the profit in the accounts.

Accounting regulators who wish to curb creative accounting have to tackle each of these approaches in a different way:

1) The scope for choice between accounting methods can be reduced by limiting the number of permitted accounting methods or by specifying circumstances in which each method should be used. Requiring consistency of use of methods also helps here, since a company choosing a method which produces the desired impression in one year will then be forced to use the same method in future circumstances where the result may be less favourable.

2) The abuse of judgment can be curbed in two ways. One is to draft rules that minimise the use of judgment. Thus, in the UK, company accountants tended to include among 'extraordinary items' in the profit and loss account those items that they wished to exclude from operating profit. The UK Accounting Standards Board (ASB) responded by effectively abolishing the category of 'extraordinary items'. Secondly, auditors also have a part to play in identifying dishonest estimates.

3) Artificial transactions can be tackled by invoking the concept of 'substance over form', whereby the economic substance rather than the legal form of transactions determines their accountingtreatment. Thus, linked transactions would be accounted for as one whole.

4) The timing of genuine transactions is clearly a matter for the discretion of management. However, the opportunities to exercise discretion can be limited by requiring regular revaluations of items in the accounts so that gains or

losses on value changes are identified in the accounts each year as they occur, rather than only appearing in total in the year that a disposal occurs. It is interesting to observe that, in their recent draft conceptual framework, the ASB in the UK have stated the desire to move towards an increased use of revaluation in accounts rather than the historic cost principle.

We have seen above that creative accounting is considered to be a particular feature of the Anglo-American approach to accounting, with its scope for flexibility and judgment, rather than the continental European model, with its tradition of detailed prescription. However, as we show in Table 9 1, each of the two approaches offers greater support for the control of creative accounting in some respects and conversely, therefore, greater opportunity to engage in creative accounting in others. The more prescriptive and inflexible approach of the continental European model makes it easier to reduce the scope for abuse of choice of accounting policy and manipulation of accounting estimates. The orientation of the Anglo-American model is less towards the law and more conducive to the use of substance over form and revaluation.

Table 9.1 Opportunities for creative accounting

OPPORTUNITY FOR CREATIVE ACCOUNTING	SOLUTION AVAILABLE TO ACCOUNTING REGULATOR	ACCOUNTING TRADITION WHERE SOLUTION IS MOST EASILY APPLIED
Choice of accounting method	Reduce permitted choice	Continental European
Bias estimates and prediction	Reduce scope for estimation	Continental European
Enter into artificial transactions	Substance over form	Anglo-American
Timing of genuine transactions	Prescribe revaluation	Anglo-American

THE MOTIVATION FOR CREATIVE ACCOUNTING

Discussion surrounding creative accounting in the UK has focused mainly on the impact on the decisions of investors in the stock market. A number of reasons why the directors of listed companies may seek to manipulate the accounts are:

- Companies attempt to smoothe their income, as they generally prefer to report a steady trend of growth in profit rather than to show volatile profits with a series of dramatic rises and falls. Income smoothing is achieved by making unnecessarily high provisions for liabilities and against asset values in good years so that these provisions can be reduced, thereby improving reported profits, in bad years. Advocates of this approach argue that income smoothing is a measure against the 'short termism' of judging an investment on the basis of the yields achieved in the immediate following years. It also avoids raising expectations so high in good years that the company is unable to deliver what is required subsequently. Against this, it is argued that, if the trading conditions of a business are in fact volatile, then investors have a right to know this; and that ncome smoothing may conceal long term changes in the profit trend. This type of creative accounting is not special to the UK. In countries with highly conservative accounting systems, the 'income smoothing' effect can be particularly pronounced because of the high level of provisions that accumulate: Blake *et al* (1995) discuss a German example. Another bias that sometimes arises is called 'big bath' accounting, where a company making a substantial loss seeks to maximise the reported loss in that year so that performance in future years will appear to be better.

- Creative accounting may help to maintain or boost the share price both by reducing the apparent levels of borrowing, so making the company appear to be subject to less risk, and by creating the appearance of a healthy trend in profits. In particular, this helps the company to raise capital from new share issues, to offer its own shares in takeover bids, and to resist takeover by other companies.

- If directors engage in 'insider dealing' in their company's shares, they can use creative accounting to delay the release of information to the market, thereby enhancing their own opportunity to benefit from inside knowledge.

Ethically, the first of the three reasons identified above is open to honest debate. The other two, particularly the last, are ethically unacceptable. In contrast, another set of reasons for creative accounting applies to all companies, and arises because they are subject to various forms of contractual rights, obligations, and other constraints based on the amounts reported in the accounts. Some examples of such contractual issues are as follows:

- It is common for loan agreements to include a restriction on the total amount that a company is entitled to borrow computed as a multiple of the total share capital and reserves. Where a company has borrowings that are near this limit, there is an incentive to choose accounting methods that increase reported profit, and consequently the reserves, and also to arrange financing in a way that will not be reflected as a liability on the balance sheet.

- Some companies, such as public utilities like electricity and telephone companies, are subject to the authority of a government regulator who prescribes the maximum amounts that the companies may charge. If such companies report high profits, then the regulator is likely to respond by curbing prices. These companies, therefore, have an interest in choosing accounting methods that tend to reduce their reported profits.

- A directors' bonus scheme may be linked to profits or to the company share price; where the link is to the share price, then clearly the directors will be motivated to present accounts that will impress the stock market. Where a bonus is based on reported profit, the scheme often stipulates that the bonus is a percentage of profit above a minimum level, and is paid up to a maximum level. Thus, if the profit figure is between the two levels then directors will choose accounting methods that lift profit towards the maximum. If the profit is below the minimum level, directors will choose accounting methods that maximise provisions made so that in future years these provisions can be written back to boost profits as and when it is advantageous to do so. Finally, if the profit is above the maximum level, directors will seek to bring the figure down to that level, again providing opportunities to boost profits in later years.

EVIDENCE OF CURRENT PRACTICE

There are some practical difficulties in ascertaining and defining the extent of creative accounting in a country:

- There is a high degree of subjectivity involved in deciding whether the accounting policy choices made by a company are the outcome of an honest effort to achieve a true and fair view (the qualitative standard laid down for company reporting in both Spain and the UK), or of deliberate manipulation designed to mislead the reader of the accounts.
- The practice of creative accounting involves, by its nature, elements of concealment and deceit. Thus, it will not necessarily be apparent in the published accounts.
- The practice of creative accounting is inherently disreputable. Thus company financial managers are unlikely to admit their involvement, explain their motives, or disclose their methods. Indeed, in an early survey of company financial managers' attitudes to one tool in creative accounting (the use of leasing for off balance sheet finance), Fawthrop & Terry (1975) reported that such practices were common but that, generally, respondents denied having this motive themselves.

In view of these difficulties, particularly in approaching companies directly, we decided instead to investigate the views of auditors. Auditors have the opportunity to observe and evaluate in depth the behaviour of a range of clients. They have the technical skills to understand the creative accounting methods used. They also have an incentive to identify, and to assist in designing, measures to control creative accounting. Interestingly, this interest was confirmed by the number of respondents who asked for a copy of our findings.

In fact, research into auditor experience in this respect has been undertaken in the UK (see Naser & Pendlebury, 1992; Naser, 1993). Accordingly, we undertook a similar survey of the Spanish experience.

A questionnaire was sent to 100 auditors in practice in Spain. Of these, 29 replied, a response rate of 29%. This is well above the normal response rate for

Spain (Garcia *et al*, 1993, p.285). Naser (1993) reports on two surveys of auditors in the UK, one sample of 22 and the other of 20. Where applicable, a comparison is made between our sample in Spain and the combined total of Naser's two samples in the UK.

The questionnaire covered four broad areas:

1) Respondents' attitudes to the broad issue of creative accounting.
2) Respondents' beliefs as to the extent of creative accounting in Spain.
3) Respondents' views on the motivation for creative accounting in Spain.
4) Respondents' views on the main areas of the accounts subject to creative accounting.

Three of the questions concerned respondents' own attitudes to creative accounting. Table 9.2 reports on attitudes towards the legitimacy of creative

Table 9.2 '*Do you consider that the use of creative accounting is a legitimate business tool?*'

	SPANISH SURVEY		UK SURVEY	
	Number	%	Number	%
Strongly agree	3	10.3	2	4.7
Agree	6	20.7	13	31.0
No opinion	2	6.9	2	4.7
Disagree	13	44.8	23	54.9
Strongly disagree	5	17.3	2	4.7
	29	100	42	100

accounting. In the UK, some 36% of respondents apparently saw this as a legitimate business tool. In Spain, auditors take a slightly more strict view with only 31% taking this position.

Table 9.3 shows respondents' views on whether creative accounting is a serious

Table 9.3 '*Do you consider the use of creative accounting to be a serious problem?*'

	SPANISH SURVEY		UK SURVEY	
	Number	%	Number	%
Strongly agree	2	17.2	1	2.4
Agree	14	48.3	26	61.9
No opinion	2	6.9	5	11.9
Disagree	7	24.1	10	23.8
Strongly disagree	1	3.5		
	29	100	42	100

problem. Some 66% of Spanish respondents take this view, compared to some 64% in the UK who indicate a similar level of concern.

Table 9.4 reports on responses to the suggestion that the problem of creative accounting can never be solved. Over 85% of the UK auditors accepted this proposition, in contrast to Spanish auditors who seem almost evenly divided in their view.

Table 9.4 *'Do you consider that the use of creative accounting is a problem that can never be solved?'*

	SPANISH SURVEY		UK SURVEY*	
	Number	%	Number	%
Strongly agree	3	10.3	15	35.7
Agree	8	27.6	25	59.5
No opinion	6	20.7	1	2.4
Disagree	10	34.5	1	2.4
Strongly disagree	2	6.9		
	29	100	42	100

Note The UK questionnaire used the words 'never be *completely* solved'.

The overall picture, therefore, is that Spanish auditors are similar to those in the UK in their tolerance of creative accounting, equally prone to see it as a problem, but more optimistic that the problem can be solved than their UK counterparts.

Table 9.5 *The extent of creative acounting in Spain*

	STRONGLY AGREE	AGREE	NO VIEW	DISAGREE	STRONGLY DISAGREE
Creative accounting is becoming more popular in Spain	1 3%	10 34%	6 21%	11 38%	1 4%
Creative accounting is more common in listed companies	3 10%	6 21%	13 45%	6 21%	1 3%
Creative accounting is more common in large than in small companies	1 3%	11 38%	4 14%	11 38%	2 7%
Creative accounting is more common in small than in large companies	3 10%	6 21%	4 14%	14 48%	2 7%

Table 9.5 shows respondents' opinions as to the current extent of creative accounting in Spain. While, as we saw above, an overwhelming majority take the view that the problem is an important one, our respondents seemed more or less evenly divided as to whether creative accounting is actually on the increase. Similarly, no clear trend emerges as to the size or listing status of companies engaging in creative accounting.

Table 9.6 shows the importance of various factors in the decision to use creative accounting.

Table 9.6 *'How important do you think each of the following is as a factor in the decision to use creative accounting?'*

	VERY IMPORTANT (1)		IMPORTANT (2)		NO OPINION (3)		NOT IMPORTANT (1)		COMPARABLE UK RESPONSES (1 & 2)	
	No.	%	No.	%	No.	%	No.	%	No.	%
To improve gearing ratios	9	31	17	59	1	3	2	7	40	95
To reduce taxation	18	62	8	28	0		3	10	22	52
To control dividends	4	14	15	52	6	21	4	13	5	12
To impress investors with high profits	6	21	15	52	3	10	5	17		
To impress investors with a consistent increase in profit	4	14	22	76	3	10	0			
To avoid high wage claims by showing a reduced profit	1	3	13	45	3	10	12	42		
To hide high profits from competitors	2	7	7	24	3		17	59		

It is interesting to note that taxation is much more important as a factor in Spain than in the UK, perhaps because the separation between tax and accounting rules is so strong in the UK. In 1990, a formal break between tax rules and accounting rules was made in Spain (Labatüt, 1993). Nevertheless, for convenience, Spanish accountants still tend to favour following tax rules in the published accounts. Thus, Gonzalo and Gallizo (1992) report that, although depreciation for tax purposes no longer has to be provided on the same basis in the accounts, many Spanish companies continue this practice.

Table 9.7 shows the experience of respondents in observing creative accounting applied to specific items.

Table 9.7. *Respondents' experiences of number of instances of creative accounting*

	0	1	2	3 OR MORE	TOTAL (TREATING 3 OR MORE AS 3)
Pension provision	15	2	0	5	17
Research and development	6	7	2	8	35
Goodwill	9	7	0	7	28
Leasing	8	6	2	6	28
Capitalisation of interest costs	4	3	7	10	47
Stock valuation	1	1	3	19	64
Bad debt provision	2	2	1	18	58
Consolidation provision	11	4	1	5	21
Foreign currency translation	14	2	2	5	21

CONCLUSIONS

Although creative accounting has been identified as a particular problem of the Anglo-American style of accounting, we have seen that both the opportunity and the motivation for creative accounting can arise equally in the continental European context. Comparing the UK and Spain, as examples of each tradition, we have found a similar level of concern over the issue of creative accounting in each country, albeit with Spanish auditors being somewhat more optimistic about the prospects of resolving the problem. The strong traditional link between tax and accounting rules in Spain actually appears to increase the motivation for creative accounting as compared to the UK. We find that auditors consider that Spanish companies creatively interpret the rules on a range of topics in order to manipulate their accounts. Both analysts and accounting regulators should be aware of this opportunity for creative accounting in the continental accounting framework.

REFERENCES

Amat, O., Blake, J., & Farran, E. (1997). La contabilidad creativa, *Harvard-Deusto Finanzas & Contabilidad*, March-April, pp.14-8.

Blake, J., Amat, O., Martinez, D., and Garcia Palau, E. (1995). The continuing problem of international accounting diversity, *Company Accountant*, April, pp.23-5.

Da Costa, R.C., Bourgeois, J.C., and Lawson, W. (1978). A classification of international financial accounting practices, *International Journal of Accounting*, Spring, pp.73-85.

Fawthrop, R., and Terry, B. (1975). Debt management and the use of leasing finance in UK corporate financing strategies, *Journal of Business Finance and Accounting*, Vol.2, No.3, pp.295-314.

Garcia, M.A., Humphrey, C., Moizer, P., and Turley, S. (1993). Auditing expectations and performance in Spain and Britain: a comparative analysis, *International Journal of Accounting*, Vol.28, pp.281-307.

Giner, B. (1992). La contabilidad creativa, *Partida Doble*, March, p.4.

Gonzalo, J.A., and Gallizo, J.L. (1992). *European Financial Reporting: Spain*. London: Routledge.

Griffiths, I. (1986) *Creative Accounting*, London: Sidgwick & Jackson.

Hatfield, H.R. (1966). Some variations in accounting practices in England, France, Germany and the United States, *Journal of Accounting Research*, Autumn, pp.160-82.

Jameson, M. (1988). *A practical guide to creative accounting*. London: Kogan Page.

Labatüt, G. (1993). Problemática actual de las relaciones contabilidad - fiscalidad al cierre del ejercicio 1992: diferencias permanentes y temporales per aplicación del método del efecto impositivo, *Tecnica Contable*, March, pp.199-252.

Nair, R.D., and Frank, W.G. (1980). The impact of disclosure and measurement practices on international accounting classifications, *Accounting Review*, July, pp.426-50.

Nair, R.D. (1982). Empirical guidelines for comparing International accounting data, *Journal of International Business Studies*, Winter, pp.85-98.

Naser, K., & Pendlebury, M. (1992a). A note on the use of creative accounting, *British Accounting Review*, July, pp.111-8.

Naser, K., and Pendlebury, M. (1992b). Creative touch, *Certified Accountant*, November, pp.36-8.

Naser, K. (1993). *Creative Financial Accounting: Its Nature and Use*, London: Prentice Hall.

Nobes, C.; (1992). The prospects for harmonisation, *Certified Accountant*, December, pp.27-9.

Rojo, L.A. (1993). Tendencias de contabilidad y contabilidad creativa, *Boletin AECA*, No 36, pp.4-7.

Smith, T. (1992). *Accounting for Growth*, London: Century Business.

Waller,D. (1990). Time to get rid of true and fair view?, *Accountants Magazine*, December, p.53.

10

DEREGULATION OF SMALL COMPANY FINANCIAL REPORTING IN THE UK

Jill Collis, David Dugdale and Robin Jarvis

INTRODUCTION

Since the 1970s, the regulation of financial reporting and accounting by limited companies in the UK has increased considerably. Not only have successive Companies Acts required greater disclosure of information, but accounting standards have proliferated since the establishment of a standard-setting body in 1970.

It has been argued that these developments have placed a disproportionately heavy burden on small companies and calls have been made for some relaxation of the regulations for such businesses. These demands have been based partly on the contention that the financial information contained in the statutory accounts of smaller entities is of limited value to users. Generally, it is claimed that the main providers of finance to small companies are banks, which demand more detailed information than that contained in the statutory accounts. If there are shareholders, they are usually family members with an intimate knowledge of the business and therefore the annual report offers them no fresh information. Finally, small companies are typically owner-managed and use internal sources of financial information for management purposes; therefore, the annual report and accounts does not satisfy their needs. Often, the latter argument rests on the assumption that owner-managers are insufficiently financially sophisticated to understand accounts produced within the full regulatory framework.

These concerns have not gone unheard and there has been some movement towards reducing the regulatory burden placed on smaller entities. Since the 1980s, there has been a general move towards deregulation of small entities in the UK, both in respect of legislation and accounting standards.

Insofar as the legislation is concerned, Schedule 8 of the Companies Act 1985 was amended in 1992, permitting small and medium-sized companies to file either full or abbreviated accounts. In August 1994, Section 249A of the Companies Act 1985 was amended and this reduced the statutory audit requirement for small companies with a turnover of up to £350,000. In May 1995, the Department of Trade and Industry (DTI) published a consultative document (DTI, 1995) that proposed simplifying accounting disclosure requirements, raising the financial ceilings for defining small and medium-sized companies and reducing the level of manadatory disclosure in small company accounts.

In 1983 the issue of accounting standards and small entities was considered by the Accounting Standards Committee (ASC), but it was not until 1988 that a statement on the application of accounting standards to small companies was published (ASC, 1988). In November 1994, a working party of the Consultative Committee of Accountancy Bodies (CCAB), set up at the request of the ASB, issued a consultative document (CCAB, 1994) which proposed that small entities should be exempt from most non-statutory guidance. In December 1995, the CCAB published a paper (CCAB, 1995a) proposing the promulgation of a financial reporting standard. In December 1996, the ASB published an exposure draft (ASB, 1996) of the *Financial Reporting Standard for Smaller Entities* (FRSSE) which proposed that financial reporting by smaller entities should be simplified and reduced.

Finally, in November 1997, the FRSSE was issued as a standard (ASB, 1997) and allows all entities that qualify as small under the Companies Act 1985 to choose whether to adopt it or comply with the complete range of accounting standards and UITF abstracts. Those adopting it become exempt from applying all other accounting standards and UITF abstracts. The measurement bases in the FRSSE are the same as, or a simplification of, those in existing accounting standards.

Recent figures show that in 1996/7 that there were some 1,091,900 public and private companies incorporated and registered in Great Britain. Of these,

1,080,200 were private companies, compared with 11,700 public companies (DTI, 1997, Table A1). Thus, private companies accounted for 99% of the total companies on the register. Some 38% of those filing abbreviated annual accounts at Companies House were small companies and less than 1% were medium-sized companies. Therefore, it can been seen that these changes to the regulation of financial reporting by smaller companies in the UK affect a significant proportion of companies. However, the regulators admit that "*while there is a body of research into the needs of users of the accounts of large companies, particularly listed companies, much less is known about who uses the accounts of small companies and what information they are seeking*" (CCAB, 1994, p 5). If an assessment is to be made of whether the reduction in compliance costs affects the information value of the statutory accounts of smaller entities, an unambiguous statement needs to be made of their current use. That is the aim of this chapter.

The research was conducted with 89 small and medium-sized private limited companies. The three main objectives were:

to identify the non-statutory recipients of the company's annual report;

to discover whether owner-managers read the annual report and accounts of other businesses;

to investigate the usefulness of their own annual report in the context of various other sources of information for managing the company.

In conducting the analysis, a distinction is made between small and medium-sized companies to determine whether their behaviour is different.

In the next section, we discuss the main strands of the arguments for and against deregulation of financial reporting by smaller companies, together with a review of previous research. This is followed by a description of the methodology used for the present study, and a discussion of the research findings. In the final section, we draw conclusions and offer suggestions for further research.

THE DEBATE AND THE EVIDENCE

The question of whether small companies should be exempt from some aspects of generally accepted accounting practice (GAAP) has become known as the 'Big GAAP / Little GAAP' debate. At the heart of the debate lies the difficulty of determining "*the criteria that should be used to exempt companies as well as widespread concern that accounts that do not comply with accounting standards would not present a true and fair view of the company's activities*" (Hussey, 1995, p.213). The FRSSE adopts the criteria of size as given in the Companies Act 1985 (s247 and s249). However, the ceilings are arbitrary and if changes proposed by EC Directive 94/8/ED are adopted, the thresholds will be raised by 50%.[1]

Differential reporting concerns the idea that different types and sizes of entities should have different financial reporting rules: "*For many years there has been different reporting by different types of company: the requirements for listed public companies have been more onerous than for private companies and those for larger companies more onerous than for smaller companies*" (ASB, 1997, p 102). Drawing mainly from Harvey and Walton (1996), with reference to other relevant literature, the main arguments for and against differential reporting are summarised below.

Arguments for differential reporting

First, large companies have a much broader range of users than small, typically owner-managed, companies. This contention is supported by evidence from the Corporate Report (ASSC, 1975) and the studies by McMonnies (1988) and Solomons (1989). For example, it can be argued that three of the seven user groups of published reports identified in the Corporate report (the analyst-advisor group, the government, and the public) would not be users of small company reports, although the equity investor group, the loan creditor group, the employee group and the business contact group appear to be users of corporate reports irrespective of company size. Further support comes from Page (1984), who believes that the users, uses and intensity of use of financial statements is likely to vary between small and large companies. In smaller firms, *"employees have personal contact with the proprietors and the role of the analyst/advisor group is very restricted where there is no public market for the company's securities*" (Page, 1984, p.272). However, this is only partial evidence of user group differences and there is a gap in the literature regarding the precise range of users (and uses) of small company reports.

A second argument is that the financial statements of large companies are used for a wider range of decisions than those of small companies. This is related to the previous point, but until the full range of users of small company financial statements have been identified, it is impossible to attempt to compare the relative usefulness of the financial statements for decision making.

A third argument is that large companies have complex transactions and provide highly aggregated information that needs sophisticated analysis, whereas small companies have fewer and less complex transactions; moreover, the cost burden is proportionately higher for small companies. Although the latter statement is supported by the conclusions of Technical Release 690 (ASC, 1988), research by Keasey and Short (1990) produced no evidence of any association between the organisational, financial, size and accountant profiles of small firms and their perception that the preparation of accounts is burdensome.

Finally, there is the view that new differential reporting requirements could be developed that would better meet management needs and reduce compliance costs.

Arguments against differential reporting

First there is the universality argument which contends that accounting standards should be the same for all accounts intended to give a true and fair view. The statutory accounts cannot give a true and fair view of the activities of the business if there are different accounting rules for different sized companies. However, although universality may be a highly desirable goal, it is a state that does not exist at present. For example, there is a legal requirement for limited companies to comply with accounting standards yet, as already mentioned, there are some exemptions for small companies from the disclosure requirements of the Companies Act. There are also audit exemptions for small companies. In addition, it is hard to argue that there is universality when standard setters in the UK have yet to agree a conceptual framework for financial reporting.

Underlying the universality argument is the assumption that compliance with GAAP leads to a true and fair view. Since the advent of the ASB, the number of financial reporting standards have increased dramatically, thus effectively changing both the rules and the concept of what is 'true and fair'. Fears that differential reporting could impair the truth and fairness of the accounts were expressed by a number of those who submitted written comments on the CCAB's consultative document (CCAB, 1995b). However, the CCAB working party took legal advice which confirmed that there could be a different true and fair view for small and large companies.

Part of the universality argument is that, since accounting standards are intended to enhance comparability and reliability of financial statements, they should be applied universally. Empirical evidence from research into lending by banks in the UK and elsewhere tends to support this argument.[2] However, given the fact that in the UK small companies are able to choose to submit either full or abbreviated accounts and, since November 1997, adopt the FRSSE or comply with the full range of accounting standards and UITF abstracts, the extent to which accounts are comparable at present is a contentious issue.

The publicity doctrine asserts that producing and preparing published accounts is part of the price to be paid by companies for having limited liability status. This opinion has been put forward a number of times in the press and professional journals.[3] Langfield-Smith (1991) points out that, historically, limited companies tended to be formed when there was a separation of ownership and control, and it is a more recent phenomenon for small businesses to be incorporated. Therefore, many owner-managed companies today find themselves subject to rules that were not developed for them. He suggests that UK company law seems to have been more concerned with protecting the remote investor than the creditor. However, it is not clear whether differential reporting would reduce creditor protection, since small companies often file their accounts up to 12 months after the balance sheet date, and companies in difficulties may not file at all (Harvey and Walton, 1996).

It would appear that user needs can be cited by both sides in the debate. In the argument against differential reporting, it is reasoned that, if user needs of both small and large companies are similar, public interest demands the same GAAP for all companies. As already pointed out, although there is some overlap between users of small company and large company accounts, there is insufficient evidence to support the argument that user needs are similar across the full range of users.

Finally, standard setters have expressed concern that reduced disclosure by small companies will encourage larger companies to lobby for similar relaxations. There is also some anxiety in the accounting profession that differential reporting could lead to the creation of a two-tier profession and that small companies might be perceived as inferior if their accounts were prepared on a different basis.

A review by Jarvis (1996) confirms the view of the CCAB that little is known about either the users or the uses of the statutory accounts of small companies. In its consultative document, the CCAB working party expressed the opinion *that "in the case of small entities, the important users are the managers, employees, the members, the Revenue, lenders and trade creditors"* (CCAB, 1994, p.7). The lack of literature on small company users is surprising since approximately 90% of corporate reports are for small and medium sized companies (Jarvis, 1996).

The main research studies that have been conducted to date have concentrated on bank lenders, and the directors and auditors of smaller companies, and we examine these next.

A survey of banks by Berry, Citron and Jarvis (1987) found that the statutory accounts were used as a source of information on lending decisions, irrespective of whether the company was large or small. However, the emphasis placed on specific items of information differed according to the complexity of the business, the availability of up-to-date information and the more short-term view taken of smaller businesses. Berry, Faulkner, Hughes and Jarvis (1993) found that accounting information was important when making lending decisions relating to small businesses, but was used in different ways and given different weightings depending on various internal and external factors.

Further qualitative research by Berry, Crum and Waring (1993) attempted to assess the actual processes used by banks in evaluating corporate loan applications by enterprises that included a large proportion of small businesses. The findings showed that banks converted the information contained in the annual accounts to standard evaluation forms, but that errors were sometimes introduced through a lack of consistent definitions. The information was not used to predict trends and little or no reference was made to the risk/return trade-off in discussions with managers. Moreover, any surplus information to that required on the forms was discarded.

Berry and Waring (1995) have produced case study evidence that shows that little attention is given by the banks to data other than that shown in the profit and loss account and the balance sheet. The authors proposed caution in introducing financial reporting reforms until further research has been conducted into the reasons why other available supplementary data are not used.

In a survey of the directors of small companies, Page (1984) asked respondents to rate the importance of the uses of the annual report; Carsberg, Page, Sindall and Waring (1985) asked a similar question in interviews with small companies. Both studies found that the most important use to the participants was the provision of information to management. Surveys of auditors of small company accounts provide supportive evidence. The 1985 study by Carsberg *et al.* also included interviews with the auditors of the participating small companies and in 1996 Barker and Noonan conducted a questionnaire survey of accountancy practitioners in Ireland (North and South) with a view to providing some measure of comparison with the earlier study. Both studies found that in the view of the auditors, the three main uses of small companies' annual accounts, in order of importance, were: providing management information; supporting tax computations; and providing information to the bank and other providers of finance.

Table 10.1 ranks the results of these studies to provide a comparison of the top three important uses of the annual accounts from the point of view of the directors and the auditors.

This comparison shows considerable consensus in the views of both directors and auditors: the most important use of the annual accounts is to provide management information. However, the researchers asked only about the most

Table 10.1 Ranking of important uses of small company annual accounts

USE OF ACCOUNTS	DIRECTORS' VIEWS		AUDITORS' VIEWS	
	Page 1984	Carsberg et. al. 1985	Carsberg et. al. 1985	Barker and Noonan 1996
Providing management information	1	1	1	1
Providing information to the bank and other providers of finance	3	2	2	2
Supporting tax computations	2	3	3	3

important use (Page, 1984; Barker and Noonan, 1996) or the first and second most important uses (Carsberg *et al.* 1985). There are two problems with this approach: first, that there is an assumption that the uses are important and second that there is no measure of the degree of importance, merely a comparison within a small set of options. Moreover, in order to evaluate the relative importance of the usefulness of the statutory accounts to management, it is necessary to identify what other sources of management information are available. The present study addresses this deficiency.

METHODOLOGY

The sample for the present study was selected from the FAME database using the following criteria:

- private and independent companies;
- accounting records available on FAME for the six years 1989 to 1994;
- registered office or trading address in one of six postal regions in the South of England;
- turnover between £1 million and £11.2 million in 1994 accounts;
- incorporated between 1 January 1980 and 31 December 1986 (although the business may have been in existence before that time) - as the failure rate of small companies has always been very high, particularly within the first five years (Milne and Thomson, 1986), this ensured that the sample consisted of companies that had survived beyond that crucial period.

All the companies had participated in an earlier survey (Hussey and Hussey, 1994). This resulted in 198 companies being selected. A questionnaire was designed and piloted through telephone interviews with three companies. It was then posted, with an accompanying letter and a prepaid envelope, to the 198 companies in the first week of August 1996. A follow-up letter, enclosing a further copy of the questionnaire and prepaid envelope, was sent to non-respondents three weeks later. Despite the postal strikes which were taking place at regular intervals at that time, a total of 89 usable replies were received by the cut-off date of 30 September, giving a response rate of 45%.

The respondents were asked to indicate whether they were willing to be interviewed and individual face-to-face interviews were conducted with five owner-managers. The questionnaire responses were analysed using SPSS to obtain descriptive statistics. The interview responses were not formally analysed, but used to provide illustrations of the general findings and offer additional insights.

The sample was divided into small and medium-sized companies to allow comparisons to be made. Small companies were defined as having a turnover in their 1994 accounts of £1 million up to £2.8 million and medium-sized companies as having a turnover of between £2.8 million and £11.2 million. The sample contained 39 small companies and 50 medium-sized companies across a wide range of industries: 28% had primary activities in the manufacturing or construction sectors and the remaining 72% were in service industries.

RESEARCH FINDINGS AND DISCUSSION

In the following three sections we discuss the findings, distinguishing between small and medium-sized companies. First we examine the results relating to the non-statutory recipients of the company's annual report and the annual reports of other businesses read. This is followed by an analysis of the usefulness of the annual report in the context of other sources of information for managing the company.

Table 10.2 Non-statutory recipients of annual report and accounts

RECIPIENT	TOTAL RESPONSES		SMALL COMPANIES		MEDIUM-SIZED COMPANIES	
	No.	%	No.	%	No.	%
Bank manager	75	84.3	33	84.6	42	84.0
Directors	66	74.2	25	64.1	41	82.0
Major lenders	20	22.5	9	23.0	11	22.0
Major customers	20	22.5	4	10.3	16	32.0
Inland Revenue	19	21.3	7	17.9	12	24.0
Senior managers	17	19.1	5	12.8	12	24.0
All employees	7	7.8	3	7.7	4	8.0
Major suppliers	6	6.7	1	2.6	5	10.0

Note. More than one response was possible. The sample contained 39 small companies and 50 medium-sized companies.

Non-statutory recipients of the annual report

The respondents were asked to indicate who, apart from shareholders and the Registrar of Companies, is normally given a copy of the company's annual report and accounts. A total of 87% of small companies and 94% of medium-sized companies give a copy of the annual report and accounts to one or more non-statutory recipient. Table 10.2 compares the responses of the small and medium-sized companies where there were non-statutory recipients. Further analysis of the data shows that industrial and regional differences in the responses to this question were not statistically significant.

The table shows that, overall, the main non-statutory recipients of the annual report and accounts are: first, the bank manager; second, the directors; and in joint third place, major lenders and customers. Although these findings broadly support the evidence of previous research by Page (1984), Carsberg *et al.* (1985) and Barker and Noonan (1996), these results show that the bank and major lenders are the prime non-statutory recipients of small company accounts.

It comes as no surprise that a large majority of the respondents (nearly 85% of small companies and 84% of medium-sized companies) send a copy of their statutory accounts to the bank manager, since banks represent the main source of finance for smaller entities (Cosh, Duncan and Hughes, 1996). The importance of the bank as the principal external non-statutory recipient of smaller companies' financial statements is supported by previous research into bank lending decisions (Berry, Citron and Jarvis, 1987; Berry *et al.*, 1993; Berry, Crum and Waring, 1993; Berry and Waring, 1995). Although a direct comparison is not possible, the results relating to banks/major lenders appear to be considerably stronger than those obtained by Page (1984) or Carsberg *et al.* (1985). These studies found that only 17% and 15% of small companies respectively felt that the information to lenders/raising finance was the most important or next most important use of the annual report.

In addition, 23% of small companies and 22% of medium-sized companies send their annual report to major lenders. Although it is possible to speculate that major lenders, apart from banks, might include family members, venture capitalists, business angels, trade creditors and factoring companies, it would be valuable to identify the major lenders to small businesses in future research.

Whereas 82% of medium-sized companies send a copy of the annual report to their directors, only 64% of small companies do so. It is possible that this is distorted by the fact that the directors may also be shareholders, although shareholders were specifically excluded in the wording of this question

One likely reason for the relatively low proportion of companies sending the annual report to the Inland Revenue (18% of small companies and 24% of medium-sized companies) is that it may also be sent by the firm's accountant. This suggests that in order to obtain a global view of the users of small company accounts future research should extend the investigation to the preparers of the accounts, as in the case of the studies by Carsberg et al (1985) and Barker and Noonan (1996).

A total of 24% of medium-sized companies, compared with 13% of small companies, distribute the annual report to their senior managers, although this difference was not found to be statistically significant. One explanation may be the difference in the way small and medium-sized companies are managed: whilst the majority of the small companies are managed by one director with advice/consultation with other directors, the majority of medium-sized companies are managed by directors with some senior managers (Hussey and Hussey, 1994).

It is interesting to note that more medium-sized companies send a copy of their annual report to their major customers. Indeed, taking major customers and major suppliers together, 13% of small companies and 42% of medium-sized companies send them a copy of their accounts. The interview findings indicate that they do this to reassure them and enable them to carry out their own financial health checks. However, the extent of reliance on debt was not investigated in the study and this may help to explain the difference between the responses of the two sizes of company. The results relating to major customers and suppliers differ from those of Barker and Noonan (1996), who found that only 3% of small company auditors rated customers and suppliers as important users of small company financial statements.

Only a very small proportion distribute the annual report to all employees and further analysis reveals that all the companies were in the service sector. One explanation may be the presence of an employee share ownership scheme, profit sharing scheme, profit-related pay scheme, etc., although the study did not investigate this.

Further analysis was conducted by categorising the non-statutory recipients of the annual report into internal recipients (all employees; directors; senior managers) and external recipients (bank manager; Inland Revenue; major customers; major lenders; major suppliers) and investigating the differences between small and medium-sized companies. The details in the Appendix show that only 64% of small companies, compared with 82% of medium-sized companies, send a copy of the annual report to internal recipients. The largest proportion of companies in the two size groups send the annual report to only one category of internal recipient. Multivariate analysis shows that, for both small and medium-sized companies, this was most commonly the directors. This finding further supports evidence from previous research of the value of the statutory accounts as a source of information for managing the company.

With regard to the external recipients, the results show that 85% of small companies and 88% of medium-sized companies send a copy of the annual report to external recipients. A total of 80% of small companies and 68% of medium-sized companies send the annual report to either one or two categories of external recipient. Multivariate analysis of the data shows that for both sizes of company this was most commonly either bank manager alone or the bank manager plus one other category of external recipient. This finding further supports the evidence from previous research of the value of the statutory accounts as providing information to the bank.

Annual reports of other businesses

Developing this theme of the uses of the annual report, the respondents were asked whether they ever read the annual report and accounts of other businesses. Table 10.3 compares the responses of the small and medium-sized companies.

The results show that some 51% of small companies and 68% of medium-sized companies claim to read the statutory accounts of their major competitors; 44% of

Table 10.3 Annual report and accounts of other businesses

ANNUAL REPORT READ	SMALL COMPANIES		MEDIUM-SIZED COMPANIES	
	Number	Percentage	Number	Percentage
Major competitors	20	51.3	34	68.0
Major customers	17	43.6	31	62.0
Major suppliers	10	25.6	18	36.0

Note. More than one response was possible

small companies and 62% of medium-sized companies claim to read those of their major customers; and 26% of small companies and 36% of medium-sized companies claim to read the annual report and accounts of their major suppliers. None of these differences between the two sizes of company was found to be statistically significant.

Further analysis was conducted to investigate any links between those distributing their annual report to major customers and those reading the annual report of their major customers, as shown in Table 10.4. There was insufficient data to provide an analysis by company size. It appears that companies which send their own annual report to their major customers are also likely to read those customers' annual reports (Chi-square 7.055, df1, $p < 0.01$).

Table 10.4 Distribution of own annual report to major customers, by readership of customers' annual reports.

ANNUAL REPORT	MAJOR CUSTOMERS' ANNUAL REPORT READ		MAJOR CUSTOMERS' ANNUAL REPORT NOT READ	
	Number	*Percentage*	*Number*	*Percentage*
Own report distributed to major customers	4	10	16	33
Own report not distributed to major customers	37	90	32	67
Total	41	100	48	100

USEFULNESS OF SOURCES OF MANAGEMENT INFORMATION

The respondents were asked to indicate how useful they find certain sources of information for managing the company using the following Likert scale: very useful; quite useful; of little use; of no use. In addition, a 'not applicable/no response' box was provided. In order to aid comparison of the results for the two sizes of company, the responses were weighted and averaged (where very useful = 5 and of no use = 1) to provide the results shown in Table 10.5.

For small companies the three most useful sources of information for management purposes are, in order of importance, the management accounts for the period, the annual report and accounts and cash flow information. For medium-sized companies it is the management accounts, cash flow information and budgets respectively. Published industry data and information from credit rating agencies and were the least important for all companies. The annual report and accounts came second in importance as a source of management information for small companies, although it came fifth for medium-sized companies. Its importance as a source of management information confirms earlier studies of owner-managers by Page (1984) and Carsberg et al (1985). It also supports the findings of Barker and Noonan's (1996) survey of small practitioners.

Further analysis of this data using Spearman's *rho* (0.905, n = 8), found a significant positive correlation at the 1% level in the ordering of the sources of information for small and medium-sized companies. This means that we can be 99% certain that there are no relative differences in ranking due to company size.

However, there may be differences in the comparative usefulness attributed to

Table 10.5 Ranking of mean usefulness of sources of management information

SOURCE OF INFORMATION	SMALL COMPANIES		MEDIUM-SIZED COMPANIES	
	Mean score	Rank	Mean score	Rank
Monthly/quarterly management accounts	4.65	1	4.88	1
Annual report and accounts	4.64	2	3.71	2
Cash flow information	4.56	3	4.60	3
State of order book	4.42	4	3.96	4
Bank statements	4.18	5	4.61	5
Budgets	4.17	6	3.59	6
Published industry data	3.39	7	3.21	7
Credit rating agencies	3.13	8	3.30	8

specific sources of information by larger companies. In particular, whereas 90% of the small company respondents found the annual report very useful or quite useful, only 70% of the medium-sized companies were of this opinion. Also, with regard to bank statements, 81% of small companies found bank statements a very useful or quite useful source of management information compared with 54% of medium-sized companies.

To aid the substantive interpretation of the data, factor analysis was then used to look for interrelationships among the sources of information for managing the company shown in Table 10.5. The method reduces the data to a smaller set of common composite variables (factors) and these hypothetical constructs can be used to describe and explain patterns of relationship among the original variables (Diamantopoulos and Schlegelmilch, 1997). The analysis was conducted using SPSS for Windows. As a precursor to the factor analysis, a correlation matrix was drawn up and the figures support the constructs identified. Varimax rotated factor analysis was chosen because it maximises the tendency of each variable to load highly on only one factor. For the small companies the Varimax rotation converged in only four iterations and three factors, which account for 75% of the variance, were extracted. Table 10.6 gives details of the three factors in order of strength of correlation.

Factor 1, the most strongly correlated factor, accounted for 41% of the variance in the original variables. It groups together four variables with loadings in excess

Table 10.6 *Rotated factor matrix of sources of management information (small companies)*

VARIABLE	FACTOR 1: PLANNING/ MONITORING DATA	FACTOR 2: EVALUATIVE/ COMPARATIVE DATA	FACTOR 3: CONFIRMATORY/ VERIFYING DATA
	41% of variance	19% of variance	15% of variance
Annual report and accounts	-.13675	.34845	**.84223**
Budgets	**.77278**	.41786	.07261
Management accounts	**.81456**	.25631	.06954
Cash flow information	**.91732**	.04281	.03922
State of order book	**.77650**	-.01204	.01386
Bank statements	.34617	-.38249	**.74493**
Credit rating agencies	.28657	**.65334**	.06932
Published industry data	.07044	**.93388**	.00219

of .7 which are highlighted in the table and have been labelled intuitively as 'planning/monitoring data', since these sources of information are likely to be part of a management accounting system, the purpose of which is to help managers with these short-term tasks. In this factor the annual report and accounts was negatively correlated.

Factor 2 accounted for 19% of the variance and groups together two variables with loadings in excess of .6. It is labelled 'evaluative/comparative data' on the basis that both variables are externally published sources of company or industry data which is commonly used for these purposes. In this factor the state of order book and bank statements were negatively correlated.

Factor 3 is the least strongly correlated factor and accounted for 15% of the variance. It groups together two variables with loadings in excess of .7 which have been labelled 'confirmatory/verifying data'. The rationale for this is that they relate to historical information corroborated by external agents, which may serve to confirm and verify internal financial records.

For the medium-sized companies the rotation converged in five iterations and three factors (accounting for 63% of the variance) were extracted. Table 10.7 gives details of the three factors in order of strength of correlation. The intuitive naming of the factors and the rationale for the labels is identical to that used for the small companies.

Factor 1, the most strongly correlated factor, accounted for 24% of the variance in the original variables, and groups together four variables with loadings in excess of .5. In this factor bank statements and credit rating agency data were negatively correlated.

Table 10.7 Rotated factor matrix of sources of management information (medium-sized companies)

VARIABLE	FACTOR 1: PLANNING/ MONITORING DATA	FACTOR 2: CONFIRMATORY/ VERIFYING DATA	FACTOR 3: EVALUATIVE/ COMPARATIVE DATA
	24% of variance	22% of variance	17% of variance
Annual report and accounts	.24265	**.72104**	.14640
Budgets	**.83797**	-.03196	-.02961
Management accounts	**.80016**	-.01891	.18187
Cash flow information	**.69812**	-.00070	-.39438
State of order book	.09100	.43502	-.49863
Bank statements	-.19407	**.68151**	-.40658
Credit rating agencies	-.19637	**.77117**	.15690
Published industry data	.03255	.22925	**.87095**

Factor 2 accounted for 22% of the variance and groups together three variables with loadings in excess of .6. In this factor budgets, management accounts and cash flow statements were negatively correlated

Factor 3, the least strongly correlated factor, 3 accounted for 17% of the variance. There is only one variable with a loading of over .5 (in this case .7). In this factor cash flow information, the state of order book and bank statements were negatively correlated.

Comparing the separate results of the factor analysis for the small and medium-sized companies, it can be seen that there is some difference in the strength of the correlation of the composite variables and some minor shifts in the combination of the variables that form each factor. With regard to the annual report and accounts, the main difference is that for small companies it is grouped with bank statements and forms the third and least strongly correlated factor, whereas for medium-sized companies it is grouped not only with bank statements, but also with data from credit rating agencies and forms the second factor.

CONCLUSIONS

Despite a considerable gap in the literature relating to the users and uses of the statutory accounts of small companies, in the current rush towards regulatory relaxation for smaller entities policies are being formulated in ignorance. The present study addresses this deficiency, both confirming and extending previous research.

In these conclusions we return to our three main objectives. The first was to identify the non-statutory recipients of the annual report and accounts of small and medium-sized companies. Our results confirm those of Page (1984), Carsberg et al (1995) and Barker and Noonan (1996) that three main non-statutory recipients are the bank manager and other lenders, the Inland Revenue and the management. The importance of the bank is related to its role as the principal source of finance to small firms (Cosh, Duncan and Hughes, 1996) and the use of the annual report in lending decisions (Berry, Citron and Jarvis, 1987; Berry et al, 1993; Berry, Crum and Waring, 1993; Berry and Waring, 1995).

A range of both internal and external non-statutory recipients are revealed, showing that the information in the annual report is disseminated more widely than assumed by the regulators. Some of these recipients differ significantly between small and medium-sized companies. Statistical tests also show that significantly more medium-sized than small companies distribute their annual reports to major customers, one particular group of external recipients.

The research also set out to discover whether the owner-managers of small and medium-sized companies read the annual accounts of other businesses. Both sizes of company claimed to do so and a statistically significant link was found between those reading the annual report of major customers and those sending a copy of their own report to major customers. This interesting finding requires further investigation to ascertain whether it is related to company size, industry, region, owner-manager's level of financial sophistication or some other variable.

This study also adds to the previous research by beginning to compare the usefulness of the annual report to owner-managers with other sources of information for managing the company. An interesting result is revealed by ranking the results: for small companies the annual report and accounts is ranked second in terms of usefulness, whereas for medium-sized companies it is ranked fifth. Reasons for this include the possibility that small companies have fewer resources than medium-sized companies with which to invest in management accounting systems and procedures; the familiarity of the annual report may lead to their greater use by small companies; the credibility of the information provided by the auditor may make it more useful to small companies than to medium-sized companies. These hypotheses require further investigation.

The composite variables suggested by multivariate analysis show that for both small and medium-sized companies the sources of information can be grouped together according to purpose: planning/monitoring, evaluating/comparing, or confirming/verifying. These hypotheses also offer scope for further research, particularly the extent to which small companies use the information in the annual report for confirmation/verification purposes or in place of a reliable management accounting system. In addition, the specific uses and the specific information in the accounts being used needs to be investigated.

The FRSSE was developed with little knowledge of the role played by small company annual reports. This is of considerable concern since *"emphasis on reducing the information required in order to meet deregulation aims or to reduce compliance costs, has the effect of making financial reports less useful to users"* (Jarvis, 1996, p 27). This research provides evidence to suggest that in relaxing the regulation of financial reporting by smaller entities, the emphasis should not be on reducing compliance costs, but on ensuring that changes in accounting regulation lead to accounts that are more useful to users.

APPENDIX

1. Present and proposed qualifying conditions for small and medium-sized companies

Measure	Small, not exceeding:	Medium-sized, not exceeding:
Turnover:		
Present level	£2.8m	£11.2m
Proposed EU amendment	£4.2m	£16.8m
Balance sheet total:		
Present level	£1.4m	£5.6m
Proposed EU amendment	£2.1m	£8.4m
Average number of employees:	50	250

2. Number of internal recipients of annual report (N = 39 small companies, 50 medium-sized companies)

Internal recipients	Small companies		Medium-sized companies	
	Number	Percentage	Number	Percentage
1	18	46	28	56
2	6	15	10	20
3	1	3	3	6
Total	25	64	41	82

3. Number of external recipients of annual report (N = 39 small companies, 50 medium-sized companies)

External recipients	Small companies		Medium-sized companies	
	Number	Percentage	Number	Percentage
1	16	41	16	32
2	15	39	18	36
3	0	0	9	18
4	2	5	0	0
5	0	0	1	2
Total	33	85	44	88

4. Usefulness of annual report as a source of management information: Chi-square 4.83, df 1, p < 0.03

Annual report	Small companies		Medium-sized companies	
	Number	Percentage	Number	Percentage
Very/quite useful	34	90	35	70
Of little/no use	4	11	15	30
Total	38	100	50	100

5. Usefulness of bank statements as a source of management information: Chi-square 6.16, df 1, p < 0.02

Bank statements	Small companies		Medium-sized companies	
	Number	Percentage	Number	Percentage
Very/quite useful	29	81	25	54
Of little/no use	7	19	21	46
Total	36	100	46	100

NOTES

[1] Further details of present and proposed thresholds are provided in the first section of the Appendix. Certain companies, such as banks, insurance companies or an authorised person under the Financial Services Act 1986, are excluded from the small company criteria of the grounds of public interest.
[2] For example, Falk, Godbel and Naus (1976); Abdel-Khalik, Rashad, Collins, Shields, Snowball, Stephens and Wragge (1983); Berry, Citron and Jarvis (1987).
[3] For example, Holgate (1995)

REFERENCES

Abdel-Khalik, A. Rashad, Collins, W. A., Shields, P. D., Snowball, D. H., Stephens, R. G. and Wragge, J. H. (1983). *Financial Reporting by Private Companies: Analysis and Diagnosis*. USA: Financial Accounting Standards Board.

Accounting Standards Board (1996). *Financial Reporting Standard for Smaller Entities*. Exposure Draft. London: ASB.

Accounting Standards Board (1997). *Financial Reporting Standard for Smaller Entities*. London: ASB.

Accounting Standards Committee (1988). *Statement by the Accounting Standards Committee on the Application of Accounting Standards to Small Companies*. Technical Release 690, London: ASC.

Accounting Standards Steering Committee (1975). *The Corporate Report*. London: ASSC.

Barker, P. C., and Noonan, C. (1996). *Small Company Compliance with Accounting Standards*. Dublin: Dublin City University Business School.

Berry, A., Citron, D., and Jarvis, R. (1987). *The Information Needs of Bankers Dealing with Large and Small Companies*. Research Report 7. London: ACCA.

Berry, A., Faulkner, S., Hughes M. and Jarvis, R. (1993). *Bank Lending: Beyond the Theory*. London: Chapman and Hall.

Berry, R. H., Crum, R. E. and Waring, A. (1993). *Corporate Performance Appraisal in Bank Lending Decisions*. London: CIMA.

Berry, R. H. and Waring, A. (1995). A user perspective on 'Making Corporate Reports Valuable, *British Accounting Review*, 27, pp. 139-52.

Carsberg, B. V., Page, M. J., Sindall, A. J. and Waring, I. D. (1985). *Small Company Financial Reporting*. London: Prentice Hall International.

Companies Act 1985. London: HMSO.

Consultative Committee of Accountancy Bodies (1994). Working Party Consultative Document, *Exemptions from Standards on Grounds of Size or Public Interest*. London: CCAB.

Consultative Committee of Accountancy Bodies (1995a). *Designed to Fit - a Financial Reporting Standard for Smaller Entities*. Working Party Paper. London: CCAB.

Consultative Committee of Accountancy Bodies (1995b). Comments on the Consultative Document, *Exemptions from Standards on Grounds of Size or Public Interest*. London: CCAB.

Cosh, A., Duncan, J., and Hughes, A. (1996). Profitability and Finance, in Cosh, A. and Hughes, A. (eds.), *The Changing State of British Enterprise*. ESRC Centre for Business Research, Cambridge: Cambridge University.

Department of Trade and Industry (1995). *Accounting Simplifications*. Consultative Document, London: DTI.

Department of Trade and Industry (1997). *Companies in 1996-97*. London: The Stationery Office.

Diamantopoulos, A., and Schlegelmilch, B. B. (1997). *Taking the Fear Out of Data Analysis*. London: Dryden Press.

Falk, H., Godbel, B. C., and Naus, J. H. (1976). Disclosure for closely held corporations, *Journal of Accountancy*, October.

Harvey, D., and Walton, P. (1996). *Differential Reporting - An Analysis*. The Foundation for Manufacturing and Industry, January, London.

Holgate, P. (1995). Big chance, little effort, lots of benefits, *Accountancy*, April, pp. 93-94.

Hussey, J. and Hussey, R. (1994). *How Companies Succeeded in the Recession*. London: Kingston Smith.

Hussey, R. ed. (1995). *A Dictionary of Accounting*. Oxford: Oxford University Press.

Jarvis, R. (1996). *Users and Uses of Unlisted Companies' Financial Statements - A Literature Review*. London: ICAEW.

Keasey, K., and Short, H. (1990). The accounting burdens facing small firms: an empirical research note, *Accounting and Business Research*, Vol. 20, No. 80, pp.307-13.

Langfield-Smith, I. A. (1991). *The Reporting Entity Concept: Implementation under the Corporations Law*. AARF.

McMonnies, P. N., ed. (1988). *Making Corporate Reports Valuable*. Discussion Document by the Research Committee of the Institute of Chartered Accountants in Scotland, London: Kogan Page.

Milne, T., and Thomson, M. (1986). Patterns of successful business start up, in Faulkner, T., Gower, G., Lewis, J., and Gibbs, A. (eds.), *Readings in Small Business*. London: Gower.

Page, M. J. (1984). Corporate Financial Reporting and the Small Independent Company, *Accounting and Business Research*, Vol. 14, No.55, pp. 271-82.

Solomons, D. (1989). *Guidelines for Financial Reporting Standards*. London: ICAEW.

11

THE IMPACT OF PRICE CONTROLS ON ACCOUNTING POLICY CHOICE: AN INTERNATIONAL STUDY OF DEPRECIATION METHODS IN THE ELECTRICITY INDUSTRY

Gillian Butler and Louise Crawford

INTRODUCTION

The aim of the study discussed in this chapter is to establish whether there is a link between price control regulation in the electricity generating industry and the accounting policy adopted for the depreciation of hydro electricity generating assets (HEGAs). We also take into account the existence of cross-subsidies between electricity generation and the electricity networks, as well as the ownership and structure of the companies involved. The hydro electricity generating companies investigated operate in the UK, New Zealand, continental Europe (Austria, France, Germany, Italy, Spain and Switzerland) and Nordic Europe (Finland, Norway and Sweden).

The accounting policy adopted by a company for depreciation will impact on levels of reported profits of that company. Price controls in operation in the electricity industry are often influenced by profit calculation (Centre for the Study of Regulated Industries, 1996), and the cross-subsidy between hydro electricity generation and the electricity network may also be affected (Scottish Hydro Electric plc, 1995). If such economic consequences are considered in choosing the depreciation policy, then the resultant policy may be influenced by certain factors such as whether the company is state owned or privately owned and whether the company structure is vertically integrated or vertically separated.

State owned companies will be influenced by Government objectives whereas private owned companies will be influenced by corporate and investor objectives. The purpose of this paper is not to discuss these objectives in any great detail. However, it is sufficient to note that corporate and investor objectives are often argued to be concerned more so with profit measurement than Government objectives which are often argued to be concerned more so with economy, efficiency and effective use of resources (Accounts Commission for Scotland, 1998). When considering the economic consequences of accounting policies, vertically integrated companies may place more emphasis on the profitability of the entire company, encompassing electricity generation and electricity networks, whereas vertically separated companies will only need to consider the profitability of electricity generation. There may also be more scope for the existence of cross-subsidies within vertically integrated companies than between vertically separated companies and this may also influence the choice of accounting policy.

The choice of depreciation policy may also be influenced by electricity price control regulation in operation in the country concerned. If price controls are linked to profit determination (Centre for the Study of Regulated Industries, 1996; SHE 1995), then the company could influence profit measurement through its choice of accounting policy (*e.g.* for depreciation) and so influence the price obtained for electricity generated.

A comparison of this nature is important from the point of view of both the national electricity consumer and the international equity investor. As discussed earlier, the level of depreciation directly affects profit calculation. This, in turn, can affect electricity price controls and the level of any cross-subsidy operating within the electricity industry (Centre for the Study of Regulated Industries, 1996; SHE, 1995). In the UK, electricity price controls and cross-subsidies are calculated in the public interest in accordance with the Electricity Act 1989 in order to protect the consumer from high electricity charges. Arguably, therefore, the depreciation policy adopted for HEGAs will indirectly impact on electricity charges to the consumer. From the point of view of the international investor, it is well documented that there is a growing need to take cognisance of international accounting differences when comparing the profitability of similar companies operating in different countries (Weetman and Gray, 1991; Lawrence, 1996). Clearly, the depreciation policy adopted by a company will directly impact on the profitability of that company.

SOURCES OF DATA AND METHODOLOGY

Companies considered to be relevant to this research were identified from various sources. Many of the European companies were identified by country and then by industry sector (Eastwood, 1995; Hast, 1992). Other European companies were identified from information provided by European companies already identified or, together with the identification of New Zealand hydro electricity generating companies, through the Internet.

The focus of comparison between the UK, continental Europe, Nordic Europe and New Zealand is motivated by various studies of financial reporting measurement practices which classify the UK, continental Europe, Nordic Europe and New Zealand separately. In a qualitative study, Nobes (1989) classifies the UK and New Zealand reporting practice as micro-based, influenced by business practice; continental Europe (being Italy, France, Belgium and Spain) as macro-uniform, influenced by government and tax legislation; and Nordic Europe (being Sweden) as macro-uniform, influenced by government economic policies. Weetman and Gray (1991) quantitatively discern UK financial reporting practices as less conservative than financial reporting practices in Nordic Europe.

Nordic Europe has also been identified separately from continental Europe because, within Europe, the Nordic countries collectively constitute the largest hydro electricity producing countries, with Norway and Sweden being amongst the top ten largest world-wide (Norwegian Water Resources and Energy Administration, 1997). Within continental Europe, only France generates hydro-electricity to anywhere near the same level as Nordic Europe. This reflects the fact that the geography and climate of the Nordic countries is considered to be more similar to northern UK, where the major UK hydro electricity generating company is located, in comparison to other continental European countries. It is also generally accepted that the Nordic countries are considered to be culturally similar, although their accounting practices are not harmonised (Lawrence, 1996).

For each hydro electricity generating company, information regarding the price controls operating in the country concerned, evidence of the existence of cross-subsidies between hydro electricity generation and the electricity network, the ownership of the company, and the structure of the company was collected. This information was extracted not only from the annual reports analysed but also from other sources (Gray, 1996; Eastwood, 1995).

Details of accounting policies on depreciation and maintenance costs are given in Table 11.1 for each company and for each of the various categories of assets specified, together with other characteristics of the companies. A summary of depreciation methods is provided in Table 11.2, and an analysis with regard to price controls, company structure and ownership in Table 11.3.

Hydro electricity generating companies which specifically disclose their depreciation policy for hydro electricity generating assets (HEGAs) have been tabulated separately in Table 11.4, together with the period of time over which such assets are to be depreciated. This has been done in order to examine more thoroughly potential links between the depreciation policy adopted and the environment in which the company operates.

In total, 22 sets of company annual reports were analysed: one from the UK, 13 from continental Europe, six from Nordic Europe and two from New Zealand. Details of which company annual reports were analysed are given in the Appendix.

ANALYSIS OF RESULTS

Out of the twenty-two sets of accounts analysed, it was found that nine did not specifically disclose their depreciation policy for HEGAs, but disclosed a more general policy for the depreciation of plant, property and equipment or tangible fixed assets. Given that the companies being investigated all generate hydro electricity, it has been assumed that these general categories of assets disclosed include HEGAs. Also, regardless of whether the depreciation policy adopted specifically relates to HEGAs, disclosure of the period of time over which such assets are to be depreciated was not always stated. These factors, together with the limited number of annual reports analysed, limited the extent to which clear links, if any, between the depreciation policy adopted and the environment within which the company operates could be established.

Depreciation and maintenance policies for hydro electricity generating assets

Referring to Table 11.1, it can be seen that all of the continental European companies disclose a policy for the depreciation of HEGAs. One company in the UK (SHE) and one company in France (Electricité de France) distinguish between hydro civil assets (such as dams, reservoirs and aqueducts) and hydro power plants. The French company depreciates both categories of asset, whereas the UK company considers hydro civil assets to have an infinite life and as such these assets are not depreciated. Where the depreciation policy is stated specifically for HEGAs, the method of depreciation is predominantly straight line although the depreciable life of such assets ranges from 20 to 75 years (Table 11.2).

Hydro electricity generating companies operating in Nordic Europe and New Zealand also depreciate their HEGAs and do not distinguish between hydro civil assets and other HEGAs. Where the depreciation policy disclosed relates

Table 11.1 Depreciation policy and the environment in which the company operates

COUNTRY	COMPANY	ASSET CATEGORY (1)	DEPRECIATION POLICY (MAINTENANCE POLICY) (2)	COMPANY STRUCTURE (3)/(4)	PRICE CONTROL (3)	OWNERSHIP (3)
UK	SHE	HCA	No depreciation (Provisioning)	VI	Competition	Private
		HPP	Straight line - 20-60 years (NA)	V/I	Competition	Private
Austria	Verbund	PPE	Straight line - power plants (NA) Accelerated method - moveable assets (NA) Rates = 4-66.7 years	NA	NA	NA
France	Electricité de France	DCP	Straight line and declining balance – 75 years (NA)	VI	Regulated	State owned
		HPP	Straight line and declining balance – 50 years (NA)	VI	Regulated	State owned
Germany	Bayernwerk	TFA	Declining balance, then straight line – no rates given (NA)	VI	Regulated	Private
	Preussen Elektra	TFA	Straight line – buildings - 10-50 years (NA) Declining balance - moveable assets – 4-35 years (NA)	VI	Regulated	Private
	RWE Aktiengesellschaft	TFA	Declining balance, then straight line – 4-50 years (Expensed)	VI	Regulated	Private
	RWE Energie	HPP	Declining balance, hen straight line – 20-60 years (NA)	VI	Regulated	Private
	VEBA	PPE	Declining balance, then straight line – 5-50 years (Expensed)	VI	Regulated	Private
	VEW Aktiengesellschaft	TFA	Straight line-some power plants & reservoirs-ro rates given (NA) Declining balance for other TFA - no rates given (NA)	VI	Regulated	Private
Italy	ENEL	TFA	Straight line - no rates given (Expensed)	NA	NA	NA
Spain	Empresa Nacional de Electricidad SA	HPP	Straight line - 35-65 years (Expensed)	VI and V/S	Regulated	Mixed
	Empresa Nacional Hidroelectrica del Ribagorzana SA	HPP	Straight line - 35-65 years (Expensed)	VI and V/S	Regulated	Mixed
	Hidroelectrica Del Cantabrico SA	HPP	Straight line method - 65 years (Expensed)	V/I and V/S	Regulated	Mixed
Switzerland	Electrowatt	HPP	Annuity method charged over duration of the licence (NA)	NA	NA	NA
Finland	Imatron Voima Oy	HA	Straight line - 40-50 years (NA)	V/S	Competition	60% state
Norway	Statkraft	PPE	Straight line - 3-60 years (Expensed)	V/S	Competition	82% state
	Graninge	HPP	Systematic method - 67 years (NA)	V/S	Competition	70% state
Sweden	Stockholm Energi	TFA	In accordance with industry - 3-50 years (NA)	V/S	Competition	70% state
	Stora	PA	Original cost method - 60-120 years (NA)	V/S	Competition	70% state
	Vattenfall	HA	Straight line - 25-50 years (NA)	V/S	Competition	70% state
New Zealand	Contact Energy Ltd	GP	Straight line - weighted average 3.8% (Expensed)	V/S	State monopoly	State owned
	Electricity Corporation of New Zealand	GP	Straight line - weighted average 2.6% (Expensed)	V/S	State monopoly	State owned

Notes. (1) HCA = Hydro civil assets; HPP = Hydro power plants; PPE = Plant, property & equipment; TFA = Tangible fixed assets; HA = Hydro assets; PA = Power assets; DCP = Dams, canals & pipelines; GP = Generation plant. (2) Maintenance costs: either expensed as incurred, or provision made for major works. NA = Not available (3) Source of data : Gray (1996). (4) V/I = Vertically integrated. V/S = Vertically separated. (5) For Nordic companies, state ownership includes municipal ownership.

Table 11.2 Hydro electricity generating assets - depreciation methods

	ANNUAL REPORTS ANALYSED	SPECIFIC DEPRECIATION POLICY	STRAIGHT LINE METHOD	DECLINING BALANCE METHOD	PERIOD OVER WHICH DEPRECIATED
UK	1	1	No depreciation	No depreciation	--
Continental Europe	13	6	4.5[1]	1.5[1]	20-75 years
Nordic Europe	6	3[2]	2	1	25-67 years
New Zealand	2	2	2	-	26-38 years[3]

Notes. [1] *0.5 represents Electricité de France's "straight line or declining-balance method".* [2] *Stora has not been included as depreciation policy is "original cost method".* [3] *Approximate useful lives derived from weighted average figures.*

specifically to HEGAs, the method of depreciation varies between straight-line method and declining balance method.

The UK company, SHE, discloses that it provides for the maintenance of major hydro civil works, whereas none of the continental Europe, Nordic Europe or New Zealand companies investigated disclosed a specific policy on the maintenance of HEGAs. Nine companies disclose a general policy covering all fixed assets whereby maintenance is recorded annually as an expense (unless extending the useful life of the asset) and twelve companies do not disclose a maintenance policy.

It is worth considering the potential impact jointly of both the depreciation policy and the maintenance policy on the reported profits of the company. Although SHE does not depreciate hydro civil assets, SHE does provide for maintenance of such assets, whereas the other companies studied, which do depreciate HEGAs, do not disclose information that indicates that they provide for such specific maintenance costs. Without quantitative analysis, it is difficult to interpret whether the non-depreciation together with provision for maintenance as seen in UK annual reports, when compared to depreciation together with no provision for maintenance as seen in other countries annual reports, results in the same net impact on reported profits.

Depreciation policy and the operating environment

Hydro electricity generating companies operating in continental Europe are predominantly part of vertically integrated companies and operate in an environment where electricity generation prices are regulated. Ownership of these companies includes private, state owned and mixed ownership.

Hydro electricity generating companies operating in Nordic Europe are vertically separated and electricity generation prices are regulated by open competition. Vertical separation of companies arguably reduces monopolistic behaviour and so is consistent with the environment of regulation by open competition, whereas vertical integration of companies is consistent with the environment of regulated price controls. New Zealand hydro electricity generating companies are also vertically separated and are state owned but the price control policy is unclear from the literature sourced. Apart from the UK company, none disclosed information about the existence of cross-subsidies between electricity generated and the electricity network.

The environments within which UK, continental Europe, Nordic Europe and New Zealand hydro electricity companies operate differ from each other with regard to electricity generation price controls, company ownership and company structure. In trying to discern whether there is a relationship between any of these factors and the depreciation policy chosen, Table 11.3 summarises the relevant data. The table indicates that there is no clear link between electricity generation price controls, company ownership, company structure and the depreciation policy adopted by the company.

Table 11.3   *Depreciation methods compared to price control regulation, structure and ownership*

	STRAIGHT LINE	DECLINING BALANCE
Price Control Regulation		
Open to competition	4	1
Regulated	5.5	4.5
Company Structure		
Vertically integrated	3.5	4.5
Vertically separated	5	1
Mixed	3	-
Ownership		
Private	3	4
State	2.5	0.5
Mixed	6	1

Note. Includes Electricité de France 'straight line or declining balance method' (see Table 11.1), 0.5 each. This table does not include information from Stockholm Energi or Stora because the policy disclosed was too vague to categorise as straight line or declining balance. Austria, Italy and Switzerland are also excluded because the relevant information was not available.

Companies that disclose a depreciation policy specifically for HEGAs are presented separately in Table 11.4. These companies have been ordered according to the length of period over which HEGAs are depreciated. This ordering is clearly limited as the weighted average of the depreciable lives is not disclosed in the company annual reports analysed, except in the case of New Zealand companies.

Table 11.4 Depreciation policy for specific hydro asset categories

COMPANY (1)	ASSET CATEGORY (2)	DEPRECIATION POLICY	COMPANY STRUCTURE (2)(3)(4)	PRICE CONTROL (3)	OWNERSHIP (3)
SHE (UK)	HCA	No depreciation	V/I	Competition	Private
Electricité de France	DCP	Straight line and declining balance - 75 years	V/I	Regulated	State owned
Graninge (Sweden)	HPP	Systematic method - 67 years	V/S	Competition	70% state
Hidroelectrica Del Cantabrico SA (Spain)	HPP	Straight line method - 65 years	V/I and V/S	Regulated	Mixed
Stora (Sweden)	PA	Original cost method - 60-120 years	V/S	Competition	70% state
Electricité de France	HPP	Straight line and declining balance - 50 years	V/I	Regulated	State owned
Imatron Voima Oy (Finland)	HA	Straight line - 40-50 years	V/S	Competition	60% state
Electricity Corporation of New Zealand	GP	Straight line - weighted average 2.6%	V/S	State monopoly	State owned
Empresa Nacional de Electricidad SA (Spain)	HPP	Straight line - 35-65 years.	V/I and V/S	Regulated	Mixed
Empresa Nacional Hidroelectrica del Ribagorzana SA (Spain)	HPP	Straight line - 35-65 years	V/I and V/S	Regulated	Mixed
Contact Energy Ltd (New Zealand)	GP	Straight line - weighted average 3.8%	V/S	State monopoly	State owned
Vattenfall (Sweden)	HA	Straight line - 25-50 years	V/S	Competition	70% state
RWE Energie (Germany)	HPP	Declining balance then straight line - 20-60 years	V/I	Regulated	Private
SHE (UK)	HPP	Straight line - 20-60 years	V/I	Competition	Private

Notes. . *(1) Excluding Electrowatt (Switzerland) – insufficient data. (2) HCA = Hydro civil assets; HPP = Hydro power plants; HA = Hydro assets;*
PA = Power assets; DCP = Dams, canals & pipelines; GP = Generation plant (3) Source of data : Gray (1996). (4) V/I = Vertically integrated. V/S
= Vertically separated. (5) For Nordic companies, state ownership includes municipal ownership.

All declining balance depreciation methods relate to companies operating in countries classified as macro-uniform, whereas straight line depreciation methods relate to companies operating in either macro-uniform or micro-based environments. The depreciable life of specific HEGAs, however, does not appear to be linked to any of the variables being considered nor to financial reporting classifications.

DISCUSSION

The causes of international differences in accounting practices have been widely discussed (Lawrence, 1996; Nobes and Parker, 1991; Nobes, 1992) and various factors have shaped accounting differently world-wide. These factors include legal systems, ownership of corporate entities, tax systems and the accountancy profession itself. These differences make it difficult for investors, managers and others who operate internationally to assess and compare financial statements.

Within the electricity generation sector we have explored the extent to which the accounting practices adopted by hydro electricity generating companies operating in different countries may be influenced by the specific background within which the company operates. From the research presented, there appears to be no link between the accounting policy adopted for depreciation and the price control regulation operating in the country concerned, the existence of cross-subsidies between electricity generation and electricity networks, the ownership of the company or the structure of the company. Apart from the adoption of the declining balance method of depreciation for HEGAs in macro-uniform countries, there is little evidence to link the depreciation policy adopted with Nobes' (1989) classification system. In all cases, with the exception of the UK, the method of depreciation adopted varies between straight line method and declining balance method, although for those companies where the depreciation policy is stated specifically for HEGAs, the method is predominantly straight line. This method is arguably less precise in allocating depreciation over the useful life of the asset and the adoption of this method may reflect the long lives, from twenty to seventy-five years, over which HEGAs are depreciated. Taking all observations into consideration, it is therefore argued that the accounting policy adopted by companies operating in the countries studied for the depreciation of HEGAs is arbitrary, in the context of the variables investigated.

The accounting policy adopted by non-UK companies for the depreciation of HEGAs appears to be consistent with national accounting requirements in the individual countries concerned (Coopers and Lybrand, 1993) and international accounting requirements (International Accounting Standards Committee, 1993, 1994). The national accounting requirements all state that tangible fixed assets with a useful life should be depreciated (Coopers & Lybrand, 1993). International Accounting Standard 4 'Depreciation Accounting' states that, *"depreciable assets are assets which are expected to be used during more than one accounting period have a limited useful life and are held by an entity for use in the production and supply of goods and services*". International Accounting Standard 16 'Property, Plant and Equipment' states that, "*depreciation is the systematic allocation of the depreciable amount of an asset over its useful life*", and "*useful life is ... the period of time over which an asset is expected to be used....*". Clearly, the European and New Zealand companies studied deem their HEGAs to have a finite life and depreciate them accordingly, and consistently with national and international accounting requirements.

Within the UK, however, certain HEGAs called hydro civil assets, such as dams, reservoirs and aqueducts are not depreciated. This treatment is arguably consistent with UK national accounting standards and inconsistent with international accounting standards. From our analysis, it would seem that SHE's policy of non-depreciation of hydro civil assets is also inconsistent with accounting practices adopted by other European and New Zealand hydro electricity generating companies. In the UK, Statement of Standard Accounting Practice 12 (SSAP 12) 'Accounting for Depreciation' states that, "*provision for depreciation of fixed assets having a finite useful economic life should be made*" (Accounting Standards Committee, 1987). Due to a statutory obligation bestowed on SHE to maintain hydro civil assets in perpetuity in The Reservoirs Act of 1975, SHE deems such assets to have an *infinite* useful economic life and therefore does not depreciate them. The emphasis would therefore be on deeming such assets to have an infinite useful economic life and thus SHE can justify non-depreciation of hydro civil assets and therefore depart from the mandatory requirements of SSAP 12. Interestingly though, the Reservoirs Act 1975 does not specifically prevent SHE from depreciating hydro civil assets and addresses the issue of maintaining hydro civil assets rather than the issue of depreciating such assets.

As well as SHE's policy of non-depreciation of certain HEGAs being inconsistent with international accounting standards, this policy appears to be inconsistent with current thinking and generally accepted accounting practice in the UK. In October 1997, the Accounting Standards Board in the UK issued Financial Reporting Exposure Draft 17 'Measurement of Tangible Fixed Assets'. Amongst other issues, it seeks to clarify the interpretation of certain points in SSAP 12. Due to the practice of some companies in the UK not depreciating their tangible fixed assets, on the basis that "*maintenance or refurbishment is carried out regularly*", the exposure draft states that this should not obviate the need to charge depreciation. Furthermore, FRED 17 proposes that the physical life of a tangible fixed asset (other than land) cannot be indefinite. SHE may therefore find it difficult in the future to justify the non-depreciation of hydro civil assets on the basis that such assets are maintained in perpetuity, if and when FRED 17 is published as a mandatory accounting standard.

The depreciation (and maintenance) accounting policy chosen for specific HEGAs will directly affect the level of reported profits disclosed within a company's annual reports. Our investigation into some of the potential determinants of accounting choice indicates that price control regulations, the existence of cross-subsidies, company structure and company ownership are not related to the choice of depreciation accounting policy. Quantitatively, it is difficult to assess with accuracy what impact the chosen depreciation policy may have on price controls and cross subsidies and ultimately the electricity consumer. Qualitatively, however, such disclosure of disparate accounting policies within industrially-similar companies will impact on the understandability and comparability of annual reports and so diminish their usefulness to the international investor.

APPENDIX

COUNTRY	COMPANY	YEAR
UK	SHE	1995/96
Austria	Verbund	1994/95
France	Electricité de France	1995/96
Germany	Bayernwerk	1994/95
Germany	Preussen Elektra	1994/95
Germany	RWE Aktiengesellschaft	1995/96
Germany	RWE Energie	1995/96
Germany	VEBA	1994/95
Germany	VEW Aktiengesellschaft	1994/95
Italy	ENEL	1994/95
Spain	Empresa Nacional de Electricidad SA	1994/95
Spain	Empresa Nacional Hidroelectrica del Ribagorzana SA	1994/95
Spain	Hidroelectrica Del Cantabrico SA	1994/95
Switzerland	Electrowatt	1995/96
Finland	Imatron Voima Oy	1995/96
Norway	Statkraft	1995/96
Sweden	Graninge	1995/96
Sweden	Stockholm Energi	1995/96
Sweden	Stora	1995/96
Sweden	Vattenfall	1995/96
New Zealand	Contact Energy Ltd	1995/96
New Zealand	Electricity Corporation of New Zealand Ltd (ECNZ)	1995/96

REFERENCES

Accounting Standards Board (1997). *Financial Reporting Exposure Draft no. 17: Measurement of Tangible Fixed Assets.* London: ASB.

Accounting Standards Committee (1987). *Statement of Standard Accounting Practice no. 12: Accounting for Depreciation.* London: ASC.

Accounts Commission for Scotland (1998). *A Quick Guide to the Accounts Commission for Scotland 1997/98.* Edinburgh: ACS.

Centre for the Study of Regulated Industries (1996). *Regulated Industries - The UK Framework.* London: CIPFA.

Coopers and Lybrand (1993). *International Accounting Summaries: A Guide for Interpretation and Comparison.* New York: John Wiley & Sons.

Eastwood, M. (1995). *Major Companies of Europe 1995/96.* Vol.1-3. London: Graham and Whiteside.
Gray, P. (1996). *Industry Structure and Regulation in Infrastructure: a Cross-Country Survey.* The World Bank.
Hast, A. (1992). *International Directory of Company Histories.* Vol.V. London: St James Press.
International Accounting Standards Board (1993). *International Accounting Standard no. 4: Accounting for Depreciation.* London: IASC.
International Accounting Standards Board (1994). *International Accounting Standard no 16: Property, Plant and Equipment.* London: IASC.
Lawrence, S. (1996). *International Accounting.* London: Thomson International Business Press.
Nobes, C. W. (1989). *Interpreting European Financial Statements: Towards 1992.* London: Butterworths.
Nobes, C. W. (1992). *Accounting Comparisons: UK – Europe.* London: Coopers and Lybrand.
Nobes, C. W., and Parker, R. (1991). *Comparative International Accounting.* Hemel Hempstead: Prentice-Hall.
Norwegian Water Resources and Energy Administration (1997). *Energy in Norway.*
Scottish Hydro Electric plc (1995). *A report on a reference under section 12 of the Electricity Act 1989, Monopolies and Mergers Commission.*
Weetman, P., and Gray, S. J., (1991). A comparative international analysis of the impact of accounting principles on profits: the USA versus the UK, Sweden and the Netherlands, *Accounting and Business Research*, Vol.21, No.84, pp.363-79.

Author Index

Subject Index

Page numbers followed by "t" indicate tables.